Gracelets Endorsements

Regardless of your current unde............................., Gracelets will give you a new perspective on the subject. As you dive into Gracelets, Dr. Winn Griffin acts as your trained and highly experienced Optometrist, helping you to identify and diagnose what part of your view comes from experience vs. Scripture. He dives deep into Paul's worldview and the original language, essentially recreating Paul's lenses and letting you view the subject as Paul may have.

He argues, fairly convincingly, that the terms that we have used to understand the spiritual gifts have been so continually misused and misunderstood and that so much baggage comes along with the use of these terms, that we should adopt the new language of "Gracelets."

Even if you don't end up fully embracing his full Gracelets View, it is hard not to find your existing view(s) modified and reformed through this process.

—Adam Arndt
God Wrestler in the Ring of Modern Context
Woodinville, WA

∽

My theology (and life) was changed when I met Dr. Winn Griffin. In conversation with him about being "filled with the Spirit," Winn rocked my thinking by asking a simple, yet profound question; "What if Holy Spirit filling is less like emptying out and more like adding something, like a soda fountain adds CO_2 to the syrup?" I haven't been the same since.

Like a wise uncle or Yoda-like sage, Winn writes as if the reader is having the same sort of conversation I did years ago. Winn's style is engaging and light, but packs a punch that will keep the reader wrestling with the profound implications.

In his latest book, *Gracelets*, Winn takes hold of the concept of Spiritual Gifts and turns conventional thinking on its head, defining the term as "gracelets," gifts of the Spirit given when needed, not something believers possess.

For those of us raised in the church who've taken (and given) spiritual gift inventories, this concept takes some getting used to. Fortunately, Winn guides the reader through this journey as a wise sage as he mines a new way of thinking about the Holy Spirit in the life of the Church.

Through careful exegesis of the "gifts-list" passages in the New Testament, he demonstrates to the reader that a different way of thinking is possible. Winn also has amazing personal stories that he weaves throughout the book. His life in the Pentecostal movement and inside connections with the Vineyard adds color to the book.

As I mentioned, I'm a fan of Dr. Winn's work and I'm grateful to add this excellent resource to the ministry toolbox.

—Rick Bartlett
Director of Theological Education, Associate Professor of Ministry
Tabor College, Kansas

∽

As I see it, the whole approach to spiritual gifts in the westernized church leaves much to be desired. First of all, there are many in the church who deny the modern-day existence of some of the more powerful gifts of the Spirit. Second, even when God's people are encouraged to explore the spiritual gifts, many teach that we should focus on only one gift per person. Then to top it off, once a saint "finds" their unique giftedness in Christ, that prideful and competitive spirit that lies deep within us rises up, tempting us to own and operate "our gift" in our own time and at our own bidding!

Thank God for Winn Griffin, who comes along just at the right time to set us straight on this important topic! As my mentor John Wimber used to say, the gifts of the Spirit belong to the Spirit…they are only on loan from God! Winn's approach to the spiritual gifts, defining them as Gracelets, is revolutionary. This book is an excellent primer for any twenty-first century follower of Jesus who is truly serious about making a Spirit-led impact in our world today!

—Marty Boller
Author: *The Wisdom of Wimber*
Cedar Rapids, Iowa

∽

It's time to start a bonfire and burn all of the spiritual gifts inventories ever created! So says Dr. Winn Griffin, author of *Gracelets: Being Conduits of the Extravagant Acts of God's Grace*. In this provocative and fascinating volume, Griffin takes on the deeply established understanding of spiritual gifts as supernatural abilities given to individual believers and replaces it with an approach that is more biblical, more honoring of the Spirit's work, and more freeing to Christians. What we have called spiritual gifts is really about "being conduits of the grace of God to others."

This fresh understanding is based on his concept of "gracelets," which are temporary acts of the Spirit working in and through human beings but are not possessions or permanent attributes of those individuals. Dr. Griffin persuasively supports his argument by exploring the meaning of the word "charismata," by re-reading the "gifts passages" of the New Testament, and by offering a theologically astute understanding of the work of the Holy Spirit in the Church and in the world. He illustrates his work with fascinating personal stories and keen biblical exegesis.

This work will benefit those from any theological persuasion–Pentecostals and charismatics who understand certain spiritual gifts as evidence of the baptism of the Holy Spirit, mainstream evangelicals who hold to the dominant view of spiritual gifts, cessationists who believe that some of the gifts have disappeared while others remain as supernatural ministry skills, and others who are confused or uninformed about these gifts of grace from the Spirit of God. But all should be prepared to have their minds changed!

—Tony Blair
President and Professor of Leadership and Historical Studies
Evangelical Seminary
Myerstown, Pennsylvania
Co-Senior Pastor
Hosanna! A Fellowship of Christians
Lititz, Pennsylvania

∽

A good book should read easily, inform, and encourage. This book does all three. Winn's thoughtful and thorough research on the subject of the gifts of the Spirit has refreshed and energized me to look again at this topic. I resonate with his premise that our role is to be conduits for these "Gracelets" to flow through us to those we meet. As an example, while I was writing this endorsement, a dear friend and church family member revealed that she has been diagnosed with cancer. Yet, another opportunity to be his conduit of his gracelets to my friend and many others alike.

—Bev Molineaux
Practice Nurse Springfield Surgery Canalside Bingley
Bingley, United Kingdom

∞

Using gifts of the Spirit as exhibit A, Dr. Winn Griffin exposes the false natural /supernatural dichotomy Christians have come to think as normative. Like Winn, I've long suspected that spiritual gifts are meant for every part of life – not just in church. Also, in spite of Paul's breadth of teaching on the gifts of the Spirit, I've often wondered, if they were that important, why didn't Jesus make a bigger deal out of them? In Gracelets, Dr. Winn solves that problem by introducing a way of practicing the gifts of the Spirit in the way of Jesus. How? By doing what Jesus did, focusing on others, rather than himself.

—Jim Henderson
Producer | JimHendersonPresents.com
Seattle, WA

Winn Griffin blows a cleansing autumn wind to clear away debris of the past, followed by a fresh spring wind to reinvigorate the parched church. His gracelets speak to nourish the people of God with the grace of God. The Spirit is alive and well in these pages, filled with wit and insight. As an insider within groups that advocate the ongoing work of the Spirit, Winn brings the rest of the story, to fill out a robust picture of how to enter conversations regarding what the Spirit is doing today. This book is an invitation to think again, to shed old models of spirituality that elevate the human, and to join the Spirit activity that causes us to up our sails and catch the Wind.

—Marty Folsom
Executive Director (USA)
Pacific Association for Theological Studies

∞

I have known Winn Griffin as teacher, mentor, and friend for thirty-five years. Thus, I've been exposed to his ever evolving understanding of gracelets almost from the inception of his theological thinking on the subject. Now you have the opportunity to explore the results of one of Winn's life projects. Take the time. You won't be disappointed. Winn's exposition has theological and hermeneutical chops but it is offered in classic Winn style: humorous, insightful, provocative, and practical. Gracelets exemplifies Winn's unique ability to get the church to think rather than blindly follow what we're being taught, often by people who really haven't thought their supposed area of expertise through. Hang on for the ride. Hopefully you'll enjoy it.

—Ed Cook
Coach | Author | Jesus Follower
Buckeye, AZ

∞

I have known Winn Griffin as a teacher, mentor, and friend for over 30 years. I have been deeply impacted by his teaching on the Gracelets of the Spirit throughout that time and reading this book has demonstrated that Winn has not rested in exploring and developing this intriguing and vital concept. Winn travels a path that questions all sides of the "Spiritual Gifts" debate and finds an alternative that is both profound in its conclusions and freeing in its application. You will need an open mind as he challenges preconceptions that some claim have settled this topic, but you will find his humorous and engaging personal stories and exploration of culture, translation, scholarship, and theology a provocative read well worth pondering. I found Winn's breakdown of what the Gracelets are and how they should work extremely useful and opens the door to find other Gracelets that aren't included in the lists. His emphasis on harmony between experience and theology, rather than trying to balance the two, has inspired me to seek a broader view of my relationship with the Trinity in all areas of my life. I hope you will join me in the journey of discovery that Winn invites us on.

—Mark H. Evans
Non-Profit IT Geek, Author, Member of "the Dones"
Tucson, Arizona

∞

In our pithy culture of social media, snippets of quotes designed to disarm the status quo compete with images and clips gone viral; Gracelets has that same potential. Sentence after sentence of the book produces the same sort of viral implications. This book has line after line of assessments that if they are correct, and I think Dr. Griffin makes the theological case they are, will reshape the way church does Church.

The context of the story, which Winn includes in his discussion and the high level of academic investment he has brought to this book make it both an invaluable tool for all Jesus followers: those studying for professional ministry in seminary; those who work as professional ministers, those who are active pew setters, or those who are inactive pew sitters. Winn seeks a re-shaping of our language; an influencing of our thoughts with such broad, long-term implications that if we can make the shift, readjust our mindset, and re-grid our theological expressions to act upon the concepts of "Gracelets," then the Church will stop getting caught up with the idea of who owns what gift and focus more on bringing "Gracelets" into the community in which they live.

—Eric Keck
Assistant Principal | Public School Administrator | Educator
Farmer | The Salt Farm
Northfield NH

∽

As someone who is on the "outside" of the Pentecostal experience or understanding of the gifts of the spirit, I find Dr. Winn's conversational style and in depth look at this topic both deeply engaging and at times quite disturbing. I applaud his lifelong inquiry of the Scriptures and deeply appreciate his stated desire to "spare some of the abuse that attends the subject of spiritual gifts." You will want to dwell with this material.

—Nancy Murphy
Therapist | Supervisor | Educator
Executive Director: Northwest Family Life

∽

Too often teachings on spiritual gifts have either dismissed them, conflated them with natural talents, or categorized them in terms of personal ownership. In Gracelets, Dr. Winn Griffin, through biblical exploration, theological interpretation, and stories of faith and humor, offers to the reader the possibility of freeing God's generous gifts from self-created boxes of predictability and into the mystery of God's intentions, desires, and love.

This book is a must-read for leaders and communities of faith that desire to open their personal and communal lives to the wonder and awe that are yet to be discovered in the gracious outpouring of God's gracelets.

—Mike McNichols
Director, Fuller Seminary Orange County
Affiliate Assistant Professor of Intercultural Studies
Fuller Theological Seminary
Pasadena, CA

∞

Not only is this a fine academic work, but Dr. Winn has produced a very readable piece that will satisfy anyone interested in issues regarding the Spirit of God. His early work with John Wimber has laid a credible foundation for him to write about this topic. His honesty about less-than-clear language and word usage adds to his credibility. He is unafraid to tackle this subject with the rigor one would expect from a commentary but with the casual tone of writing to a friend. I found his diligent commitment to the truth extremely helpful while exposing myths and traditions with gentle candor. Very interesting to me was his section on "How Words Work" and the great way he leads us through word dynamics and the evolution of their definitions over time. Any serious Bible student would be wise to include this book in their library. Dr. Winn continues to impact many with his book on Gracelets. I am one of the impacted.

—Mark T. Eaton
Master of Art in Global Urban Leadership
President, Eaton Leadership Foundation
Vice President, Susie McEntire LLC
Atoka, Oklahoma

∞

Utilizing rich spiritual ingredients tested over a lifetime of theological chopping and dicing, Dr. Griffin's newest book on *Gracelets* is a hearty chicken soup for the Church that can be enjoyed by expert and novice alike. While new wine continues to pour out of the broken wine skins of many modern congregations, this timely survey of the spiritual 'gifts' challenges the perceived duality between laity and clergy by proclaiming the level playing field of God's Extravagant Grace.

—Joe Ricciardi
Husband, Father, and Itinerant Jester to the King
Fort Collins, CO

Winn Griffin is out to change the church's thinking about spiritual gifts…in fact, he wants us to stop using that term altogether…and start spraying our world with drops of God's grace, his gracelets.

Tired of trying to figure out which "gift" you "have"? Let Winn Griffin suggest a whole new way of letting God's grace work through you…discover his gracelets.

When he's not trying to slay sacred cows (cessationism, gifts as abilities, etc.), he's combining top scholarship with plenty of his own personal stories to make you think in new ways about how God's Spirit might want to work through you for others.

—Kent Yinger
George Fox Evangelical Seminary

GRACELETS

Being Conduits of the
Extravagant Acts of God's Grace

WINN GRIFFIN

Harmon Press

Seedling Thought about Gracelets

As Jesus followers, we are the conduits for his gracelets. We are carriers of the gracelets. We don't own them, thus we cannot use them at our discretion. The gracelets are owned and operated by the Trinity. In any life circumstance, the Trinity might flow a drop or two of grace through us to give to someone else. When that gracelet reaches its destination, our part is complete. The giver of the gracelets decides how to make what we have delivered flourish in the recipient. The gracelets are always housed in the Trinity, never residing in an individual.

∞

Fish don't know they're in water.

If you tried to explain it, they'd say, "Water? What's water?"

They're so surrounded by it, that it's impossible to see.

They can't see it until they get outside of it.

– Derek Sivers: Founder: CD Baby | Writer | Entrepreneur

∞

...charis, grace:

charidzomai, I act graciously;

and *charisma*, the outcome of such an action.

—Russell P. Spittler

Dedication

To Russell P. Spittler
Who provided me with the word concept of Gracelets and first
mentored me to think critically.

∽

To John Wimber
Who provided me with the place to write and reflect
on the idea of Gracelets.

∽

To Donna Faith Griffin
Who has been a conduit of God's gracelets
to me over the years.

∽

...highlighting the Lord's grace as the *source* and the neighbor's needs as the *destination* of charismatic practices can surely be welcomed widely and warmly.
—Russell P. Spittler

GRACELETS

Contents

GRACELETS

Foreword by Russell P. Spittler

The vocabulary of the English language expands, in large part, by contagion. There already were common words like booklet, islet, leaflet, starlet, even piglet, or more digitally recent, applet—all miniature manifestations of their parent terms. In the Greek language that underlies the New Testament, there is a grammatical feature whereby a Greek word for a consequence of a verbal action is often signified by a two-letter suffix that comes into English as *–ma*. *Zeteo*, for example, means "I interrogate," *zetema* is the word for a "question." The word *hiaomai* means "I heal"; a *hiama* refers to the capacity to effect a cure. The verb dikaioo, for "I justify," leads to the noun *dikaioma*, "justification."

In a similar language development, the word *charisma* labels a concrete manifestation of *charidzomai*—to bestow something graciously, that is, an asymmetrical grant in which the giver in an act of pure kindness was under no obligation to make the gift and extracts no cost or condition from the recipient. Both words stem from a parent term, *charis*, grace: *charidzomai*, I act graciously; and *charisma*, the outcome of such an action.

So it seems naturally warranted to blend the English suffix for concrete miniaturization with the splendorous New Testament concept of grace, hence *gracelet*. A *gracelet*, then, is a droplet of divine grace, a tiny and often temporary manifestation of God's unmerited favor given to an individual believer mostly for the benefit of others in the congregation. Such droplets are mediated by the Holy Spirit, who inhabits the gathered people of God. Spiritual gifts, this author understands, shouldn't be viewed as permanent individual abilities: instead, individuals are *conduits* of molecules, you could say, of God's grace intended for the common good. A *charisma* is a miniature manifestation of divine grace.

A firm in Texas offers a line of hand-crafted jewelry with symbols reflecting divine grace: these special bracelets become *gracelets*.

In this book, Winn Griffin, long a student and teacher of Scripture, uses the term *gracelet* to spell out his views of what commonly have been called "spiritual gifts." Unsatisfied with notions of becoming a Christian that set out the process in two or three essential landmark waystations— history reveals some went beyond, to four or five marked stages in becoming a full-fledged Christian—the author stakes everything on God's gracious act in conversion, whatever the particulars, however varied the personal histories, whether instantaneous and disruptive (as Paul) or gradual and unspectacular (as Timothy).

Readers will be met with informative, engaging, and often entertaining, personal accounts of the author's experience over decades both as a student of Scripture and as a minister of the gospel. These incidents explain the course and the contours of his thinking as it developed over the years.

Here then comes a book with a fresh perspective on "spiritual gifts." In some details, the approach may not pass for orthodoxy within the classical Pentecostal circles. But highlighting the Lord's grace as the *source* and the neighbor's needs as the *destination* of charismatic practices can surely be welcomed widely and warmly.

Russell P. Spittler
Professor of New Testament, Emeritus
and Provost, Emeritus
Fuller Theological Seminary
Pasadena, California

Preface

➠ **Check Your GPS: Where We Are Going!**
- Where Are We Going?
- The Premise of This Book
- Thanks to Some Very Special Folks
- Hi, I'm Winn
- Question?
- Answer
- Using This Book

"The Holy Spirit is not the private property of Christians."
—Amy Plantinga Pauw

Where Are We Going?

We all know that in order to get to where you are going, you need a map of sorts, even if the destination is not on the map. When I was a kid, my mom and dad would take a family vacation every summer. Dad loved to drive. His idea of a vacation was to sleep in a different bed every night and get up in the morning and not have to worry about making up the bed. I think that I inherited the latter from my dad to the dismay of my wife. In addition, he thought that eating three meals a day in a different restaurant or café along the way was just superb. We usually went somewhere different each summer, a real road trip. He would spend weeks gathering up the maps he needed and sit in his favorite chair in the evenings after work and plot out how he was going to get to his destination. He had an internal compass. He seemed to instinctively know where he was and which way to go, but he still needed a map to help him achieve his much sought after two weeks away from the grind of his daily barber chair.

The book you are about to read provides a primer of sorts about the concept of gracelets. In each of the chapters, there is a small outline called "Check Your GPS" that offers a small overview of what is in the chapter about to be read. The following is a general map that will point you toward the destination. Let's see where it really takes us.

- The Spirit, whose gracelets we will be discussing, is described by many metaphors. In Chapter 1, we look at one of these metaphors: "wind." I use a small passage from the book of John (3.1-8) to introduce this concept.

- In Chapter 2, the concept of change is discussed. The church must know her story and to that end she must be invigorated during the cultural change in which she is living, learning to hold on to her story while changing her theater.

- Chapter 3 follows with a discussion of three different views of the so-called spiritual gifts. We look at the gracelets view, then the common view, and finally the ministry view.

- In Chapter 4, I build a foundation for understanding how "words" work in our language. Therein, we look at the four original words that are sometimes expressed by the translation "spiritual gifts." A word of caution: while this chapter is a bit more technical than others, it is imperative to interact with the concepts to think through the concept of using the word gracelets vs. spiritual gifts.

- Chapter 5 brings us to theologize (to reflect on theology) about the difference between the gift of the Spirit and the gifts of the Spirit. The gift of the Spirit is undisputed by today's Evangelical church. The church loosely believes that the Spirit is still ministering in today's world. What is held in contention is: do certain so-called gifts of the Spirit continue to be available to the Body of Christ or did they stop being available at some point in the past?

- In Chapter 6, we introduce the first of two important clues that are helpful in order for us to unlock a full grasp of the subject matter at hand. The first is the interpretative clue and the second, which follows in Chapter 12, is the hierarchical clue. Also, in Chapter 6, I share an important idea that any readers should be aware of before reading. In order to read the next chapters about the individual gracelets and the list of gracelets in 1 Corinthians, we provide an overview of 1 Corinthians and zero in on the interpretive clue and the need to understand the body metaphor that Paul provides.

- Chapter 7 begins our walk through the texts that mention possible gracelets. We address the concept of supernatural and meet the first gracelet that Paul shares.

- As we continue, Chapter 8 briefly works through the concept of diversity in unity and presents the first two gracelets in the first list in 1 Corinthians 12: an utterance of wisdom and an issuance of knowledge, differentiating between the common usage of the idea behind these two gracelets and the popular meaning attributed to them.

- Chapter 9 continues our voyage through the next three gracelets in the first list of 1 Corinthians 12. We set out the concepts of the gracelets of faith, the gracelets of healings, and the effects of miracles, suggesting that they are gracelets that the Spirit uses to facilitate his ongoing work in the restoration of the world.

- Chapter 10 turns to the final four gracelets that Paul presents in this first list in 1 Corinthians 12: prophecy, discernings of spirits, tongues, and interpretation of tongues. We close out this chapter with two other gracelets mentioned in a second list at the conclusion of 1 Corinthians 12.

- Chapter 11 discusses the list that Paul shares in Romans 12. We provide an overview of Romans to set up the list, which includes prophecy, service, teachers, exhortation, giving, aiding, and showing mercy.

- In Chapter 12, we share the second interpretative clue, hierarchy, and why that clue may help us understand the list that is found in Ephesians that are often called office gifts.

- In Chapter 13, we encounter our final list that is found in Ephesians 4, which concludes our study. We begin with an overview of Ephesians. Then, in Chapter 14, a discussion of apostles. Chapter 15 is concerned with the gracelet of prophets. Chapter 16 rounds out the list covering evangelists, and, finally, pastors and teachers. Because pastor may be the new tongues problem in many churches in this day and age, the chapter closes with a discussion of Psalm 23.

- The book ends with a wrap up chapter, three appendices, and a bibliography of books that are referenced in the footnotes.

That's a whirlwind tour of where you are going. I trust that you will find all this information helpful and encouraging as you participate as a conduit for the gracelets.

GRACELETS

The Premise of This Book

The church has its cycles about what it believes concerning what is sometimes called gifts of the Spirit. Since the time of the Reformation, the idea that all believers are priests has penetrated the *theology* of Protestantism. However, this idea has had a difficult time penetrating the *practice* of Protestantism. While we may believe that "everybody gets to play,"[1] we don't practice what we say we believe!

We tend to practice our theology only in crisis mode instead of practicing it daily as a continual process of growth and journeying as Eugene Peterson suggests in his book: *A Long Obedience in the Same Direction.*[2] We tend to be *reactive* instead of *active*! Thus, one group becomes involved in a certain practice and another group doesn't because it believes that its own theology condemns that very practice. This describes the ongoing dilemma around the so-called spiritual gifts, especially tongues, which has been a lightning rod over the years in this active-reactive portrait. No wonder followers of Jesus are often confused in their process of trying to understand and practice their theology about ministering with the empowerment of the Spirit.

The premise of this book is that our understanding of the ministry of the Spirit with so-called spiritual gifts is built on an English definition of the word "gift" rather than a concept built on the words used in the sacred text. There are three definitions in most dictionaries of which two are important. First, a gift is a "notable capacity, talent, or endowment." Second, gift is "something voluntarily transferred by one person to another without compensation."[3] This book rejects the first definition, which is employed by the great majority of books that are written about spiritual gifts. Rather I find biblical support for the second definition and work toward the presentation of a theological insight that suggests that the Spirit gives gracelets (to be explained anon) without compensation and they are given through an individual and received by another individual much like one gives a birthday gift and it is received by another.

---

1. This phrase was one of Vineyard Founder John Wimber's playful ways of saying to folks that the "priesthood of all believers," reframed by the Reformation, was a reality that every follower of Jesus could experience during her/his lifetime.

2. Eugene Peterson, *A Long Obedience in the Same Direction: Discipleship in an Instant Society* (Grand Rapids, MI: InterVarsity Press, 2000).

3. Webster, "Merriam-Webster Dictionary," Merriam-Webster, Inc. http://www.merriam-webster.com/dictionary/gift (accessed October 21, 2015).

Preface

The primary purpose then is to help the reader begin the process to re-language the concept often called spiritual gifts. Our English language is so impregnated with the present view of "gifts" or "spiritual gifts," it is an uphill battle to adopt a new story while continuing to use the words/concepts of an old story. When the old language is replaced, the new concepts can have an opportunity to find life.

In the present atmosphere of the church, there are at least two basic belief systems concerning so-called gifts. One system believes that only certain gifts are available today and those gifts can be discovered, developed, and deployed in one's life. This traditional view stems from a presupposition that gifts are "abilities" (following the first English definition). The second system says that all of the so-called gifts are still available today and that each believer has at least one. One or the other of these two systems of interpretation usually provides the boundaries for the books that present instruction about gifts of the Spirit, even though there are many variances of views within their boundaries.

It strikes me that both these views suffer from a wrongheaded systemic theology, which affects the outcome of their differing but to some degree the same point of view. What makes them different is that one system has determined that certain gifts are no longer available to the followers of Jesus while the other one disagrees and says all so-called gifts are available.

I think that there is a different way of thinking about gifts, which I will pursue in this book. To understand, to make this leap, this view will ask the reader to think about taking on a different language system and a different set of presuppositions.

Thanks to Some Very Special Folks

I would like to thank Dr. Russ Spittler who is the past Provost of Fuller Seminary in Pasadena, California, and Vanguard University in Costa Mesa, California, now retired, for his strong influence on my life and ministry of teaching. He has challenged me on more than one occasion to rethink my theological positions. He cautioned me often that the categories that I create were probably not the categories of the author who penned the material that I was studying. When I attended Southern California College (now Vanguard University), I took a course from Dr. Spittler on 1 Corinthians in the fall of 1969. As I remember, that was my first exposure to the concept of "gracelets" as a different way of thinking about spiritual gifts. He provided formation as well as information for this material. However, I must say that I am responsible for the final thoughts penned on these pages.

Years later after I graduated from Fuller, I returned in the Spring of 1982 to take a course on Spiritual Gifts from Dr. Spittler and Dr. Mel Robeck.[4] Wow, that sounds like a long time ago. I would also like to thank Dr. Mel Robeck for his interaction on this subject while I was a student at Fuller Seminary some three decades ago. He took time to help me think about the implications of this theme. On one occasion, while he was in the then Fuller Bookstore, I approached him and he paused in his search for books and chatted with me about a question that I posed to him. Both Dr. Spittler and Dr. Robeck have sought to bring some harmony into the lives and ministry of those whom they have taught.

I would be remiss if I didn't thank the late John Wimber who gave me an opportunity to write and reflect on this subject. In the early '80s, I was employed by John Wimber and one of my first research projects was on the concept of spiritual gifts. The material that was produced for Wimber was first taught in a small home group setting at Vineyard Anaheim and the original teaching document that I produced for that teaching was offered for sale in a booklet form along with a series of tapes. That material was reduced to a TV format to be seen on Trinity Broadcasting Network in Southern California in 1985.

I have labored with this material since that time clarifying it in places where I believed that Wimber had made up his mind prematurely, as with the "word of knowledge" concept that is still pervasive in the Vineyard[5] movement today. I have refined it, rewritten it with my own insights, and now present it for your learning and edification.

But, alas, now in the winter of my life, I offer this book that began all those years ago with taking courses and doing a research project. My hope is that in reading and reflecting on the contents that you would be enticed to become his conduit for his gracelets.

In addition, there are three other friends to mention: Dr. Steve Robbins, Ron Ford, and Dr. Don Williams, who have also helped in molding my thoughts and from whose material and conversations I have gleaned. Thanks to each of you!

To that list of folks, I must add the works of Dr. Gordon Fee and Dr. James D. G. Dunn who have been influential. Of course, as with any research project, I have used many other resources along the way that are reflected in the bibliography.

4. Russ Spittler and Mel Robeck. "Spiritual Gifts." Spring Quarter. 1982.
5. Association of Vineyard Churches. Stafford, TX 77497.

Preface

Let me confess at the beginning: there are many books and articles on the subject of the gifts of the Spirit. I googled the words "spiritual gifts" and received 882,000 hits.[6] At amazon.com there were 19,861 books listed. It would take a lifetime to interact with all those resources. So, at this writing, my bibliography has 164 books and articles referenced. They are selective. There are few things that I am certain about: one of them is that I don't know what everyone thinks or believes about the gifts of the Spirit. So, you will need to be aware that this is a limited view of a vast amount of resources. I have selected resources that have different views from my own, along with those that have similar views but not the exact one that I have come to hold. These books form my conversation partners for the material you are about to read. These mentors and teachers, while responsible for their own material, are not responsible for the final reflections that are presented in this book. Those conclusions are mine. Of course, their brows might furrow at such a reading of this subject; therefore, I take full responsibility for writing and believing this material.

Hi, I'm Winn

Now there's a statement that you don't often find at the beginning of a book! Why is this important? It is always good to know a bit about the writer you are reading. This knowledge often helps understand a point of view with which she/he is working. As an example, if you were reading in a book about someone's view of water baptism and knew that the person was a Southern Baptist, you would probably recognize that the person writing most likely would mean water baptism by immersion. If, however, you were reading a book by an Episcopalian, and she mentioned water baptism, you might understand that she may mean sprinkling and if you were a Southern Baptist, you might even have a problem that the Episcopalian lady had a right to even speak or write about such a thing, unless, of course, she was writing to children or other women. Of course, these are broad brush strokes and not necessarily true in every situation of language, but they do serve as an illustration. To know something about an author you are reading helps parse out some of the language. That's one of the purposes of small bios on the back of books, but those are usually written with marketing in mind and not necessarily to help the prospective reader to know the author any better.

So, I take this occasion to give you a whirlwind tour of information about me. Tongue in cheek, I tell folks that I have been in the

---

6. Searched google.com and amazon.com for "spiritual gifts" on September 17, 2015.

Pentecostal church (including the Charismatic, what would include the Third Wave and Empowered Evangelicals churches) since nine months before I was born and I am pretty sure that I was in church the Sunday after my conception. I grew up on the knees of two Pentecostal parents, one a bit more radical than the other. In my youth, I saw many revivalist preachers walk the aisles preaching and, on occasion, climb atop the pews and pulpit to shout out their message. On one memorable occasion, an almost sixty-year-old pastor jumped up on his pulpit, the stage was about ten to twelve feet above the floor on which the pews were located and the pulpit added another four feet or so. From that perched position, he took off his coat, rolled up his long sleeves, and began to whirl his coat in a circle around his head all the time balancing himself and shouting from the top of his lungs. It was great entertainment! My journey took me from a denomination that believed in three different works of the Spirit, saved, sanctified (wholly), and filled with the Holy Ghost and fire, to a denomination that only believed in two specific works of grace, saved and baptism in the Holy Spirit with the initial evidence of speaking in tongues to a group that believed that there was just one work of grace, becoming a follower of Jesus. It is in the latter theological position that I still stand or on this occasion sit, as I write this book.

While afflicted with dispensational theology and fundamentalism from birth forward, I have spent my life trying to get unshackled from the toxic prison of those theological beliefs. I have the scars to show for the journey and, on occasion, part of that luggage finds a moment of resuscitation in my life and I turn my attention to digging its grave once again.

So, I come to the theme of God's gracelets as we will call spiritual gifts from a non-dispensational/fundamentalist point of view. I don't believe that any of the gracelets mentioned in the Bible have ceased in their existence and that there may be more of them than God has seen fit to tell us about in our sacred text. I do not believe that we "have," in the sense of possessing, a gracelet or a cluster of gracelets that are ours, but believe that the gracelets are *ad hoc* drops of God's grace given through us and to us as we live out our call to be the new humanity of God for the sake of his creation. He gives gracelets *through* us for his fame and for the benefit of others.

I believe that every follower of Jesus is a candidate to be used as a conduit or vessel for God to present his gracelets to his creation. I also believe that God is not limited to just flowing his gracelets through followers of Jesus. They are, after all, his to distribute as he wills.

Preface

My years of education have broadened my imagination while sharpening my beliefs about this theme in the Story of God. Herein, I share some of my theological journey for you to think about and consider and maybe, just maybe, you can be spared some of the abuse that attends the subject of spiritual gifts. To that end, I write this book.

Winn Griffin
Woodinville, WA
October 2015

Question?

Questions and Answers is one way of learning new information that gives us new journeys to take in our ongoing transformation process. One of the books that I read as I continued to study this subject matter began with the following sentence, "Another book on Spiritual Gifts?" What can be said that hasn't already been said many times?[7] Let me offer an answer to that question.

I met Barry one day when he walked into a church where I was functioning as a pastor. In our ensuing conversation, I discovered that he was a bus driver. He was anxious to tell me that he was a Christian and that he had been "saved" in a Bible study that a group of bus drivers held once a week. He wanted to know right away if I believed in the rapture of the church. I suggested that we set up a time to have coffee and we could discuss his question and if he had any more questions to bring, he could feel free to ask them. I assured him that I wasn't a "Bible answer man," but that I would take a stab at answering his questions. We agreed on a time and place.

When the day arrived and we were sitting in a local café (there was no Starbucks in those days in my neck of the woods or anyone's neck of the woods for that matter; wow, does that date me), as we were talking, I asked him if he was married and did he have any children. He told me that he had been married for several years, had no kids, but it looked to him like he was going to face a divorce because of his new found faith.

Barry's eyes moistened as he said, "she tells me that she wants the man she married back, not the man I have become since I met Jesus."

That was an intriguing response. I asked him if I could begin to pray with him about that issue, he responded, "yes."

He had shared something very intimate about his life situation right off the bat. I didn't want to press him so the talk turned to his questions that he had brought to this meeting. He had asked me the previous Sunday in the foyer of the church building, "Do you believe in the rapture of the church?" I repeated his question

---

7. Kenneth Berding, *What Are Spiritual Gifts? Rethinking the Conventional View* (Grand Rapids, MI: Kregel Publications, 2006), 7.

and then asked, "I assume that you believe in the rapture of the church and if so, how did you come to hold that belief and why is it important to you?"

He looked at me a bit puzzled being asked a question instead of my answering his. He thought for a few moments and said, "I was saved a little over a year ago in a Bible study at work. As I entered the study with my newfound friends, they were studying the 'rapture of the church.' The study was presented very simply: the study leader would read a couple of verses from the Bible and then make some comments, and then he asked others to share and provide any thoughts they had about the passage that had been read. We have spent the better part of this year studying that theme. It has become very important because it is a way that I can enter into conversations with others as I try to reach them for Jesus."

So what I was hearing was that this lad had been given a steady diet of rapture teaching for the purpose of doing better evangelism.

That day we began an ongoing conversation with Barry that lasted for months. During those months, I simply sidestepped his theological advances with light probing questions about why he believed what he believed without challenging what he believed. He had all the dispensational theology stuff down. That theological position had been drilled into his head for a whole year and was the only voice that he had heard. As our weekly conversations continued, he finally revealed that he had a fear that if he changed his beliefs that God would be angry and condemn him to an eternity in hell.

Over the months, I met with him at the café and at his home where I had the privilege of meeting his wife. She confirmed in a conversation that he had changed from the man she had married to a man who preached a certain kind of religion that condemned her for her lifestyle, always with the message that if she didn't change, she would be "left behind" when Jesus came and would be doomed to hell.

She admitted that since we met several months before, he was gradually changing into a different more gentle and kinder man and admitted to me that whatever was going on in our conversations was saving their marriage. She still longed for the original Barry while sharing that she despised the second version, i.e., the I'm saved and you need to think the way I do in order to get saved or suffer hell as the consequences of your rejection. She opined that she was becoming at peace with becoming more like the last version of Barry, the one he was becoming.

Answer

I'm making the assumption that most of you reading this book did not expect a story as the answer to the stated question above. But, stories are great for conveying answers to sometimes complex questions. Many of you who venture to read this book about gracelets have already formed a deep seated belief system about spiritual gifts, not unlike Barry had done about the rapture of the church. While there are some varieties in the story about the so-called spiritual gifts that you have chosen to follow, there is most likely one central belief that is basic to your general and specific belief about this subject from the books that you have collected and read, the sermons you have heard, the seminars or conferences that you have attended that possibly formed your beliefs. I will share more about that in the pages anon.

What you will read in the following pages will sometimes, maybe even most times, run counter to your long held beliefs. You may even experience some feelings of not being loyal to the Bible as you read. I know the feeling; I've been there before you. Actually, I'm there often. However, my hope is that you would suspend your judgment (often called a "suspension of disbelief") and read the whole book before drawing your final conclusions. And even then, pause and ask the Trinity if there is anything of value that you should think about and eventually do something about in your journey of transformation.

Paul implores his readers to think differently in the new world that has been inaugurated by Jesus, to think differently as a newly being-formed-human in this new world. So as you read here, begin to think about grace and God's gracelets differently.

I must hasten to say that the study of Scripture is not for accumulation of knowledge but for playing your part in ministry in the great Story of God. However, the Holy Spirit should be the final word for how you live into God's Story. Listen to what he may be saying to you personally while you are studying. Allow yourself for the moments that you are reading to read with fresh eyes and to think about this subject with a fresh mind. Remember this easy rule of thumb: one meaning, many different ways that one meaning may be lived out in the life of your community of faith and in your life. The biblical text provides a firm footing on which you walk out being a Jesus follower.

Preface

Using This Book

This book about gracelets will cover the concept and passages on what has been traditionally called spiritual gifts in the Second Testament. It will hopefully make reading and studying Scripture easier and more fun. I propose that you will be able to read and be introduced or challenged about the subject of gracelets in just a few short hours. In order to get the most from your reading of this book, it is important that you read the biblical text along with it. It would be tragic if this book was substituted for reading the sacred text. *The New International Version* (2011 version) is the English text on which the studies are built, unless otherwise identified.

In addition to personal reading and study, you might want to try some of the following ways of using this book. You may use it in gatherings such as:

- New Jesus Follower's Class
- Bible Study (Home or Elsewhere)
- Mid-Week Study Classes (if that is in your tradition)
- New Members Class
- Retreats
- Youth Groups
- Sunday Evening Service Study (if that is in your tradition)
- Sermon and Teaching Preparation

You may use it outside of the traditional institutionalized church in any creative way in which you see fit for personal edification or meeting with friends. Your imagination is the limit. Surely, there are other creative ways that you can use this study to gain a working knowledge of the subject matter at hand. Go ahead, be creative!

∽

It is fair to reflect that Scripture is firm about the notion that one can't advance the kingdom or build the kingdom; one can only be birthed into the kingdom.

GRACELETS

Chapter 1: Facing the Wind

➠ **Check Your GPS: Where We Are Going!**
- The Spirit Blows Where He Pleases
- The Background of John 3.1-8
- The Teaching of John 3.1-8
- So What?

The Spirit Blows Where He Pleases

There are volumes of books about the Holy Spirit.[1] In Scripture, Luke who is known for being a historian is also known as the Theologian of the Holy Spirit.[2] But we turn to John to catch a glimpse of the work of the Holy Spirit and how he may be at work with the so-called gifts of the Spirit.

I was first going to name this book *Chasing the Wind* because in my own early church background, and to some degree my ongoing church background, is where church folks were and are often found chasing after the latest move of the Spirit. Often when asked what these folks were doing, I would say, "They are looking for the spout where the glory is coming out," with a kind of wry grin on my face. It is true that the Spirit blows where he pleases. But, instead of eternally chasing an experience of the Spirit, we need to allow ourselves to turn into and face the Wind. God is moving all the time. He is not static. He does not just work when a group of people have gathered in a building to sing a few songs and hear someone speak. He is not to be identified with one of the latest fads, as of this writing, called "Strange Fire," which is a strange book by John MacArthur, which author Craig Keener suggests "that MacArthur suppresses some biblical truth on the basis of a postbiblical doctrine, the very offense with which he charges others.[3]"

1. There were 16,902 books/products listed on amazon.com with the two words Holy Spirit in the title as of June 20, 2015. On google on the same date, there were 39,000,000 entries found for the exact search of Holy Spirit.

2. Ben Witherington, *The Indelible Image: The Theological and Ethical Thought World of the New Testament (Volume 2)* (Downers Grove, IL: InterVarsity, 2010), 278.

3. Craig S. Keener, "John Macarthur's Strange Fire, Reviewed by Craig S. Keener," The Pneuma Review http://pneumareview.com/john-macarthurs-strange-fire-

The Spirit is dynamic. The Wind "blowing where he pleases" is a metaphor to help us grasp his dynamism.

It may seem curious that I suggest that we face the wind. That just seems counter intuitive. So, why face the wind? One illustration is the takeoff position of an airplane. Pilots like to take off into a headwind because it helps them achieve wheels-up faster as they yield to the physics of flight.[4] Another illustration of why this is important is to look at the behavior of seagulls. Seagulls, like most birds, stand towards the wind (otherwise, a gust could blow their feathers up and tip them over). It appears that even nature knows the value of facing the wind. One benefit for Jesus followers could be that facing the wind provides them with balance while being blown away by "every wind of teaching," which provides imbalance. It just may be that God can flow through you with his gracelets when you are facing the wind instead of the instability that comes when you are being blown by the wind from behind or chasing after the wind as it blows.

Here is a small devotional to begin our study about *facing the wind* from the Gospel of John.

The Background of John 3.1-8

The story in John 3.1-8 reads as follows:

Now there was a Pharisee, a man named Nicodemus who was a member of the Jewish ruling council. He came to Jesus at night and said, "Rabbi, we know that you are a teacher who has come from God. For no one could perform the signs you are doing if God were not with him."

Jesus replied, "Very truly I tell you, no one can see the kingdom of God unless they are born again."

"How can someone be born when they are old?" Nicodemus asked. "Surely they cannot enter a second time into their mother's womb to be born!"

---

reviewed-by-craig-s-keener/ (accessed November 2, 2015).

4. Condé Nast Traveler, "Explainer: Why Do Airplanes Take Off into the Wind?," Condé Nast Traveler http://www.cntraveler.com/daily-traveler/2012/06/airplane-flying-wind-storm (accessed September 21, 2013).

Chapter 1

Jesus answered, "Very truly I tell you, no one can enter the kingdom of God unless they are born of water and the Spirit. Flesh gives birth to flesh, but the Spirit gives birth to spirit. You should not be surprised at my saying, 'You must be born again.' The wind blows wherever it pleases. You hear its sound, but you cannot tell where it comes from or where it is going. So it is with everyone born of the Spirit" (John 3.1-8).

Having a bit of background is always better than having no background when reading the text of Scripture. While this section may seem a bit technical, it is necessary to understand and get a better grasp on the meaning of the text, which is offered in the next section only eight paragraphs away. So hang in there.

The passage above is the first part of three sections in John 3.1-21. In this brief story, there are two characters, Jesus and Nicodemus, who are chatting about who Jesus is. The scene feels warm, just like when two friends might sit around in Starbucks after a day's work and just chat about different subjects. The name Nicodemus was Greek and was not normal among the Jews in the timeframe of this story. He is only mentioned in the Second Testament five times and all in John's Gospel (John 3.1, 4, 9; 7.50; 19.39, these are presumably the same person). He was a member of the Sanhedrin, which was the highest governing body of the Jewish people and made up of Sadducees (priests), Pharisees (scribes), and others of the ruling nobility of Judaism of the day.

The text suggests that he came to Jesus at night. More than likely, *night* is a metaphor for evil in John's Gospel.[5] While it may well have been during the evening that the two met, its message is missed, if a reader only sees in this report the absence of sunlight. John's *light and darkness* comparisons should not be lost by the reader in favor of seeing Nicodemus as some kind of coward fearfully sneaking around after dark so as not to be seen by others when he visited Jesus.[6]

In the conversation when Jesus says, "...no one can see the kingdom of God...," the word *see* probably carries the meaning of *to experience, encounter, or participate in* and is repeated differently just a few words later with "...no one can enter the kingdom of God..." where *enter* is to be understood as its parallel in a brief form of parallelism, which is

---

5. Leon Morris, *The Gospel According to John* (Grand Rapids, MI: William B. Eerdmans Publishing Co., 1971), 211.

6. Daniel Burke, "Nicodemus, the Mystery Man of Holy Week," RNS (Religious News Service) http://www.religionnews.com/2013/03/27/nicodemus-the-mystery-man-of-holy-week/ (accessed August 2, 2013).

19

a Jewish form of poetry where the second line in a poem says the same thing as the first line but uses different words. To get a feel for this kind of Jewish poetry, think about the Psalm that begins:

Bless the Lord, O my soul
and all that is within me, bless his holy name (KJV).

The second line of this Psalm 103 says the same thing as the first line does using different words to express the same thought. For the Hebrew, the *soul* was the whole of the individual not some part of an individual, which is a form of Greek dualism that has slipped into the mindset of the Western world through Plato and has lodged firmly in the church. The Psalmist was simply saying that the whole person should bless God.

This kingdom saying in John is the same kind of thing; the second line about "entering" is saying the same thing as the first line, which says "seeing." The phrase kingdom of God is only used two times in the Gospel of John (3.3, 5), which are both in this passage. John wants his readers to know that folks entered the kingdom (rule) by birth. It is fair to reflect that Scripture is firm about the notion that one can't advance the kingdom or build the kingdom;[7] one can only be birthed into the kingdom.

A bit of grammar is needed here. Sounds like an English course, huh? In the text, the phrase *water and spirit* has no article and only one preposition and it can be translated *spiritual water,* where *water* is a metaphor for *seed,* thus a rendering of the text as *spiritual seed* would be appropriate.[8] Seed could be thought of as a euphemism for sperm-bearing semen. The meaning, then, of "born again of water and seed" could be as what my friend Dr. Ed Cook calls a "divine pregnancy." As we enter the kingdom, God gets us pregnant with his Spirit and we become a work of "new humanity," gestating into the new creation that we are constantly becoming, having been "born from above."[9]

The word *wind* in the translation can mean *wind* or *spirit* in Greek and Hebrew. It appears that here John is using a clever play on both meanings, a double entendre, if you please, but a play on both meanings

---

7. Darrell L. Guder (Editor), *Missional Church: A Vision for the Sending of the Church in North America (The Gospel and Our Culture Series)* (Grand Rapids, MI: Wm. B. Eerdmans Publishing Co, 1998), 92.

8. Morris, *The Gospel According to John,* 215-216.

9. From a conversation with Dr. Ed Cook via email: November 2, 2015.

Chapter 1

that cannot be easily translated into English. The word *sound* is literally *voice* and is part of the extended double entente, the *voice* of the wind, i.e., the *voice* of the Spirit.[10]

The Teaching of John 3.1-8

It is not quite clear in the text what the purpose of Nicodemus was when he came to Jesus. There are many suggestions, one of which was that he was the spokesperson for the Jewish ruling council. This may or may not be the case. He is introduced and when he speaks, he announces that Jesus is a "teacher sent from God." However, Jesus did not come from God in the sense that Nicodemus was portraying, i.e., one who was performing signs among them. By the end of the extended passage (3.16), we discover that Jesus came from God to provide the eschatological life for which the Jews had been waiting.

In the conversation with Nicodemus recorded by John, Jesus says, "The wind blows where it pleases." This story is set at night, a useful metaphor, as we said above, used by John to remind his readers of the evils at work in the world. It is often thought that Nicodemus came at night because of fear. But at the conclusion of the book of John, we are told that Judas left the light and went out into the night. So, in this first story, John suggests that Nicodemus came from the darkness into the light, which may be the story arc of John about light and darkness.

The most remembered phrase in this story is "you must be born again" (v. 7). While most modern translations translate it as such, it could and probably should be translated as "you must be born from above," realizing that the word "you" in this passage is plural, referring to more than just Nicodemus. In the parallelism of the passage, Jesus says two things about the kingdom of God, "no one can *see* the kingdom of God without being born from above," and "no one can *enter* the kingdom of God without being born of water and the Spirit." In these two parallel sayings, Jesus says the same thing. Without being *born from above*, or of *spiritual seed*, you cannot participate in the kingdom (rule) of God. The two words "water and spirit" may be translated "spiritual seed" a term that Nicodemus as a Pharisee and a teacher himself (v. 10) would have recognized. Being born "from above" and being born of "spiritual seed" is saying the same thing. After telling Nicodemus that he shouldn't be surprised by such

10. Raymond Edward Brown, *The Gospel According to John*, [1st ed., 2 vols., vol. I-XII (Garden City, NY: Doubleday, 1966)., 128-141. Leon Morris, *The Gospel According to John* (Grand Rapids, MI: Eerdmans Publishing Company, 1971), 208-220.

21

rhetoric, he says, "The wind blows wherever it pleases. You hear its sound, but you cannot tell where it comes from or where it is going. So it is with everyone born of the Spirit." So, to be born from above, is to be born of the Spirit.

So What?

The wind blows where it wills provides a clue as to how the Spirit operates. That idea could provide a possible "how to" moment of how to repackage the idea of spiritual gifts as momentary drops of God's grace given through or passing through an individual to another, rather than thinking about a gift of the spirit being possessed or permanently residing in an individual, i.e., I have the gift of faith. It could reasonably follow that the spirit decides through whom his gracelets flow and to whom they will be delivered. Our job: to be a conduit.

One might say that those born of the Spirit might wish to turn facing the Wind during this time of cultural change. So, when you sense that small breeze blowing against your cheeks, know that in facing the Wind, you can breathe in his presence allowing him to blow through you with his bountiful gracelets as he directs them to others for their, as well as your, benefit.

The rest of this book is about how this might possibly work out in the life of your community and in your personal life.

∽

Chapter 2: Times They Are a Changing...

Where We Have Been

In the previous chapter, we reviewed the idea of the Spirit doing what he pleases and glanced at the background and teaching of John 3. We suggested that a good posture for us is to "face the wind" to gain maximium benefit for being God's conduits of grace.

The Chill of Change

Bob Dylan wrote a song that was released in February 1964 about how the times were changing. Sometimes songsters prophesy. In USAmerica and around the world, one can feel the chill of change almost on a daily basis. Some date the beginning of the postmodern period, in which we may presently be living, as having its beginning in the mid-1960s. Knowing where one is on the cultural map is helpful in understanding any subject that you approach.

Why is that important? Understanding culture and the shifts in culture may help us interact with what is happening around us. When one looks at the culture today, it is obvious that things are different than they were ten years ago and surely different than they were twenty-five or fifty years ago. In the year of my birth, a mere seventy-two years ago as of this writing, a new car was $1,100, a house costs $6,950, a loaf of bread costs nine cents, milk was sixty cents a gallon, you could send a letter for three cents, minimum wage was thirty cents an hour, and the annual average salary was $2,400. Yep! Things have changed.

Because modernity was created out of the bowels of the Enlightenment Project, truth claims are at risk. *What is truth* is the buzz in conversations with those who think of themselves as postmodern.

Questions abound like: Is truth absolute? Can we know the absolute truth? Ask the different generations that form the divide of modernity and postmodernity and you will surely come up with several different answers. Truth has been shifting from scientific proof to experiential proof in the last fifty or so years. In the church realm, the Pentecostal varieties of the church have lived with this "experience notion" of faith for much longer than that period.

In history, it seems that every few hundred years the church emerges in some fashion. It transforms. The present church is not your father's Oldsmobile! The late Stan Grenz said:

> Many social observers agree that the Western world is in the midst of change. In fact, we are apparently experiencing a cultural shift that rivals the invitations that marked the birth of modernity out of the decay of the Middle Ages: We are in the midst of a transition from the modern to the postmodern era.[1]

Culture is measured by change. Surely one doesn't have to look far to discover the difference between the Bronze Age (ca. 3500-1100 BC) and the Enlightenment Period of the last 500 years or so and its movement called Modernity. The Modern Era has as its foundation an emphasis of scientific proof. Everything can be known by reducing it down to a scientific provability. In addition, this period elevated the importance of the individual over family/community that has led to a consumerist era with the focus on the individual and what the individual can receive from an encounter.

The Western Culture has had several major cultural changes since the Christ-Event[2] of the first century. The Romans Period, which ended approximately AD 600, saw a world dominated by Roman power and Greek culture. In the Middle Ages (AD 600-1500), the Western Roman Empire crumbled and no dominant power took its place. This period lasted into the period of the Renaissance. The transition into the Modern Age from the Medieval included economic expansion, political centralization, and secularization.[3] Next, came the Enlightenment/Modern Period and the usual dates given are

1. Stanley J. Grenz, *A Primer on Postmodernism* (Grand Rapids, MI: William B. Eerdmans Pub. Co., 1996), 2.

2. This is a term used by theologians to speak of the complete story of Jesus during his earthly life as seen in his Birth, Life, Death, Resurrection, and Ascension.

3. infoplease, "Middle Ages: Transition to the Modern World," infoplease http://www.infoplease.com/encyclopedia/history/middle-ages-transition-to-modern-world.html (accessed November 11, 2015).

Chapter 2

AD 1500-2000. This period was a shift that saw the influence of philosophers/theologians and is usually thought to be summarized by Descartes in his statement "I think, therefore I am" that suggested the rise of the autonomous self. The postmodern era is usually slated as having its start in the late 1960s of the twentieth century and has seen a shift away from the autonomous individual to the concept of community relationship. However, it is fair to say that a newer brand of individualism has arrived during this period in seeking community. Community is often the place where individuals show off their individualism. Truth has taken on a new way of being thought about; it has moved from certainty to relativism.[4]

I think Dylan was correct. Times have and continue to change. Maybe a part of that change is to move on from the standard concepts of the so-called spiritual gifts to a different way of thinking. That's part of the purpose of this book, to present a different way of thinking about this subject matter that influences all those who are Jesus followers.

Times Have Changed

My dad was born in 1893 on a small farm in Southern Georgia. It was the year of the World's Fair in Chicago in May. It was the year of Gandhi's first act of civil disobedience in June. It was the year Jimmy Durante (February 10) and Mae West (August 17) were born. The actress-comedienne Georgiana Drew Barrymore, mother of Ethel, Lionel, and John Barrymore, died (July 2). It was the year that Thomas Edison finished the first motion picture studio in West Orange, New Jersey, and received two patents; one of which was for a cut out for incandescent electric lamps. It was the end of the Presidency of Benjamin Harrison and the beginning of the Presidency of Grover Cleveland. It was a year of legal triumph; The United States Supreme Court legally declared the tomato to be a vegetable. Go figure!

My dad would be ten years old before the Ford Motor company was launched in 1903. In his early years, he only knew the horse and buggy. We had chats when I was a young lad about all the change that he had experienced in his lifetime. He lived into his '70s and close to the end of his life flew on a jet from Orlando, Florida, to Chicago, Illinois. It was an amazing trip for him, so much so that he wanted to stay on the plane and go to its next stop. He witnessed along with thousands of others the first man on the moon. Of course, it is only fair to say that

4. Relativism is a theory, especially in ethics, which believes that conceptions of truth and moral values are not absolute. Rather, values are *relative* to the persons or groups holding them.

he did not believe that it really happened but that it was concocted by Hollywood. His thought pattern was sort of a prequel to Capricorn One (1978) about a Mars landing hoax. During his lifetime, things changed radically. Shift happens!

One thing is for sure, dad didn't go to bed one night and rise the next morning and the world around him had completely changed. Rather, it emerged. Emerging is natural. It occurs all the time. Since you began reading this page, you have emerged to something different than you were when you began reading this page. While change is a common occurrence, when addressed, it is often viewed with some suspicion. We are a paradox. We like for things to stay the same while all around us things are changing, emerging.

This is certainly true of the church. The church today in the twenty-first century is different than the one in the first century. It seems strange that in today's church, there seem to be movements that want to carry us back to the first-century church as if that was a "holy" model for doing church. The truth be known, there was not one model of church in the first century for the twenty-first century or any other century, for that matter, to imitate.[5] Just read Acts where that picture is clear. We have a fascination with returning back in time, as one could note for the movie industry and their ongoing plots and characters from the past being renovated on today's screen. One wonders why we don't focus on where we may be going rather than where we have been. Of course, that happens in literature and the big screen as well. I'm not saying that where we have come from is unimportant, it surely informs us. In the study of Scripture, it is incredibly important. But, it seems reasonable that the past as it was is not the goal, not even with God. Humankind started in the Garden but the story is ever moving forward to a New Garden, a New Jerusalem.

So What?

So what, I can possibly hear you saying. What does all this have to do with so-called spiritual gifts or, what you will soon discover, we are calling gracelets? Glad you asked. In the emerging culture, while there are only a few books being written about the theology of the Spirit's participation in the church, there are many books that are written about how an individual experiences the Spirit in the church or in most cases

---

5. My friend Dr. Ed Cook shared with me that at the beginning of a course he took at Fuller offered by the late Dr. Ray Anderson that Andersons said: "God lost all interest in the first-century church on the first day of the second century." That rather nicely sums it up.

in special meetings or conferences held by a parachurch organization. Living in a postmodern world where the experience of an individual is paramount, it is no wonder that this subject captivates publishers. It seems to be the new interest. Of course, most of the church is just catching up with the Pentecostal part of the family who has had their eye on experience for more than a century now. There are all kinds of renewed emphases. There is a renewed emphasis on the Trinity, as well there should be. There is a renewed interest on the life and times of Jesus with authors like Tom Wright. There is a renewed interest on the theology of the kingdom of God. There is renewed interest on Paul as seen in the "New Perspective on Paul." While there is an abundance of interest in the Pentecostal/Charismatic/Third Wave churches in the experience of the Spirit, there is less interest about a theology of the ministry and work of the Spirit in the church. Why is that? The old saying, the squeaky wheel gets the oil, is prominent here. There is simply more interest in experiencing the Spirit than in a theology of the Spirit. One wonders why experience and theology aren't on the same playing field together instead of pitted against one another. One possible reason: we are given to reflecting in a Greek dualistic way of thinking. Instead of looking for harmony between experience and theology, where both are needed to have a well-rounded "new humanity" lifestyle, we separate them and pick a winner. When you think of the Spirit, which do you think of first, theology, experience, or a harmony of theology and experience? For the church to be invigorated during the cultural change in which she is living, she must learn to hold on to her story while changing her theater. The church has a Story that is presented in her sacred text. It was played out in the cultural theater of the First and Second Testaments. The theater of the church, as we read about it in the Second Testament, was lived out from the birth of Jesus till about AD 100. That culture was a different time. The church now lives in a culture that is even different from just fifty years ago. The story is the same, but the theater is now a multiplex.

So, what does all this have to do with gracelets? We have come through a time in recent culture in which the teaching about gracelets has been heavily influenced by Modernity and its scientific certainty. We have been taught that the so-called gifts have specific definitions (usually created without any association with the specific biblical context in which their names appear) and that you can discover, develop, and deploy these gifts as you will. They are seen as special abilities, thought to be owned by modernity's autonomous individual and with scientific certainty. These so-called spiritual gifts can be personally improved upon in their usage. Contrary to that opinion, and in my opinion, a better view is that of Amy Plantinga Pauw who suggests, "The Holy Spirit is not the private property of Christians."[6]

All this seems to miss the text in John that suggests that the Spirit will blow where he wills, when he wills, and on whom he wills. We are not directors of our own gifts, most likely because we don't own them. We are responders to the wind of the Spirit. The church in the emerging culture is perfectly positioned to be able to respond to a more biblical view of the gracelets of the Spirit. So, to this end, we write this book with hopes that everyone can turn in this postmodern culture and face the Wind and allow the gracelets of God to provide a liftoff, to flow to them and through them for the sake of the world around them.

∽

6. Dr. Pauw, a professor at Louisville Seminary, made this statement while presenting a paper at the Society of Vineyard Scholars, April 2014, held in Columbus, OH.

GRACELETS

Chapter 3: Three Views of the So-Called Spiritual Gifts

Check Your GPS: Where We Are Going!
- Where We Have Been
- Introduction
- The Gracelets View
- The Common View
- The Ministry View
- Balance or Harmony
- So What?

Where We Have Been

In the previous chapter, we made reference to how times change and with that comes other changes. Because we have come through Modernity which heavily influenced our view of the so-called spiritual gifts, it is time to take a fresh look at another view that we will offer in this chapter after reviewing the two basic views that have dominated thinking and praxis of gifts of the Spirit.

Introduction

Over the years, a high percentage of books on what is commonly called spiritual gifts have been written from a theological position called cessation (some gifts ended at the end of the first century or when all the books of the Bible were accepted by the church). Other books have been written from a theological position called continuation (all gifts continue into the present era). Many of these books were written from a popular position often from the experience of the author or the experience of others who wrote before them. Some were written with and some without any scholarship to back up the claims of the authors on their pages.

The primary position of these books is that "gifts are given to every follower of Jesus and each follower possesses the gift and it is her or his job to discover, develop, and deploy that gift or cluster of gifts."

Many scholars have written on the subject, but far too little of what they have had to say has filtered into the pew. My friend-at-a-distance and early mentor, Dr. Russ Spittler, once told me that his interest in training at the seminary level was to get scholarship into the pew. Since that conversation, I have spent many years trying to do just that. This present book is an attempt to view the subject of the so-called spiritual gifts and present a different way of looking at this theme in Scripture. Hopefully, present-day followers of Jesus can be released from the views of their past about this subject and find more freedom in the ministry in which they participate.

About thirty years ago when the Vineyard movement was just beginning to crawl its way into public awareness, John Wimber, its pronounced leader,[1] provided folks from all kinds of denominational churches a way to participate with the Spirit without all the hype that usually attended a Pentecostal or charismatic star in a church, an auditorium, or a group of stars sitting on a TV set sharing about their experiences. For Wimber, some of their theology and some of their practices were a problem. My hope is that the material in this book would make every Jesus follower who reads it, understand that the Spirit is not about hype. He has no favorites in the ministry. He is interested in delivering his gracelets to intended receivers through those who simply say, "yes, I can deliver that gracelet." I want followers of Jesus to comprehend that there are no superstars, not even any stars in the body of Christ.

There are at least three views on how individuals and gifts are viewed. They are: the Gracelets View, the Common View, and the Ministry View. The second of these views, i.e., the Common View, dominates the so-called spiritual gifts topic in books, sermons, seminars, and conferences. Let me begin with the Gracelets View that I am endeavoring to work out in this book.

The Gracelets View

The Gracelets View will give you a beginning overview of the idea of gracelets as a substitute word for spiritual gifts. My own research in this area was sparked by two individuals. The first is a way of thinking about the words *spiritual gifts* that I learned from Dr. Russ Spittler with the use of the word *gracelet* and his discussion of the "gifts of healings." This view will be further developed in the chapters below. But, quickly, the Greek word translated "spiritual gifts" comes from the root word for "grace" in the original language. So a gracelet is like a small drop of grace

---

1. The beginning of the Vineyard movement and its name came into existence through Kenn Gulliksen in 1975. John Wimber entered the Vineyard at the request of Gulliksen in the early 1980s. The official recognition of the movement occurred in 1982.

given by God through his children to others. A second line of reasoning comes from Dr. James D. G. Dunn in his book *Jesus and the Spirit* where he wrote about prophecy and suggests that prophecy is not a skill or aptitude or talent. It is the actual speaking forth of words given by the Spirit in a particular situation and ceases when the words cease.[2] The idea that prophecy seemed to flow through a person to another and that gracelets were "drops of God's" grace given to his people allowed me to think about the so-called gifts in a different paradigm. In this thinking process, the word "conduit" came to be the "water bucket" to carry the idea that gracelets are given through us to others and the others are the ones that receive the gracelet. I will flesh this idea out below as it relates to how God provides gracelets to his people.

The Common View

The common view suggests that the commonly called spiritual gifts are special abilities that are given by God to every Jesus follower. This is at least as old as J. V. McGarvey who wrote, "…by those in possession of spiritual gifts," in his book *A Commentary on Acts of Apostles* that was published in 1863.[3]

In this view, folks are urged to discover their spiritual gift through a spiritual gifts inventory. This spiritual gifts inventory idea may have been invented in 1976 by Dr. Richard F. Houts, who was a professor in the North American Baptist Theological Seminary and the inventory was later modified by Dr. C. Peter Wagner.[4] This same idea was published in a book entitled *Discovering Your Spiritual Gifts: A Personal Inventory Method* by Kenneth Cain Kinghorn in which he says that spiritual gifts are "special abilities."[5] Dr. Kinghorn wrote an earlier book on this subject

2. James D. G. Dunn, *Jesus and the Spirit: A Study of the Religious and Charismatic Experience of Jesus and the First Christians as Reflected in the New Testament* (Grand Rapids, MI: W.B. Eerdmans Publishing Company, 1997), 229.

3. J. V. McGarvey, "A Commentary on Acts of Apostles," StudyLight.com http://www.studylight.org/com/oca/view.cgi?bk=43&ch=3 (accessed September 28, 2013). The quote in his commentary is in his comments in Acts 3.16. Others who have pressed this view were Henry Eyster Jacobs edited version of *The Lutheran Commentary: A Plain Exposition of the Holy Scriptures* (Volume VIII, 1897: 82, 107); and *The Epistles of St. Paul with Introductions and Commentary for Priests and Students, Volume I: Romans, First and Second Corinthians, Galatians* (1922: 384).

4. Charles E. Fuller Institute of Evangelism and Church Growth, "Wagner-Modified Houts Questionnaire," Charles E. Fuller Institute of Evangelism and Church Growth http://exchristian.net/images//wagner_modified_houts.pdf (accessed September 28, 2013).

5. Kenneth Cain Kinghorn, *Discovering Your Spiritual Gifts: A Personal Inventory Method* (Grand Rapids, MI: Zondervan, 1981), 7.

entitled: *Gifts of the Spirit* that was published at the beginning of 1976 by Abington Press, where he writes: "Technically though, a spiritual gift refers to a supernatural[6] enabling of the Holy Spirit, which equips a Christian for his work of service and ministry."[7]

The pollster George Barna falls into this camp. His survey of 2001 called "Awareness of Spiritual Gifts Is Changing" reports:

> There has been a substantial deterioration regarding people's understanding of spiritual gifts, with a five-fold increase in born again adults who are aware of gifts saying God did not give them one, and half of all born again adults listing gifts they possess, which are not among the spiritual gifts listed in the Bible. Even one-quarter of all Protestant pastors listed one or more gifts that they possess, which are not identified in the Bible.[8]

Barna continues in that report to say, "Imagine what might happen if nearly half of all believers had a clear and firm conviction that God has given them a supernatural ability to serve Him in a specific manner."[9]

This idea of spiritual abilities is still current. As recent as 2009 in a Barna survey,[10] the report begins with "The Bible teaches that all followers of Christ are given supernatural abilities by God to serve Him better, known as spiritual gifts."

This way of thinking is in part of the title reflected in the words, "...the Spiritual Gifts That Christians Say They Have." The survey also pointed out what it called "False Gifts," which included a sense of humor, singing, health, life, happiness, patience, a job, a house, compromise, premonition, creativity, and clairvoyance. Go figure!

---

6. I will discuss the subject matter of supernatural below in Chapter 7.

7. Kenneth Cain Kinghorn, *Gifts of the Spirit* (Nashville, TN: Abingdon Press, 1976), 20.

8. George Barna, "The Year's Most Intriguing Findings, from Barna Research Studies," Barna Group https://www.barna.org/barna-update/5-barna-update/64-the-years-most-intriguing-findings-from-barna-research-studies#.UkjjIDaTh8E (accessed September 29, 2013).

9. George Barna, "Awareness of Spiritual Gifts Is Changing," Barna Group https://www.barna.org/barna-update/5-barna-update/32-awareness-of-spiritual-gifts-is-changing#.UkjneDaTh8E (accessed September 29, 2013).

10. George Barna, "Survey Describes the Spiritual Gifts That Christians Say They Have," Barna Group https://www.barna.org/barna-update/faith-spirituality/211-survey-describes-the-spiritual-gifts-that-christians-say-they-have#.UkjkXDaTh8E (accessed September 29, 2013).

Chapter 3

In a recent book by Robert Cornwall entitled *Unfettered Spirit*, he affirms the view that followers of Jesus are given gifts and have the freedom to choose how, when, and where we use them.[11] However, he has somewhat of a hybrid view of the operation of gifts when he talks about gifts being constitutional or occasional.[12] Even then, these gifts are discoverable by an individual.[13]

In another recently published book, as of this writing, called *The Beginner's Guide to Spiritual Gifts*, the author telegraphs his position on the cover with the selling point: "Discover You Own Unique Gifting."[14] While Storms is only covering the first list of the list-passages of 1 Corinthians 12, he confirms the outer cover's promise by stating: "The apostle Paul says that to 'each one' male and female, young and old (1 Cor. 12:7a) has been given a manifestation of the Spirit."[15]

It is fair to say that the common view of the so-called spiritual gifts is alive and well in the Western church and possibly because we export our Christianity everywhere else in the world, it is alive and well globally. Just check it out yourself. The next time you are with a group of Jesus followers in a small group or a church building service, ask them if they believe that "everyone possesses at least one spiritual gift."

I suggest that it is highly probable that most followers of Jesus hanging out in the pews on any given Sunday perceive spiritual gifts as special abilities that they possess given to them by the Spirit . Why? Because that's the way in which they have been trained in a myriad of sermons, seminars, and conferences that have been presented.

A question that is fair to ask at this point is: Why do Jesus followers keep trying to discover what special ability they have, or so-called spiritual gift, when there aren't any special abilities being handed out? What's up with that?

Discover and Develop or Occasional?

A major question to talk about is: Do the gracelets belong to a believer

---

11. Robert D. Cornwall, *Unfettered Spirit: Spiritual Gifts for the New Great Awakening* (Gonzalez, FL: Energion Publications, 2013), 38.

12. Ibid.

13. Ibid., 56.

14. Sam Storms, *The Beginner's Guide to Spiritual Gifts* (Ventura, CA: Regal Books | Gospel Light, 2012).

15. Ibid., 22.

or are the gracelets provided occasionally and given through a believer? Do individual believers possess a gracelet given to them so that they can use the 3D approach: discover, develop, and then deploy? Or, on the other hand, are the gifts occasional? Can you be used by God at any moment to share a gracelet?

In broad brush strokes, the segment of the Evangelical church, which holds that the *sign gifts* have disappeared, usually teaches that one can *discover* those remaining gifts and *develop* and *deploy* them in his or her own personal ministry. The other segment of the church, which believes that all the gifts remain today, usually believes that each believer is eligible for God to use him or her at any time that he sees fit, but often still ascribe to the belief that the gift being used through them belongs to them rather than to the person in need to whom the gift is sent through them. In my opinion, the value of adhering to the 3D approach puts the onus on the individual. If I can discover my gracelet, develop it, and deploy "my" gift, then, it seems that belief would produce a certainty that the gracelets are mine, when, in fact, they belong to the Holy Spirit and are only mine in the actual moments that they are flowing through me to others.

Here is a possible problem with adopting the 3D approach. Let's say that you discover that you have three gifts and you work really hard to develop them and then you look for times when you can deploy them. You believe that those three gifts are yours. One day, God suggests that he wants you to use a gift that is not on your list of three. I've seen this happen. I've lived it myself. Here is the beginning of a story about thinking that I knew what my gifts were, even while living in a pneumatic community and how God broke me of that theological premise. I was in a Denny's restaurant in Bakersfield, CA, after a long day of teaching when I saw an older lady who was having breathing problems approach my table and I sensed this strange sense to pray for her. I had just taught an eight hour Second Testament seminar in a local church. I thought it was God nudging me and I reminded him of what I had taught for years. I have the gift of teaching not the gift of healing. However, I had a quick turnaround and decided to pray for her. I will share the complete story below in the section on The Gracelets of Healings.

The Ministry View

An alternative view is offered by Dr. Kenneth Berding in his book *What Are Spiritual Gifts?*[16] He presents the idea that Paul's central concern

---

16. Berding, *What Are Spiritual Gifts?*

is building up the Body of Christ through the ministries of its members.[17] He suggests that in the varied passage-lists that Paul is not referring to special abilities but to spirit given ministries.[18] He suggests that "every believer has been assigned by the Holy Spirit to specific positions and activities of service small and large, short-term and long-term." Individuals who have been assigned ministries in the church are gifts to the church.[19] Berding's view does not completely reside in a "ministry appointment." He suggests that at least in one category, the miraculous, that there are both ministries and special enablements.[20] That is an unfortunate and unhelpful dichotomy in his alternative view.[21]

Berding suggests in a fiction Q&A session recorded in his book that there are many reasons why his view is correct.

- The Greek word *charisma* does not mean special ability.
- Paul's goal was the building of the body, the community of faith, by every believer fulfilling his or her role in ministry. The Corinthians seemed to be interested in special abilities.
- Paul's body illustration is all about the roles or ministries of various members of the body.
- The activities in the various list-passages can all be described as ministries but cannot be described as special abilities.
- In eighty percent of accumulative lists that Paul writes, he uses a word or phrase to indicate the nature of the list. In the four main list-passages, which surround the idea of spiritual gifts, these indicators help read the lists as referring to ministries.
- When Paul uses the word "grace" and "given" together, he is discussing ministry assignments within the context where they are found.
- Paul uses his own ministry assignment as a model for others in the Body of Christ.

17. Ibid., 71.
18. Ibid., 32.
19. Ibid.
20. Ibid., 33.
21. It has been pointed out that the concept of special enablements is also a part of the Common view that we have discussed. Some don't see the concept of "special enablements" as unfortunate in these views and point to the idea that it is required by the other two views in order to match the experience of a large percentage of people to that view's theology. The difficulty that I see with this argument is that maybe we should change the mindset and suggest a theology that challenges the experience model. Is it not possible that one has experienced the idea of enablements because the other two views (Common and Ministry) have taught such so the natural outcome would be to call something that approximates an enablement, an enablement?

- While the spiritual abilities idea often assumes that using a spiritual gift flows out of our own strength, i.e., we discover and develop them, that ministry is called to work out of our weakness.[22]

I think that Berding heads out of the pack but doesn't catch the nuance of the idea of gracelets that the final recipient receives the gracelet as it flows through another believer who is like a conduit from the Spirit to the final recipient. This is different than seeing gifts as tools for ministry or special abilities that are given to an individual that they then possess. Surely the flowing of a gracelet through an individual to a final recipient is ministry, but it does not assume that it is an ongoing ministry that is permanently given to a Jesus follower. My hope is to dispel the common and ministry views and offer the gracelets view as a replacement.

Balance or Harmony

Some readers might think that there is certainly a continual balance needed between *theology-only* and *experience-only* believers. A reader should be driven toward some middle ground in which a foundation of theology and the availability of experience can find a happy balance. I rather dislike the idea of balance. Rather, I would rather say that what we should seek to obtain is some note of harmony. Balance suggests equality between two opposing ideas or situations. Harmony, on the other hand, suggests that both seemingly opposing sides (think notes in a music scale) can be played at the same time. It takes two notes to play harmony. Usually one will be major and the other could be minor in terms of emphasis, but both are played. Theology and experience are both needed. Sometimes theology trumps experience while other times experience may trump theology. Toward such harmony, I present this material. As you will see, God's gracelets are meant to bring his grace to humankind during our day-to-day life and ministry.

So What?

If you are already firmly situated in the "special ability to everyone" view of this topic, then there is in reality no reason for you to read any further. If you ascribe to the "appointed ministry" view as a replacement to the "special ability" view, then you might want to pick up Berding's book and soak yourself in that view. But, if you are ready to at least give an ear to an alternative view to either of the above, read on and try to wrap your head around this alternative paradigm.

22. Ibid., 39–40.

Chapter 3

With that in mind, here are some, but not all of the things that I hope to build a case for in this book.

1. That the Greek word charisma — often translated by the English word "gift" — does not intrinsically mean a Spirit-given ability given to an individual, i.e., s/he is a prophet.
2. That charisma should be defined in its own context and that definition should not necessarily be transported to all other contexts.
3. That charisma means a concrete way that God expresses his grace. For that Spirit activity, I have chosen to call these concrete events gracelets, i.e., small drops of grace distributed by God to others through a human conduit.
4. That the list passages in Paul (1 Cor 12; Rom 12.3–8; Eph 4.11–13) discuss Spirit activities rather than individual abilities, which an individual possesses.
5. That Jesus followers should not sit around waiting until they have figured out *what* special ability they have or don't have because they have taken a *Spiritual Gift* test or appraisal.
6. That there should be an Acts-like event in which all the *Spiritual Gifts tests/assessments* are burned.
7. That followers of Jesus should stop using the word "gift" or "spiritual gifts" and start talking about gracelets as a Spirit activity, which flows through a person to another for the latter's benefit.
8. That everyone teaching a spiritual gifts course should cancel it and replace it with a course entitled something like *GRACELETS: Being Conduits of the Extravagant Acts of God's Grace.*

∽

In order to communicate using a language, everyone needs words.

Chapter 4: How Words Work

➡ **Check Your GPS: Where We Are Going!**
- Where We Have Been
- Words and Concepts
- Defining Words
- The Second Testament Language of Gracelets
- What Is a Gracelet?
- So What?

Where We Have Been

In the last chapter, we reviewed the basic three views of the subject matter at hand: The Gracelets View, The Common View, and the Ministry View. So, in order to understand the gracelet view that I am proposing, we must take a small excursion into the realm of word meanings. With that information in hand, we can have a better grasp of what a gracelet is.

Words and Concepts

In order to communicate using a language, everyone needs words.[1] When we communicate ideas to each other, we use words and combine them together into a larger unit of thought. Without the use of words, we would be limited in our ability to express our thoughts with any precision. In fact, without words, one wonders if a person could even think as we currently understand and experience thinking. Words are central in language communication. Therefore, it becomes important to understand the idea of concepts. The best interpretation of Scripture happens when the meaning required by the normal meaning of the words used in the context in which they occur are understood. The meaning of a word is not determined from a resource tool like a dictionary or word study book. We only receive a definition there. The meaning of a word comes from the context in which it appears. Therefore, the same Hebrew or Greek word may

---

1. Or in sign language, which is a system of communication using visual gestures and signs, as used by people having impaired hearing.

have a different meaning when found in a different context. So, a word has a range of meaning.

Range of Meaning

A specific word, spelled the same, can have many totally different meanings. Let's illustrate using the English word *hand*. We have a *hand*, which is a part of our body. A clock has a *hand*. A card player holds a *hand* in his *hand*. *Hand* is a unit of measurement for horses. We hear phrases like, "all *hands* on deck." We may be asked at some point in time to "give someone a *hand*." In each of these cases, the word is the same. It is spelled the same, but the meaning is different. The different meanings of the word *hand* make up a range of meaning, sometimes called a semantic domain.[2] Under normal circumstances, such a range of meaning does not cause misunderstanding or confusion. A native speaker of the language, aided by the context in which the word appears, will pick up on the correct meaning of the word. The ideas, which are expressed in the larger context in which the word appears, will, for the most part, clarify the intended meaning of the word in use. A non-native speaker of a language may need some help to grasp the meaning of a word in a certain context.

Years ago, when providing oversight for a church in Southern California, the church hosted a group of four young ladies for about a month. They were on mission from a youth organization. They shared with me that part of their ministry requirements was to take a daily assigned passage of Scripture and then use Strong's Concordance to find out every place in the Bible that each word in that passage appeared in the King James Version and then apply the meaning supplied by Strong's to every other place that word occurred in the Bible. When they explained this process to me, I asked them if that was how they used language in their everyday speech. They all answered that they did not treat English that way as they were out and about on their daily mission. I decided to try and help them understand that the same ways in which they used language daily was also true in usage of the words in the Bible. This idea caused some tension with them because they had been taught that the English words in the KJV were special, not to be tampered with. When I suggested that they weren't tampering by investigating a different way of thinking, the tension grew. Then, over the next few evenings as they gathered to do their regimented Strong's study, I pushed back on the whole premise of what they were doing. Little by little, their shell showed some cracks and they finally, but not

---

2. Or, a specific area of cultural emphasis.

without resistance, began to comprehend that a word used by John in his gospel and the same word used by Paul in one of his letters could have different meanings, let alone that the English word may have been the same but the Greek word may have been different. Before they left town to go to their next place, they presented me with a small figure of a priest favoring Friar Tuck, which they indicated as being a kind hearted priest and a good friend. It is still displayed in my office. Their way of thinking is still an epidemic among those who read and study the Bible. I call it *neuteritis*, which is the deadly disease of making words that are diverse mean the same thing; in short, neutering them of their contextual meaning.

On another occasion, a friend presented me with a sign for my desk on which was engraved "Head Hermeneutical Hack," which I still display in my office. It was his response to my constant "needling" him about words and context.

I do realize that even as you may be reading this section that you may be seeing this information in this context for the first time. Thinking about it can be painful. Take heart! While there may be pain during the night, joy can break out in the morning.

Change of Meaning

The meaning of a word does not remain fixed. Therefore, it is important to pursue what the original words in a passage meant at the time they were written and in the context they occur. A new meaning occurs because a word begins to be used in a certain way. The KJV is a classic illustration of how English words have changed their meaning since 1611. As an example, the word *conversation* appears in 2 Corinthains 1.12, Galatians 1.13; Ephesians 2.3; 4.22; and Philippians 1.27. When we use the word *conversation,* we usually mean two individuals who are talking to each other face to face or these days via eMail or on Facebook. However, it meant something totally different in 1611. Today we use words like *conduct* or *way of life* to convey the same idea that *conversation* conveyed in 1611. Another example in KJV is its translation of 1 Thessalonians 4.15 as, *We who are alive and remain until the coming of the Lord will not prevent those who have fallen asleep.* The word *prevent* in 1611 meant "to go before" while today it means to *stop* or *hinder.* I once purchased a KJV produced by American Bible Society about thirty years ago, as of this writing, that had a list of words in an appendix that had changed since KJV was translated. The list contained several hundred words. Today we would call the words archaic. What this may teach us is that what served as a good translation in the seventeenth century, no longer communicates what Paul originally meant. BTW: The New King James Version (NKJV) has simply been reworked by a publisher who commissioned a group of scholars to remove the archaic English words and replace them with more current words. It is fair to remember that the earliest of the Second Testament books, Galatians, was written in AD 49, while the last one, Revelation, was written in the mid '90s of the first century. Just as English words change meanings over time, so do the words in the biblical languages during that timeframe.[3]

Characteristic and Figurative Meaning

A word has a *characteristic* meaning, which is the usual meaning of the word. In addition, the same word can have a *figurative* meaning. The word *dog* usually has the characteristic meaning of a four-legged, hairy little or, in some cases, big animal. However, if you used it in reference to a person, "You dog!" it communicates something quite different. The figurative meaning used this way is usually derogatory.

All the words that you have been reading in this book are symbols. They are like signs that point to something else. When I was younger, I had a dog named Tippy. The name was not actually the dog, but the name I used to indicate my dog from other dogs in the neighborhood. So if I asked several folks to use the word dog in a sentence, I might receive something like this: My friend is dogging me about fixing his TV. He told me that his TV had gone to the dogs. To demonstrate that he needed his TV fixed, he put on the dog. My friend told me that while he was watching TV, he liked to eat hot dogs. While he was watching TV and relaxing, his wife walked into the room and said, "you lucky dog!" My friend turned to me as we watched the president deliver a speech on TV and said, "That speech is a dog."

In Scripture, Paul uses the word *dog* when he writes to the believers at Philippi. He says, "Watch out for those dogs, those men who do evil, those mutilators of the flesh" (Phil. 3.2). As a historical note, first century Jews considered dogs as detestable animals. Jews expressed their dislike for Gentiles by calling them dogs. Paul uses the word *dog* to throw back at the Jewish troublemakers in Philippi their own contemptuous use of the term. When Matthew and Mark use the term in the story of the Syrophoenician woman, *dog* carries its characteristic meaning.

---

3. It should be pointed out that the very popular paraphrase by Eugene Peterson called *The Message* will be somewhat obsolete most likely within a generation as the English language continues to change and new translations of the original languages will come to fore translating the concepts of the original text into more current language forms.

Chapter 4

As we read and interpret Scripture, we must study words carefully to determine if the word is being used characteristically or figuratively.

Good reading will help one arrive at the meaning the original hearer could have heard when there is also an awareness of *context* and *content*.[4]

Below, we will examine the words that lie behind our English translation for "spiritual gifts."

Arbitrary and Flexible

Words as symbols have flexibility while at the same time they are arbitrary or whimsical. Think about this scenario. You give eight folks of varied ages a piece of paper with a box of colored crayons and ask them to describe a two car accident at an intersection. Chances are you will get eight different pictures of the accident. All of the drawings would be arbitrary. If one was a fireman, he might draw a large fireball coming from one of the cars. If one was a military person, he or she might try to put sound into the picture using word balloons to represent the loud noise that occurred when the accident occurred. If a doctor or nurse was drawing a picture, they may have drawn the people who were in the cars receiving medical attention. Different folks with different baggage would simply draw different pictures of the same event using whatever symbols/words were at hand. The pictures drawn and the accident being described are, however, two different things.

As we said above, words change over time. They don't remain the same. They are used in different ways from one period to another. Anyone can pick up a sponge and wipe down a counter with several different kinds and colors of liquid. Symbols/words are like sponges. As you saw in the paragraphs above, the word "hand" and "dog" have picked up lots of different meanings all due to the context in which each was used. This kind of flexibility produces the range of meaning.

An Illustration

Over the years, I have noticed that our tendency in reading the Bible is depleted because we are unaware of the information like the information about words just presented. We have developed the habit, when reading, of taking an English word, finding a meaning in a word study book or concordance sometimes based on the etymology of the

---

4. Winn Griffin, *Learning to Think and Teach Biblically* (Woodinville, WA: Seeing the Bible Live Publishing, 1998), 37-38.

word, and giving the word that meaning as was the case with the young ladies in the story above. Think of the word butterfly. It is made up of two different English words, i.e., butter and fly. If one tried to forge a definition from the two words, then you would most likely come away with a greasy buzzing little insect that is a nuisance, instead of a beautiful multicolored two winged insect. How many words can you think of that have changed their meaning over the years? Go ahead, stop reading for a moment and write down as many as you can think of. It will most likely surprise you.

Defining Words

In 1961, James Barr, a Scottish First Testament[5] specialist, wrote a book entitled *The Semantics of Biblical Language*[6] in which he critiqued the way biblical scholarship had come to define words. His complaint was that a word definition did not take into consideration the difference between the symbol/word and the concept that it represented. He was keen to point out that theological wordsmiths were dumping meanings onto words and making them static, which ignored the context in which a word might appear. The biblical specialist of the day understood his points well. Larry Hurtado, a Second Testament specialist, has written, "I fear that this [misunderstanding] remains the same [today].[7] Hurtado goes on to suggest that too many scholars (and so their students) still take an approach in which Hebrew or Greek words are treated as having fixed meanings, and so understanding texts as being essentially a process of totting up a suitable dictionary meaning of all the words of their sentences. It is still news to many that the fundamental semantic unit is not the "word" but the sentence, and that "words" (lexical entries) acquire a specific meaning when deployed in sentences. Likewise, scholars often still don't understand that word constructions often take on their own meaning that is not the sum of the parts (e.g., "hot dog" isn't the sum of the meanings of "hot" and "dog"!).[8]

5. We might want to think about using the term First Testament instead of Old. Old implies out of date and to some degree not useful. "First," implies the beginning of something that might have a "second," which is the function of the Second Testament, i.e., what is usually called the New Testament. Together they present the whole Story of God from the creation of the heavens and earth to the recreation of the new heavens and earth.

6. James Barr, *The Semantics of Biblical Language* (2004: Wipf and Stock Publishers, 2004). This is a reprint of Barr's book, which was originally published by Oxford Press in 1961.

7. Larry Hurtado, "50th Anniversary: Barr's "Semantics of Biblical Language," Larry Hurtado (accessed October 24, 2013).

8. Ibid.

Chapter 4

Kevin Vanhoozer, author of *Is There a Meaning in this Text?*[9] wrote the following in an article in *New Dictionary of Biblical Theology* about James Barr:

James Barr's *The Semantics of Biblical Language* (London and New York, 1961) is a formidable critique of the linguistic and hermeneutical presuppositions that lay behind several of the articles in the early volumes of G. Kittel's *TDNT*, [*Theological Dictionary of the Old Testament*] a work that, like the Biblical Theology Movement, looked to words as the primary locus of the Bible's theology. First, Barr attacks the assumption that words have certain root meanings that remain constant, even across centuries of use. It is simply not the case that the "basic" meaning of a word is present in each individual use of it. Many of the entries in *TDNT* were also guilty of what Barr called "illegitimate totality transfer." This refers to the error of reading all possible meanings of a particular term into a single occurrence of the word. While it is true that some words can have several meanings (*e.g.* in the phrase "he's hot," the word "hot" could refer to his temperature, anger, or tennis), it is wrong to think that the many possibilities are always contained in the one use.

Closely related to this first mistake is a second error: the etymological fallacy. The meaning of a word cannot be deduced from its etymology or origin. Instead, the meaning of a word must be determined in the concrete context of its use. Barr's work demonstrated that it is fallacious to move too quickly from word to concept (e.g. from biblical words to theological doctrines). The moral is clear; one cannot move from a study of words (e.g. "salvation, [or] to save") to biblical theology (e.g. soteriology).

Barr correctly observes that meaning is expressed at the level of a sentence (i.e. in the author's particular use of words) rather than at the level of the sign (i.e. in the individual words considered apart from the context of their use). The Biblical Theology Movement, we may conclude, ultimately foundered on a misleading picture of language and an inadequate theory of meaning. It is one thing to study the etymology of a word, another to study what an author meant when using it on a particular occasion. "What it meant" has less to do with the

---

9. Kevin Vanhoozer, *Is There a Meaning in This Text?* (Grand Rapids, MI: Zondervan, 2009).

origins or history of a word than with the circumstances of its actual use.[10]

In a conversation about the value of TDNT, Jon Stovell writes:

TDNT is a tool with some pretty major flaws. It isn't completely without merit, but it should only be used with caution. On the one hand, it usually does a good job presenting information about the history of use for a term and its semantic range. On the other hand, the way it takes all of the different meanings the term has carried in the various examples given and layers them on top of each other to arrive at its supposed "full meaning," as though an entire "symphony of meaning" were contained in a single word, is misled and misleading. To be clear, it's not that no one should ever read the TDNT, but that one should not rely on it as a guide.[11]

With this in mind, we can now turn to the four words that live in the swirl of the language about the gracelets of the Spirit.

The Second Testament Language of Gracelets

Charismata

In popular interpretation about the so-called spiritual gifts, the word *charismata* is associated with Paul's usage and is translated in different translations as "spiritual gifts." It has been pointed out that Paul qualifies *charisma* with *pneumatikon* (often translated spiritual). This qualification means that *charisma* should not automatically be thought of as "spiritual gifts."[12] Paul appears to be the creator of the word *charisma*. It is used outside Paul's writings only once in 1 Peter 4.10.[13] It may be possible

10. T. Desmond Alexander and Brian S. Rosner. *New Dictionary of Biblical Theology* (Downers Grove, IL: InterVarsity Press, 2000), s.v. Kevin Vanhoozer: "Exegesis and Hermeneutics." 52-63.

11. Jon Stovell, "Society of Vineyard Scholars Facebook Group [Conversation on Theological Dictionary of New Testament]," Facebook https://www.facebook.com/groups/102214556490936/permalink/601544656557921/ (accessed November 9, 2013).

12. Gerald F. Hawthrone and Ralph P. Martin. *Dictionary of Paul and His Letters* (Downers Grove, IL: InterVarsity Press, 1993), s.v. Gordon Fee: "Gifts of the Spirit." 339-347.

13. 1 Peter 4.10 could be translated: "'Like good stewards of the manifold grace of God, serve one another with whatever gift each of you has received." The sharing of the gracelets is the doing of ministry. One could understand this outlier in Peter as suggesting that whatever gracelet flows through you, be a good steward of it on its way through to the one who is the ultimate receptor. So, be generous with the different

that Peter used this word from Paul. Remember, Peter appears to have been familiar with Paul's writings (2 Pet. 3.16). However, we could probably assert that by itself, *charisma* has nothing to do with the Spirit, only picking up that overtone by context. Some NT specialists suggest that the word is formed from the word *charis* (grace) and means "a concrete expression of grace" in every instance it is used by Paul.[14] These "expressions of grace" is what I am calling *gracelets*. Gordon Fee suggests that there are some difficulties found in Paul around this word but concludes that "...there seems to be little question that the list of "manifestations" in 1 Corinthians 12:8–10 are to be understood as *charismata*, gracious bestowments of the Spirit in the gathered community for the sake of building up the people of God."[15]

Pneumatika

Another word used in this arena is the term *pneumatika*, which appears two times in the list-passages of 1 Corinthians 12-14. It seems that *pneumatika* and *charismata* are overlapping words. First Corinthians 12.1 begins with the translation: "Now let me turn to some issues about spiritual gifts, brothers and sisters. There's much you need to learn." The term "spiritual gifts" in the NIV translation (and others) should be translated "Now concerning Spirit matters." This translation of *pneumatikon*, from which *pnuematika* comes, sets the stage for Paul to talk about the abuse of the one gracelet, tongues, on which the enthusiasts in Corinth seemed to be fixated. Second Testament specialists are divided around its meaning. Some think that the words *pneumatika* and *charismata* simply mean the same thing and can be used interchangeably. Others suggest that one is more comprehensive than the other. Yet others think one of these words is a word created by the Corinthians. One solution that is proposed is to understand the root meaning of each word. *Charismata* appears to focus on the graciousness of God toward his people while *pneumatika* deals with the nature of the Spirit's activity for which the various *charismata* point.[16] As an example, with the gracelet of tongues, the Spirit is working with each individual for edification. On the other hand, with the gracelet of prophecy, the Spirit is working for common edification of the whole community. The gracelet, tongues or

---

things God flows through you, passing them around so all get in on it.

14. *Dictionary of Paul and His Letters*. Fee: 339-347. One shouldn't read "gathered community," as Sunday morning or evening services. A gathered community could be any number of folks, doing any number of things together and within that gathering, the gracelets may flow to Jesus follower and non-follower alike.

15. Ibid., 340.

16. Ibid., 341.

prophecy, demonstrates the graciousness of God while the activity of the Spirit, (*pneumatika*) focuses on the resulting activity of the *charismata*, the edification of either individual or community.

Pneumata

A third word is the word *pneumata*, which appears three times in 1 Corinthians 12-14 (12.10; 14.12; 14.32). The anthropology in these passages is the interplay between the spirit of a human and the Spirit of God. Whatever that interplay is between human and divine, the word should not be translated by the term "spiritual gift."

Dorea

Finally, the proper term for *gift* in Greek is *dorea*. It does not appear very many times in Paul's writings, but it does appear in the Ephesians 4.7 passage. Just a few verses later in Ephesians 4.11, there is another list passage. Since three of four items listed are mentioned in 1 Corinthians 12.28, some Second Testament specialists see the four as gracelets. Remember, 1 Corinthians was written before Ephesians and it would be natural to pull items from a previous list and place them in a latter list as the ad hoc circumstances required. While not using the word *charismata* specifically for the Ephesians' list, it would be natural to suggest that for Paul, the four gracelets in Ephesians were to be understood as gracelets as well.

Think of it this way. We have come to believe in our culture that where death occurs all around us on a continual basis, to think about resisting the idea of death by the use of the phrase "die hard." We have had "die hard" batteries offered by a well-known USAmerica department store. We have had the "Die Hard" movie franchise with five movies at the time of this writing with a box office take of just under 1.5 billion dollars. It would probably be okay to jest that the "Die Hard" franchise is not "dying hard."[17] In the same way, it is difficult to break our own habit of thinking about the words "spiritual gifts" without applying the baggage to them that have come along with years of usage in a certain way. However, as difficult as the habit is to break, we must break it in order to allow our imagination to see new possibilities.

What is A Gracelet?

As I wrote above, I was introduced to the word gracelet while taking

---

17. Wikipedia, "Die Hard," Wikipedia (accessed September 21, 2013).

a Spiritual Gifts course at Fuller Seminary. It is a word that supplies a way of thinking about this subject matter. The idea of gracelet is amazingly simple. Visually we can respond to the idea of a droplet of water as it falls from the sky to earth to refresh. We have the same ability to visually respond to the idea of gracelets as we see the grace of God coming through our lives to minister to others. Followers of Jesus then become a funnel or conduit through which God sends his "drop of grace" through his people to others. We will say a bit more about this below.

God's Grace

God is a speaking God. The opening pages of the Story of Scripture present God in this fashion. He spoke and the world was created. Turn all the way to the end of the book, or the many books that make up the Bible, and at the conclusion of the book of Revelation, God is still speaking. From cover to cover, we come face to face with a personal God who loves to communicate to his creation. He really is pretty talkative, but talking or speaking is not the only way to communicate.

Some readers may be familiar with a certain dichotomy that is played out in the church in which two brands of Protestant Christianity, non-charismatic or charismatic, or non-Pentecostal or Pentecostal, or pneumatic or non-pneumatic, select sides about when and how God has spoken or speaks. Those who are in a basic non-charismatic brand of American Christianity are often taught that God only speaks now through his Word, the Bible. Some in this camp might also suggest as well that he speaks through "...a still small voice," (1 Kings 19.12 KJV) or as NIV translates it: "...a gentle whisper," or as Eugene Peterson paraphrases it in *The Message*, "...a gentle and quiet whisper."

On the other side, those folks within a charismatic form of the church believe that God speaks to them all day long about everything. They have their antennas up and tuned to GOD.AM. While these are broad brush strokes of reality, they do fairly represent the idea that in the non-charismatic world, God is seen as rarely speaking; while in the charismatic world, God is seen as speaking all the time. One of the reasons that the folks in the non-charismatic world take their position about a speaking God is the exegesis of one small passage in the Corinthian Correspondence that suggested that God stopped speaking at a certain time in history in certain ways and now the church and individuals only have one way in which to listen to God, i.e., the Bible.

Scripture seems to validate that God is a speaking God.[18] Our challenge is to hear what he has said and still says. That sentence you will notice places me in the charismatic world. God loves to communicate to his creation and there seems to be nothing within the covers of his book that would cause us to believe that he has stopped speaking or only speaks in the Bible itself. As readers, we should broaden our understanding of speaking to include actions (works) as well as words.[19] You know the old saying, "Actions speak louder than words," implying that actions are more important than words. In the Story of God, however, actions speak the same message as the words. But in reality there is no difference and certainly the actions are not louder or more important than words. The actions and words of God in his Story speak abundantly and all at the same volume.

Here's an illustration: One of the ways in which God communicates is through the action of giving. The story of creation tells of a loving God who gave his children everything they needed for their daily lives. No worry, no pressures, no stress. What could be better? The story tells us that in the cool of the day, he would join his created beings for a friendly face-to-face chat.[20] In many of the stories of the First (often called the Old) Testament,[21] God is seen as a giving God. In the Second (sometimes called New) Testament, he reveals his ultimate gift, Jesus, the apex of God's own Story. It is surely beyond question that God loves to give. It is a part of his communicative character and it is well documented throughout the Story of Scripture.

18. In terms of reading and hearing Scripture see: Winn Griffin, *God Has Spoken: But What Has He Said? 3 Reasons for and 3 Approaches to Hearing God in Scripture* (Woodinville, WA: Basilia Press: An Imprint of Harmon Press, 2013).

19. The Hebrew phrase *dabar YHWH* can be translated either "word of God" or "actions of God." The word *dabar* is translated as "acts" 51 times in the OT. The concept is not just "word" and in speech, but also "acts" as in God doing something. Isaiah seems to have that intention when he chooses to use that word as it is recorded at 55.11 where he shares that "my word goes out from my mouth," and then says "but shall accomplish (do or act)," as the second line of the poetic piece reads. One of the reasons that "red letter" Bibles in the New Testament really have no value, is that they give more "value" to the words of Jesus over against the acts of Jesus. The words and works of Jesus carry the same value. In addition, they don't count the words/actions of God in the Old Testament with the same value of the words/works of Jesus in the New Testament.

20. The idea presented about God as coming in the cool of the day is anthropomorphic language, i.e., the text presenting God in human terms so the listener and readers of this story could identify with God.

21. I have chosen the designation of First and Second Testament instead of Old and New Testament to avoid the idea that the Old is not valuable for the followers of Christ today and to redeem the idea that the whole Bible from Genesis to Revelation is one complete Story of God.

Chapter 4

There is a tremendous move in some parts of the church to work for God's justice[22] in the world. This is an important aspect and often overlooked. What allows us to bring justice to a separated world? It is God's grace. Of course, we have all but destroyed this notion with our over abundant attention to the concept of God's grace or the grace of God. In a recent search on Google, Google returned 6,560,000 hits for the exact phrase "God's grace" and another 20,700,000 for the term "grace of God."[23] Those numbers imply that there is a lot of information out there about God's grace. But, information doesn't by itself provide transformation, as many have discovered.

Maybe one of the reasons that there is so much talk and writing about grace is because it is focused on one of the enduring characteristics of God, which is that he loves to give. So we have come to believe that one of the blessings God loves to give is *grace*, a blessing that we do not necessarily deserve, but out of his abundant love for us, he gives grace to us anyway. Where is this abundant grace at? Well, it can be seen and felt on a daily basis through what we have miscalled the gifts of the Spirit, which, as we have stated, are believed to be special abilities that each person is given as a possession. While we will deconstruct that notion of position, it is fair to say that these displays of his daily grace should, in my opinion, be called *gracelets*.

The Gracelets of the Spirit

The most often used Greek word for what is usually translated spiritual gifts in the Second Testament is *charismata*. The root (*char*) of this word gives us the word joy (*chara*) and grace (*charis*). *Charismata* is plural and indicates that there is a definite result of grace that occurs when it is given. One might think "acts of grace." Thus, what has been called spiritual gifts could better be translated gracelets, which are the specific displays of God's grace, which he gives through us as we serve as his conduits. Through that action, God brings a definite result to the one receiving the gift and exposes everyone in the vicinity to the loving care of God for his children.

The giving of *gracelets* works like this: in whatever situation God needs to send his grace, he uses a human vessel (you and me) as a funnel or

---

22. I think we should consider what we are saying when we make a divide in God's justice into varieties such as Social Justice. Justice is one of the main qualities of God and that includes what we call social.... So everything is about justice, i.e., the treatment of the poor, the treatment of different races, the treatment of women in ministry, the treatment of gays, the treatment of sinners, etc. To make the divide seems to me to be unnecessary and very dualistic.

23. Google search, July 6, 2015.

conduit to provide a droplet of grace into the situation. This *gracelet* is given out of the abundance of his grace that he has for any situation that one or anyone, a follower or non-follower of Jesus, may run into during the course of his or her day or life. We don't own God's gracelets; we don't possess them as we have been taught over the years. Rather, we are the UPS, USPS, or FedEx persons that deliver the gracelets to their rightful destination.

I prefer the name *gracelets* because of the temporary idea that springs from the metaphor. Like a drop of water, it comes, does its job, and then disappears from our view but allows us to see the results. Part of our job as followers of Jesus is to be aware of God's activity in the world around us as we face the wind of the Spirit ready to be launched into the moment in which he taps us on the shoulder and tells us to deliver this gracelet to one in need. I use the word gracelet in this book instead of the word gift or the phrase spiritual gift. Why? You might ask. Because the embedded terms that are in our Christian vocabulary makes it difficult, if not impossible, to overcome their entrenched meaning. Some terms have a long shelf life and need to be eviscerated of their control in our speech.

Credited as the earliest translation into English, even before the King James Version, was the Tyndale Bible in the 1500s. In his translation of 1 Corinthians 1.7, he wrote: "so that ye are behynde in no gyft and wayte for the apperynge of oure lorde Iesus Christ." This was followed by the King James translation of 1 Corinthians 1.7 with "so that ye come behind in no gift; waiting for the coming of our Lord Jesus Christ." Then to the translation of "Therefore you do not lack any spiritual gift as you eagerly wait for our Lord Jesus Christ to be revealed," in the New International Version of 1973 and 2011. The Revised Version (1901) translated this verse in 1 Corinthians 1.7 with "so that ye come behind in no gift; waiting for the revelation of our Lord Jesus Christ…." This was followed by the Revised Standard Version (Second Testament 1946) with "so that you are not lacking in any spiritual gift, as you wait for the revealing of our Lord Jesus Christ" followed by the New Revised Standard Version (1989) with the same translation except for different grammar marks in the sentence. Notice that the word "spiritual" was added to the translations in the RSV between 1901 and 1946 and the same addition was taken up by the NIV 1973 and remains in both the NRSV and the NIV 2011.

So What?

Well, it took almost 6,000 words to talk about how words work and why one should consider choosing a different word to talk about the often called gifts of the Spirit. The history provided above about how "spiritual gifts" has been translated with the English word "gift" or phrase "spiritual gift" demonstrates how deeply entrenched they are in the psyche of the English reader. So, if one wants a different experience, one might want to change the words expressing the experience that suggests a new way of thinking about the experience. That would surely be the case with using gracelets instead of spiritual gifts.

If someone asked you why are you calling what Scripture calls spiritual gifts by the word gracelets, you might answer: because the embedded term of spiritual gift that is in our Christian vocabulary makes it difficult, if not impossible, to overcome its entrenched meaning; we need a new way of thinking about how God delivers his grace to us and the word gracelets is a start in that direction.

Let's Have a Conversation

- How do the different concepts presented at the beginning of this chapter help you think about how you use words when you communicate?
- How has the way in which you define words differed from the way that is presented in the section above called "Defining Words?"
- How does the substitution of the word gracelets help you in putting away old baggage that you have carried about the topic of spiritual gifts and re-calibrate your idea of how this idea in the sacred text works in everyday life?

...the Holy Spirit is no more important or less important than any other member of the Trinity...

Chapter 5. The Gift of The Holy Spirit

➠ **Check Your GPS: Where We Are Going!**
- Where We Have Been
- The Gift of the Holy Spirit
- Baptism in the Holy Spirit
- The So-Called Gifts of the Holy Spirit
- Four Theories About the So-Called Gifts
- So What?

Where We Have Been

In the last chapter, we gave attention to the idea of how words work. We use words every day to communicate ideas. But, words do change their meaning from time to time and also have a range of menaing at any one point in time. Understanding that bit of information will help us move forward as we now discuss the Gift of the Holy Spirit

The Gift of the Holy Spirit

We begin with trying to sort out this topic by working our way through the terminology that surrounds the phrase the Gift of the Holy Spirit as it is used in the context of speaking and writing about the Holy Spirit. As an aside, it seems to me that churches that live in the Pentecostal/Charismatic/Third Wave variety sometimes provide an overfocus on the Holy Spirit. I recently heard a presentation in which a church group was celebrating their church distinctives. There were six of them of which one was the ministry of the Holy Spirit. In the time spent, the distinctive of the Holy Spirit received more time in the presentation than any of the other five. Even more interesting, the use of the word distinctive usually carries the idea of how one is different, but in this presentation while calling each of the points a distinctive, the counter point was being made that the church group should not compare themselves with other church groups. Such binary or dualistic thinking is often not well thought through. Hopefully, as we proceed, we can avoid such thinking in our presentation. So, I might say that the Holy Spirit is no more important or less important than any other member of the Trinity and as we will see later, all three are intricately involved in the functions of gracelets.

There are numerous books, both popular and theological, which discuss the doctrine or theology of the Holy Spirit in great detail. You may have noticed that I have broken the categories of books into two categories: popular and theological. Why? It is my contention that not all popular Christian books are good theologically. Some of them are based solely on an author's personal experience of a specific group of spiritual gifts such as prophecy, which is often a highly sought after gift. Experience is fine, but it must find harmony with the sacred text.

If you go into almost any Christian bookstore, there will be a section of books about the Holy Spirit being offered for your reading pleasure.[1] There is usually a group of books within that section that are devoted to the Gifts of the Holy Spirit.[2] It is not my concern to provide you with a comprehensive study of the Holy Spirit, but only to introduce you to the concept of the Gift of the Holy Spirit, which is often called the Baptism in the Holy Spirit among Pentecostals and Charismatics, and what has been called the Third Wave movement. However, it must also be said that all books dealing with the theology of the Spirit are not all understood popularly.

Some believe the beginning of the Pentecostal movement in the twentieth century was occasioned by the Pentecost gift of the Spirit with speaking in tongues. This event occurred at Stone's Folly[3] in

1. There were approximately 181,500 books with the words "Holy Spirit" listed on amazon.com when I checked on July 8, 2015. That's a lot of choices.

2. There were 7,700 plus books listed with the words "Gifts of the Spirit" in its title and another 19,500 plus books with "Spiritual Gifts" listed in its title. However, the latter also included gifts like "Treats for Troopers Snack Package," which doesn't seem to have anything to do with spiritual gifts but you can find them as you search for spiritual gifts. Go figure! These are from amazon.com searches on July 8, 2015.

3. Kansas Historical Society, "Stone's Folly, Topeka, Kansas," Kansas Historical Society http://www.kansasmemory.org/item/216413 (accessed November 23, 2012). The following is the information from the website. "An east view of Stone's Folly located at 17th and Stone Streets in Topeka, Kansas. Construction on the three-story eighteen room mansion began around 1887 when Erastus R. Stone purchased a thirty acre tract of land west of Washburn College. The castle-like structure with its ornate appearance was Stone's vision of the finest mansion in the state of Kansas. Unfortunately, an economic depression and a drought halted construction on the home. Without the financial means to finish the mansion, Stone's castle became known as Stone's Folly and was eventually sold to the American Bible Society of Philadelphia. The home, never occupied by Stone and his family, remained vacant for over a decade until 1900 when the Rev. Charles Fox Parham rented the residence for his Bethel Bible College. From October of 1900 to July of 1901, Parham and his wife Sarah used the home as a gathering place for the teachings of the Pentecostal faith. When their lease on Stone's Folly was not renewed, the mansion was sold to Harry Croft, a bootlegger, on July 20, 1901, who converted the residence into a roadhouse. Tragically, a mysterious fire destroyed the Gothic structure on December 6, 1901. Today, there are no reminders of the mansion but the site is the

Topeka, Kansas, on December 31, 1900, when Agnes Ozman was the first to "speak in tongues" at the Bible school located there.[4] This school was directed by Charles Parham, the reputed founder of the doctrine of the "initial evidence of speaking in tongues as the baptism of the Holy Spirit."

Parham moved from Topeka to Houston, TX, where a young African man who was allowed to sit in his class heard him through the door and later went to California and a Pentecostal revival began there at Azusa Street[5] where the Pentecostal movement grew deeper roots.

Fast forward to the '60s of the last century where the palpable experience of the Holy Spirit began to be seen in traditional churches like Episcopalian, Presbyterian, Roman Catholic, etc., which were often called the high church versus the low church, like Baptist, Nazarene, Pentecostal varies, etc., because of the liturgy of the church. One of the better known stories during this period was Dennis Bennett, an Episcopal priest who announced his "baptism in the Spirit" in April of 1960 to his congregation at St. Mark's Episcopalian Church in Van Nuys, California. After the announcement, he was asked to resign and he moved to St. Luke's Episcopal Church in Seattle, Washington. With this series of events, and I am painting with a broad brush, the Charismatic Renewal had its humble beginnings. How, one may ask, did Bennett come to call his experience of "speaking in tongues," the "baptism of the Holy Spirit?" It's my hunch that he only had the roadmap of the Pentecostals to guide him in this new journey and he ended up calling what had happened to him by using the same name that the Pentecostal movement had adopted as the way to talk about this experience.[6] The early Charismatics and the early Pentecostals were

---

home of the Most Pure Heart of Mary Catholic Church." You can view the picture of the church on goggle maps @ http://bit.ly/R6G7pM. It's a bit of history you should see.

4. Cecil M. Robeck Jr., *The Azusa Street Mission and Revival* (Nashville, TN: Thomas Nelson, 2006), 42-43. See also: Harold D. Hunter, "A Portrait of How the Azusa Doctrine of Spirit Baptism Shaped American Pentecostalism," Enrichment Journal: Assemblies of God http://enrichmentjournal.ag.org/200602/200602_078_azusadoctrine.cfm (accessed November 3, 2015). This article suggests that when "Agnes Ozman spoke in tongues at the opening of the 20th century in Charles Fox Parham's Bethel Bible College in Topeka, it was xenolalia (speaking in a language not necessarily learned by the speaker), rather than glossolalia, the more common term for speaking in tongues used by the Pentecostal/Charismatic groups.

5. Cecil M. Robeck Jr., *The Azusa Street Mission and Revival.* You can read the whole story in this book mentioned in the previous footnote by Mel Robeck. If you are interested in Pentecostal history, this is one of the best books to help you become informed.

6. I have thought this over the years and only recently spoke with Rick Willans, the

basically the same in the "two-step" process, even though it must be noted that historic Episcopal theology was not influenced by Wesley's theology of a second crisis experience subsequent to salvation.

The so-called Charismatic Renewal[7] in the high church soon had a sister in the low church, which began in the Pentecostal family but later used Charismatic language to speak of itself. While he had been ministering for some time, Kenneth Hagin founded the "Word of Faith" movement around 1966. Sometimes called Pentecostal, sometimes called Charismatic, Hagin's brand of Christianity had an added component that has been popularly called "the Prosperity Movement" that believed that it was God's will for every believer to be blessed with health and wealth. This teaching took on a life of its own and he wrote in his later life to try and curb some of its extreme interpretations.[8]

In roughly the same timeframe, a church ministering in Southern California to the Jesus People of the '60s and pastored by the late Chuck Smith (1927-2013) began its visibility. Smith, a former Foursquare Pastor, broke away from the Foursquare denomination and through a prophecy became the pastor of what is now Calvary Chapel. While the Spirit was important to this fledging group of churches, the open practice of the Gifts of the Spirit was not really open but was celebrated in "afterglow'"[9] services. They did not stray far from the Foursquare roots of Smith and still saw the coming of the Spirit to followers of Jesus as a second experience.

So, let me clarify the terms. Pentecostal refers to Classical Pentecostalism, which had its origins in USAmerica at the beginning of the twentieth century. Pentecostalism has its roots in the nineteenth-century Holiness movement. The name "classical" was added to the Pentecostal designation about 1970 to distinguish them from the new

---

husband of the author Jean Stone Willans, *The Acts of the Green Apples: The inside Story of the Beginning of the Charismatic Renewal* (Hong Kong: Society of Stephen, 1973). Jean worked with Dennis Bennett in the early days of his charismatic experience in Van Nuys, CA. Later, she also worked with Harald Bredesen and between them coined the term, "Charismatic Renewal." In my conversation with Rick, I ran my theory by him and he acknowledged that it was what had actually happened. The Pentecostal language was adopted by Bennett to express what his experience was.

7. Coined by Harald Bredesen and Jean Stone Willans.

8. J. Lee Grady, "Kenneth Hagin's Forgotten Warning," CBN.com http://www.cbn.com/spirituallife/churchandministry/grady_hagan_prosperity.aspx (accessed July 20, 2015).

9. Henry Gainey, "The Afterglow," The Word for Today http://www.amazon.com/Afterglow-Calvary-Basics-Henry-Gainey/dp/0936728760/ (accessed July 8, 2015).

Pentecostals in historic churches such as Episcopal, Lutheran, and Catholic, which were being called "Charismatics." A new term has arisen today to designate those who believe in the full expression of the ministry of the Holy Spirit but do not want to be identified with Classical Pentecostals or Charismatics in theology and some practices. That name is *Empowered Evangelicals*.[10] This is the subject of the book by the same title written by Rich Nathan and Ken Wilson. Peter Wagner tried at one time to develop the name "Third Wave," around 1988 for the newer churches like the Vineyard, but it did not really stick as a descriptor.

So, what language is used to describe the Gift of the Spirit?

Baptism in the Holy Spirit

The Gift of the Spirit is often spoken about in specific ways within Pentecostal and Charismatic circles. You will hear folks in that tradition say, "I got my baptism in the Spirit at a little country church," or "my uncle got his baptism in the Spirit at a revival meeting." My late father-in-law used this term in such a way. He often spoke of his father as having received his "baptism in the Spirit" at Azusa Street, the historic Pentecostal meetings that ran roughly between 1906 and 1915. My father-in-law was a product of a specific denomination, which was not only fond of the terminology, but specific in its meaning when it was used.

Depending on who you are talking to when you use the phrase *baptism in the Holy Spirit*, you will either receive an extreme amount of heat, or if you are fortunate, some light. In the two Pentecostal denominations of my youth and early adulthood, this term had a specific meaning and in one of those groups, it had a specific meaning with no flexibility at all.

The concept of being baptized in the Holy Spirit is presented in all four Gospels (Matt. 3.11; Mark 1.8; Luke 3.16; John 1.33-34). Outside the Gospels, Luke used the phrase in Acts 1.5 and 11.16. Just before his Ascension, Jesus said to his disciples, "For John baptized with water, but in a few days you will be baptized with the Holy Spirit" (Acts 1.5). The other occasion was when Peter quoted Jesus, "Then I remembered what the Lord had said: 'John baptized with water, but you will be baptized with the Holy Spirit'" (Acts 11.16). In all these passages, the term is *baptize*, not *baptism*. It must be noted that the term *baptism in the Holy*

---

10. Rich Nathan and Ken Wilson, *Empowered Evangelicals: Bringing Together the Best of the Evangelical and Charismatic Worlds* (Boise, ID: Ampelon Publishing, 1995 Reprint edition (March 3, 2009).

Spirit is not the language of Scripture. As a matter of fact, the term *baptism in the Holy Spirit* never appears in Scripture. For some groups who have built their identity around that specific distinctive phrase, those can be fightin' words.

Subsequence

There are two ways by which this Gift of the Holy Spirit is thought to be received. First, it is believed by some that the gift is given *subsequent* to salvation. Salvation is seen as the entry point; one confesses her/his sins and finds entry into a new life with the destination of heaven. The Gift of the Spirit in these groups is something one receives *after* salvation.

In some Pentecostal denominations, one must *speak in tongues* (thought to be the gift listed in 1 Corinthians 12) as the initial evidence that the gift of the Holy Spirit has been received by a believer. This *baptism in the Spirit* is usually believed to be a second work of grace, salvation being the first one. We must remember that the idea of a second work of the Spirit has its roots in the Wesley Revival in the eighteenth century and serves as the basic foundation for this teaching among Classical Pentecostals who find their roots in Wesley.

Sometimes the experience is also called being "filled with the Spirit." It should be noted for clarity that the language *filled with the Spirit* in Acts 2 is identical to the language in Luke 1 and Acts 4.31. The conclusion that can be drawn is that *subsequent* is not in the theological mindset of Luke when he was writing these texts. The *subsequent* mindset is believed by many because of their experience or the experiences of others because they have been taught to think this way about "getting into" the family of God. I have found over the years that it is a good idea to allow Scripture to nudge our presuppositions toward a more theological mindset as we consider any topic in Scripture. As we read the text, we must develop the discipline of letting the text read us. If we always read the sacred text with our button-down presuppositions, we will never find a fresh message in the text. The concept of subsequent in relationship to the Holy Spirit does not seem to be in the mind or heart of God. It is clear to me that those who preach and practice such a message may be doing so to hold to the "faith" of those who have gone before them. I can admire the value of standing on the shoulders of those who have preceded us, but doing so in a muddled way may continue to bring a static theology instead of one that is dynamic.

Contemporaneous

Second, it is believed that the gift of the Holy Spirit is given at conversion. The late Clark Pinnock, who was a Second Testament specialist, said in a chapter in *Perspectives on the New Pentecostalism*:

> Baptism is a flexible metaphor, not a technical term. Luke seems to regard it as synonymous with wholeness (Acts 2.4, cf. 11.16). Therefore, so long as we recognize conversion as truly a baptism in the Spirit, there is no reason why we cannot use baptism to refer to subsequent fillings of the Spirit as well. This major experience or experiences ought not to be tied down in a tight second blessing schema, but should be seen as an actualization of what we have already received in the initial charismatic experience which is conversion.[11]

The focus of this statement suggests that conversion and the baptism in the Spirit is the same act of God and that there are many fillings, which will follow. All of these continuing experiences are only an actualization of what was completely given and received at conversion. This understanding provides us with a liberating knowledge that says that there are no second-class believers, some who *have* received the baptism of the Holy Spirit and some who *have-not* received the baptism of the Holy Spirit.

As an illustration, picture yourself going shopping at a supermarket to buy food. As you shop, you notice that there are different labels for some food items but there is no difference in the food, except the price for the name-brand. The ingredients are the same and even the taste is the same. An illustration might be in order. Picture yourself going to the market to shop for breakfast cereal. When you arrive, you notice that there are several packages that look like Cheerios®, one of them in a bright yellow box with the word Cheerios marked clearly across the front of the box. Next to it is a clear bag of what looks like Cheerios, but the bag is entitled "Scooters" or "Toasted Oats." You pick each of them up and notice that the ingredients are the same. You have now encountered Cheerios not branded as Cheerios. The non-Cheerios are priced much less than the Cheerios package. The difference is not in the actual product but the brand markings and the price.

A friend of mine who was in the wholesale business selling to large retail box stores once told me that there was a product group that was sold that had a "white" label, a "company" label, i.e., the store brand name, and a "gold" label. The three differently packaged products were

---

11. Russell P. Spittler, *Perspectives on the New Pentecostalism* (Grand Rapids, MI: Baker Book House, 1976), 185.

the same product and all had the same identical ingredients. Some of us are given to purchasing only name-brand labels while others purchase non-brand names.

We must remember that *Baptism in the Spirit* is only a label, a brand name if you please. In *Fire in the Fireplace*, Charles Hummel says:

> The Church often faces the problem of the medicine bottle and its label. It is possible for a person's experience of God to be better than his doctrinal explanation of it. Unfortunately, the reverse can be true. Orthodox theology is often affirmed with little Christian character and service. Good medicine may be incorrectly labeled, while an accurate label can adorn an empty bottle.[12]

It has been my experience that we spend far too much time debating over the phraseology of the reception of the Gift of the Holy Spirit and too little time reaping the benefits of the gift. We have to call this experience something and we have all sorts of Christianese at our disposal. We could call it baptism, infilling, empowerment, a special touch, being zapped, overwhelmed, or any number of other metaphors. It has been observed that it is actually the same experience as what elsewhere is referred to as "born again."

So What?

We have often allowed what we observe as an experience to make conclusions about theology and then read those experiences back into the sacred text. Our experience is often a set of steps. First, we are "born again," a term used by John in his Gospel; in reality, I might add, it is really "born from above."[13] By that phrase we have declared that we are "saved." Then along comes this experience, which has been called the "baptism of the Holy Spirit," and it happens to folks who are "saved." So, we simply conclude that the experience is subsequent and because many folks who have received this experience have spoken in tongues, we conclude that this phenomenon happens when this second experience happens. What we have done is chosen one metaphor for the initial experience of following Jesus and another for a second experience. The Enlightenment's push for reductionism has helped us to reduce the experiences into a pattern and then prove our pattern with prooftexts from Luke and Paul. Could it be that because there is no recognizable

---

12. Charles E. Hummel, *Fire in the Fireplace: Contemporary Charismatic Renewal* (Downers Grove, IL: InterVarsity Press, 1978), 185.

13. See p. 20-21 above for a discussion of this phrase.

pattern in the Second Testament for Christians to follow—remember, the Spirit blows wherever he wills—that the Holy Spirit did not confirm a specific recognizable pattern as he inspired the authors of the text?

For Paul and Luke, it seems clear that *one baptism, many fillings,* is an adequate way to understand this gift. In the book of Acts, there is no one model for how an individual comes to followership of God through Jesus. There is no specific sequence of events delineated for everyone to follow. What one can say is that the Spirit blows where he desires. Russell Spittler says, "Completeness and not subsequence strikes me as a better category by which to understand the arrival of the Spirit in Acts."[14]

The good news is that you already have the gift of the Holy Spirit if you have come to believe in Jesus and have accepted him into your life. We may say that *baptism in the Spirit* is one of the many metaphors like saved, born again, justification, etc., that is used by the writers of the Second Testament to describe the different shades of the experience of receiving Jesus. From reception of the Holy Spirit (conversion) to the time you leave this world, you will be in the process of *being saved* according to Paul in 1 Corinthians 1.18. As that process continues, you will be actualizing the blessings that God gave you once-for-all in Jesus. Some of those blessings are the gracelets that flow through us to others. So be ready at any moment for God to send through you another gracelet to share with someone else for their benefit.

There is a gift of the Holy Spirit, which occurs at conversion. There are also gifts (gracelets) of the Spirit that are given. To that discussion we now turn.

The So-Called Gifts of the Holy Spirit

There seem to be two main theological positions that divide today's Jesus followers concerning the so-called *gifts of the Spirit.* One of these theological positions believes that only some of the so-called gifts remain in which followers can participate. They insist that the so-called *sign gifts* (miracles, healings, tongues, and interpretation of tongues) were rendered inoperative when the Bible was finalized at the Council of Carthage in AD 397. The other theological position believes that all gifts that are listed anywhere in the First or Second Testaments are still available today to followers of Jesus. The flaw in that ointment is that there are likely more gifts/gracelets than what are mentioned in the Bible. Remember, this book is offering an alternative to both of these

14. Spittler, *Perspectives,* 5.

positions. However, with those two positions in mind, the question is: have these so-called *sign gifts* ceased or do they continue?

Continuation or Cessation

Before we begin to offer an answer for the question above, let me assure you that it is difficult to read any piece of material when you already have your mind made up on the issue. Emotions arise that say, "If I pay attention to this material, I may let myself fall into error." I have felt those very feelings in my own study of spiritual gifts.

We must remember that we all have presuppositions. These presuppositions provide a starting point for how we view anything. If you believe that the gifts have ceased and only certain ones remain for Jesus followers today, it will truly be difficult for you to read the following material. However, I urge you to try for a few moments to set aside your present set of presuppositions and read the following pages as unbiased as you can, a hearty goal that is not always reachable. Ask God for his help. He's good at this sort of thing. If you believe that you already know what gift you have because you have discovered it by someone telling you that you have such a gift or by taking a "gift inventory," I urge you to set aside those presuppositions and give the following material a chance to possibly change the way you think and live in his Story.

Four Theories About the So-Called Gifts

There are at least four different theories about the continuation or cessation of the gifts of the Holy Spirit. The following is a brief overview of each theory.

Theory #1: The End of the Apostolic Age

This theory suggests that the gifts ceased at the end of the apostolic age (about AD 100). Any supposed gift being used today will either be spurious or it will have its origination point from Satan.

I have seen this theory in action. I once attended a small conference in Southern California with college and seminary students in attendance that had an interest in the subject of spiritual gifts. There were two biblical scholars debating the issue of continuation or cessation: one believed in continuation the other believed in cessation. At the conclusion of the debate, a student approached the scholar who believed in cessation and asked, "If I am speaking in tongues, where is it coming from?" The answer was simple and direct, "you are speaking by the power of the devil." This particular scholar had a reputation that preceded him.

Chapter 5

During summer times, college students would go away and get involved in Pentecostal meetings and come back to college in the fall "speaking in tongues," and these colleges would hire this scholar to come in and teach those students the wrongheadedness of their experience. I nicknamed him, "Dr. Defanger." I have wondered over the years what would happen if he woke up one morning "speaking in tongues," what would he do? I like to think that God has a sense of humor and that would not be out of the realm of such an attribute.

B. B. Warfield proposed this view in his book *Counterfeit Miracles*. He had the following to say:

> Everywhere, the Apostolic Church was marked out as itself a gift from God, by showing forth the possession of the Spirit in appropriate works of the Spirit—miracles of healing and miracles of power, miracles of knowledge, whether in the form of prophecy or of the discerning of spirits, miracles of speech, whether of the gift of tongues or of their interpretation. The Apostolic Church was characteristically a miracle-working church.

> How long did this state of things continue? It was the characterizing peculiarity of specifically the Apostolic Church, and it belonged therefore exclusively to the Apostolic age.... These gifts were not the possession of the primitive church as such... they were distinctively the authentication of the Apostles. They were never part of the credentials of the Apostles as the authoritative agents of God in founding the Church. Their function (i.e., healing and other miracles) thus confined them to distinctively the Apostolic Church, and they necessarily passed away with it....

> The possession of the charismata (i.e., the supernatural gifts of the Holy Spirit in the early church) were confined to the Apostolic age[15]

> They (the miracle workings) were confined to the Apostolic Age, and to a very narrow circle then."[16]

Here are some considerations to think about as you think through this theory:

15. Benjamin Breckinridge Warfield, *Counterfeit Miracles*, Thomas Smyth Lectures, Columbia Theological Seminary, Decatur, Ga ([London]: Banner of Truth Trust, 1972), 5-6.

16. Ibid., 236.

1. This theory is not supported in Scripture. Nowhere in his book does Warfield support any of his conclusions with an interpretation of Scripture. His whole theory is believed by inference. Now before we get all judgmental about Warfield's nonuse of Scripture, we must remember that we do the same thing. There are all kinds of stuff that we believe and practice in the church today that can't be found in the text of Scripture. So we would be well advised not to use this response to one who suggests that the gifts of the Spirit are from Satan. We must recognize that the same argument is used today against Classical Pentecostals and Charismatics. It is the intent of those who believe that the *sign gifts* have ceased who suggest that certain activities, which occur in the Pentecostal-Charismatic or Empowered Evangelicals circles, should not occur because there is no specific Scripture to support them. It may not be wise then to use this argument with anyone who believes as Warfield did that the gifts have ceased but delivers no Scripture to back up his or her view. In short, know your own theological backside before you become embarrassed by arguing from a point of view that you yourself hold for other ideas within the church.
2. This theory rejects the belief of the early Church Fathers. Warfield notes that the Church Fathers were men who were "outstanding scholars, theologians, and preachers...,"[17] but rejects their testimony about seeing miracles in their own ministries. It is ironic to say that they are "outstanding scholars" and reject their personal testimony. Some of these church leaders were: Justin Martyr, Irenaeus, Tertullian, Origen, Ambrose, Athanasius, Jerome, and Augustine.

At least the second reason suggests that Warfield's position should be abandoned.

Theory #2: Credential and Canon

This theory suggests that the gifts ceased because they belonged to the credentialing stage of Christianity. In these earliest centuries the leaders of the church needed to have credentials among the people they were ministering to—thus the gifts were given by God for this purpose. When the need for credentialing ceased, so did the gifts. The need for credentialing ceased when the full Canon came to be fully accepted about AD 400.

17. Ibid., 37-38.

Chapter 5

Dr. John MacArthur is one of the most visible Bible expositors of this day. In his book *The Charismatics*, John espouses the following:

As we study the Scripture, we find three categories of spiritual gifts. In Ephesians 4 there is a category of gifted men: apostles, prophets, evangelists, teaching pastors, and teachers. These gifted men are called to be leaders in the church. Second, there are the permanent edifying gifts, which would include knowledge, wisdom, prophecy, teaching, exhortation, faith (or prayer), discernment, showing mercy, giving, administration, and helps (See Romans 12.3-8, 1 Corinthians 12. 8–10, 28).

Third, there were the temporary sign gifts. These were certain enablements given to certain believers for the purpose of authenticating or confirming God's word when it was proclaimed in the early Church before the Scriptures were penned. These sign gifts were temporary. Their purpose was not primarily to edify, although sometimes edification did occur. The four temporary sign gifts had a unique purpose—to give the apostles credentials, to let the people know that these men all spoke the truth of God. But once the Word of God was inscriptured, the sign gifts were no longer needed and they ceased.

The gift of miracles and the gift of healing were both special sign gifts given for the single purpose of confirming God's revelation.

The gift of healing was one of the four miraculous sign gifts that were given to help the apostolic community to confirm their preaching of the gospel message in the early years of the Church. Once the Word of God was completed, the signs cease. Miraculous signs were no longer needed"[18]

MacArthur's contention for this view is based on his reading of Paul's writings to the Corinthian church (1 Cor. 13.8-10). We must remember when we are reading Paul's material to the Corinthians that we are reading "corrective material," not a treatise stating everything that should be known about the subject being written about.

As an illustration, our tendency is to read Scripture very literally or woodenly because we have been taught to think literally about the Bible as we read it. So, when Paul corrects the Corinthians about too

---

18. John MacArthur, *The Charismatics: A Doctrinal Perspective* (Grand Rapids, MI: Zondervan Publishing House, 1978), 131, 149.

many prophecies, we are prone to take that number literally. If one was attending a small group meeting where prophecy was allowed and there was a prophecy, then another, then another, then another, and then a fifth one. Someone would invariably suggest that the last prophetic word was out of order or must have been delivered "in the flesh." However, if a reader understands the material to be corrective, it could well have been the following scenario. The problem: when you come together, all you do is prophesy. So, think about holding it to three or four in order for others to participate with the gracelets that God may be flowing through them.

MacArthur contends that when Paul stated, "But when that which is perfect is come, then that which is in part shall be done away" (1 Cor. 13.10, KJV). The phrase *...that which is perfect...* is interpreted by him to mean the completed Canon of Scripture (including the Second Testament). For him, the phrase *that which is in part shall be done away* refers to the spiritual gifts such as miracles, healings, tongues, and interpretation. This view is widely held by both Reformed and Dispensational scholars.

Here is the rationale for his exegesis; okay, it's a wee bit technical, but I'm sure as a reader you will understand:

The word *perfect* is a neuter noun in the original language of the Second Testament (Greek) and it refers to a *thing* and not a *person*. He reasons that the word "scripture" fits the neuter reference; therefore Paul is referring to Scripture when he penned these words to the Corinthians.

The *first* weakness of this conclusion is that neuter nouns can often refer to *someone* rather than *something*. As an illustration: the word *begotten* in John 3.6 is neuter, but it refers to Jesus; the word *spirit* is neuter, but it is clear from Scripture that even though the word *spirit* is neuter in Greek, the Spirit is not an "it" but a person.

A *second* weakness is that the interpretation suggests that the reader must depart from the immediate context to determine the identity of the word *perfect*. Those who offer this as a correct interpretation turn to Paul's writing to Timothy (2 Tim. 3.15-16). In this passage the word *Scripture* is used and it is a neuter noun. The reasoning pattern that is used is as follows: because *Scripture* is a neuter noun in the Timothy passage and *perfect* is a neuter noun in the Corinthians passage they must mean the same thing. However, one must not overlook that in order for the Corinthians to understand *perfect* in this way, they must have had 2 Timothy in hand. They did not, nor did Paul, because Paul had not yet written that book to Timothy.

A *final* weakness of this theory is that this interpretation overlooks a rule of interpretation, which says, *a passage of Scripture cannot mean what it could have never meant to the first hearer.* The first hearers had no conception of the Second Testament becoming Scripture. When the Corinthians had the letter written to Paul that we call 1 Corinthians, that was it. They most likely didn't have a copy of Galatians. There was not a Christian bookstore that they could go to and purchase a scroll of Galatians. They only had their letter in hand and then only one copy of it that may have been passed around to their home gatherings. They did not think of it as the Bible, only a word of correction from a brother who functioned as their pastor for a period.

This was outside of their frame of reference. Since it could not have meant *the Second Testament* to them, then it cannot mean the Second Testament or Canon today.

Let me take a moment to examine a way of thinking about how we interpret Scripture with other Scripture. If you drew a line across a page and made a dot in the middle, which would here represent 1 Corinthians, everything to the left of that dot would be material that was created before 1 Corinthians and everything to the right of the dot would be material that was created after 1 Corinthians. What can be appropriate to use for help in understanding a text you are presently reading or studying are those writings by Paul, which he created before he created 1 Corinthians. What would not be appropriate would be to use passages from books that he, or others, had not yet created. So, to refer to 1 Timothy as a reference to help understand 1 Corinthians is completely unrealistic. How can one use something that was not in existence yet for the Corinthians to validate a specific understanding for the Corinthians? You can see how flimsy that kind of interpretative procedure is. Yet, we often resort to it in our own use of Scripture, and pastors and teachers seem to make a meal out of following such a procedure in their weekly presentations. Surely, this is an anemic way of interpreting Scripture. Anemic sermons produce anemic Jesus followers.

One might want to ask, *what is the possible meaning?* A noted Second Testament scholar, the late F. F. Bruce, suggests in his commentary on 1 and 2 Corinthians that the word *perfect* means the Second Coming of Jesus.[19] This interpretation fits the possible natural understanding of this text in light of Paul's statement in 1 Corinthians 1.7, where he stated, *Therefore you do not lack any spiritual gift as you eagerly wait for our Lord Jesus Christ to be revealed.*

---

19. F. F. Bruce, *1 and 2 Corinthians*, New Century Bible Commentary (Grand Rapids, MI: Eerdmans, 1980), 122.

Let me share with you a personal story to illustrate this theory espoused by MacArthur and others.

My own personal experience with John MacArthur brought me face to face with this line of reasoning. I attended his church for a six month period of my life and heard his teaching about this subject. On a completely different issue, I heard him say via cassette, yep, there were such things back in the day, that at the end of the previous year to the time he was speaking that the church had financially ended in the black with a large sum of funds that they had to find ways to give away. I was working at a small church plant in Thousand Oaks, CA, at that point in time. So, on my previous relationship that had developed with John that occurred during the six month journey, I picked up the phone and gave him a call to inquire if I was eligible for some of those funds his church was giving away. He suggested that we meet and talk about it.

We set a lunch appointment and when I arrived I discovered that lunch was with his whole staff at a local pizza parlor. As we munched on pizza, we talked. The conversation went something like this.

"Winn has requested that we share some of the surplus funds that Grace Community Church ended up with at the conclusion of last year," said John as he began the conversation. "I thought it would be helpful to get together with Winn and ask a few questions."

John continued, "I'll start with a bit of information about Winn and then ask him a question. Winn comes from a Pentecostal background and is a bit like Hal Lindsey in that Hal has now accepted all the gifts of the Spirit as being operable including the gift of tongues. The difference is that Hal believes that folks can speak in tongues but has not done so himself while Winn not only believes in speaking in tongues but practices such. So, Winn, my question is: have you ever seen a miracle?

I thought that was a rather peculiar place to begin the conversation, so I said, "John, can you define what you mean by miracle so I will know if what I have seen is what you understand a miracle to be."

He answered, "A miracle is something that only God can do."

My response, "Sure, I've seen miracles. I have seen them happen in your own church on Sunday morning."

To say the least, I think that caught him a bit off guard.

I continued, "On any given Sunday when you have finished preaching, you give a traditional altar call for folks who wish to be saved. And on almost every Sunday that I have attended, folks from all over the auditorium rose to their feet and walked down to the altar where you led them in a prayer to become followers of Jesus. That conversion is a miracle. Only God can do such a thing."

Without a breath, I marched on, "What I don't understand is how you can believe that God can change a person's life but he can't heal a sick body because he stopped doing that through people when the canon was set in stone."

It was quiet for a few seconds and then John responded, "Does anyone else have a question for Winn?"

There were a few and they all dealt with the so-called spiritual gifts that are mentioned in 1 Corinthians 12. By the way, you might want to know that at the conclusion of the pizza lunch, John announced that while we might find common ground in some of our theology, we were at a difference around the theology of the gifts ceasing and because of the position of the church on such matters, it would be inappropriate for them to give funds to a ministry that had a different theological focus. In short, his congregation would not understand how he could preach against such activity and then turn around and give away their funds to one who practiced such an activity.

I not only left empty handed from any surplus money the church was giving away but had to pay for my own lunch. (I am smiling at the irony of that sentence as I write it!)

So What?

If you believe that the gifts have ceased, ala MacArthur, and you interact with folks who are brothers and sisters but who hold the position that spiritual gifts are still available, how do you respond to them? On the other hand, if you believe that the gifts continue and you are talking with a brother or sister who holds the opposite view, how do you respond to him or her? When they try to tell you that you may not be accurate in your thinking and then pull out 1 Corinthians 13.10 as a prooftext, you can say to them: Let me tell you three reasons that I don't believe that this verse teaches what you have come to believe that it teaches about what you call spiritual gifts. Really, you can do that!

Theory #3: Fading Gifts

The third theory is that the gifts gradually faded from existence because the church deteriorated in its mission. Therefore, there was not a continued need for these gifts to operate.

Think about this: even if the church did deteriorate, it would not follow that the gifts would vanish. If anything, they would flourish in pockets so that God could get his message and grace across. Critical thinking[20] has taken a lapse within this theory. Not being able to think critically when reading Scripture or talking with others about Scripture is certainly a fault with which the church must contend. It seems to me that we have "dumbed down" our reading and conversation to the point that the Scripture as a grand EPIC has lost its potency among everyone sitting in the pew Sunday after Sunday thinking that what is being fed is nourishing. What seems to be deteriorating in the church is the contact with Scripture, which appears to be on the wane.

Theory #4: The Gifts Have Never Ceased

The fourth theory is that the gifts have never ceased and continue in the church today.

This appears to be the only reasonable solution. God acted in the past by sending his *gracelets* when they were needed and he still does so today. Just because one abuses the gracelets that God graciously gives is no reason to look for Scriptural support to banish them from being used in the church today. We abuse cars and food every day, but no one is rising to the occasion to banish them from our lives, except in March 2013 in New York City where the mayor outlawed large soda drinks to be served.[21]

---

20. Critical thinking is the learned ability to actively and skillfully grasp a concept, analyze and evaluate it to determine if it is worthy of further reflection leading to a guide to belief or some kind of action. It is a needed concept to practice in the church with so many different popularized beliefs passing around the pew.

21. In March of 2013, sugar-sweetened beverages over 16 ounces would no longer be legal to purchase from restaurants, movie theaters, sports venues, coffee shops, pizza shops, delis, food trucks, or street carts. This restriction will apply to both fountain and bottled beverages and include beverages like soda, sweetened coffee drinks and teas, juice drinks, and sports drinks. Diet sodas or any other calorie-free drink will be exempt and consumers can refill a beverage at a restaurant as many times as they want. Go figure! On June 26, 2014, the New York Court of Appeals, the state's highest court, ruled that the New York City Board of Health, in adopting the regulation, exceeded the scope of its regulatory authority. D. A. Carson. Consulting Editor, *New Bible Commentary: 21st Century Edition* (Downers Grove, IL: InterVarsity Press, 1994).

Chapter 5

So What?

There are those who think they have been given the gift of preserving orthodoxy. It appears that they believe that God died and left them in charge of doctrine. They have become the police of orthodoxy. They are bent on trying to control the movement of God by suggesting that the Bible does not support a continued use of the *sign gifts* in the church. Their suggested orthodoxy is often based on a closed system of beliefs. These beliefs may condemn what God may be trying to do presently while at the same time allowing for things in the church, which God is not doing. For them, his goal is only finding people and enfolding them into the Body of Christ, i.e., evangelism and then preaching to them about what God used to do. It's a wonder how much money is wasted in the church paying folks who continue to tell those in the pew what God used to do. Isn't that amazing?

Let's Have a Conversation

- Why is it important for you to understand that you already live with the presence of Holy Spirit?
- How does the above understanding improve your relationship with God?
- Which of the theories have your heard?
- To which one have you ascribed? Why?

In our contemporary world with the proliferation of different Bible translations, we are prone to read them as we would read a news entry in google, a newspaper, or modern novel set in our own timeframe.

Chapter 6: Help Me Understand!

➡ **Check Your GPS: Where We Are Going!**
- Where We Have Been
- Two Clues: Context and Hierarchy
- Preunderstanding
- First Corinthians Book Overview
- The Interpretive Clue for 1 Cor. 11.17-14.40
- The Body of Christ Metaphor
- So What?

Where We Have Been

In the last chapter, we worked through the concept of the Gift of the Holy Spirit, the idea of the Baptism of the Spirit in terms of whether it should be understood as subsequence or contemporaneous. Next, we looked at the idea of the so-called Spiritual Gifts whether they continue or have they ceased in operation. Finally, we covered at least four different theories about the continuation or cessation of the gifts of the Holy Spirit. Now, we will look at two clues to help us understand how to put the concepts that are listed into the context where they were placed by their original authors and where they live today.

Two Clues: Context and Hierarchy

For years, I have loved reading mystery stories, police procedurals, thrillers, and the like. I enjoyed the process of picking up clues and following the characters as they discovered those clues, sometimes "red herrings" to distract me, and begin to follow them in the adventure of solving their mystery. Clues move the story along.

In this chapter and chapter 8, we will focus on two very important clues that may help you the reader in your search to understand the concept of gracelets. Understanding these two clues will help you comprehend the list-passages in our sacred text and the passages in which gracelets may appear where they are not part of a list. We will begin with the first clue, which is context, and then move on to hierarchy. Each of these clues will be presented as chapters with succeeding chapters fleshing out the biblical text material that each clue points toward. So, we begin with Clue 1: Context.

Clue 1: Context

The *first clue* is the context of the content we are reading. By context, I mean the circumstance surrounding the words that you read in the sacred text. In Scripture that would at least mean the discovery of the following information to the best of one's ability. Discovering who the author of the content is of what we are reading. Then, as readers, we should be aware of the timeframe of the material we are reading, Next, we should know who the reader/listener of the words may have been. Finally, we should discover the purpose the author may have had in writing the words for the readers to whom he was writing. Knowing these concepts will help to some degree in keeping us from reading stuff into the text that the authors never meant to be there.

In our contemporary world with the proliferation of different Bible translations, we are prone to read them as we would read a news entry in google, a newspaper, or modern novel set in our own timeframe. Because the timeframe of this material is current for us, we don't spend any time thinking about any of the above issues. But if we did, we might understand the material better. As an example, if you are reading a political article on google, knowing the author's own political background will alert you to the position of the article.

When we read a period piece in a novel, authors usually provide us with setting and background information within the book we are reading. The author may also be presenting a political or cultural bias as well. Knowing this information helps us have a better read. For the Bible text, one should seek this information out. In one of my first courses in my bachelor's degree, the professor suggested that knowing a "little Greek" (language) was better than not knowing any Greek at all. So, knowing a "little information about a Bible book/passage" is better than knowing no information at all.

In our present search for the meaning of individually listed gracelets, we must secure some understanding of the close context of the lists in the passages in which those gracelets reside. We should also, in a wider circle, understand the section of the book these lists fall into. Finally, we should have some idea of the overall book in which the passages reside. There are other rings in the circle of interpretation that are also important, but for our purposes for the discussion of gracelets, we will pay attention to these three. We will attend to these three rings in the reverse order of how they are listed above. First, we will review the book in which a list resides, then, the section of the book, and finally the list. As an example, to grasp the list in 1 Corinthians, we will briefly examine the flow of the book of 1 Corinthians. Next, we will look at the unit of thought[1] in which the lists are listed. Finally, we will look at the lists themselves.

The above areas are important aspects of knowing the background that is important to help a reader understand the context of a passage being read or studied. Using the First Testament as an example, when one studies a book like Hosea, is would be useful to know who Hosea is, to whom he was delivering his message, and the situation that caused him to speak and write as he did. The same is true of all books in our sacred text.

Folks in the Western church are prone to think about the Bible in very simplistic terms. Here's an example:

I spoke on a Sunday in a church about the topic of "women in ministry." I took time in the presentation to provide information about the context so that those listening could understand my conclusions.

The week after that Sunday presentation about "women in ministry," the church offered its whole teaching time for a Q&A. One individual rose to ask this question: "Why do we need Winn to tell us all that history stuff? Why can't we just pick up the Bible and read it and let the Holy Spirit tell us what it means, after all he wrote it." I wasn't asked to respond. The response that was provided was shaky at best, an attempt to promote harmony. After the service, I went to the one who asked the question and asked:

"When you were in school, did you take a literature course?"

"Yes," he responded.

"Did you read Shakespeare?"

"Yes."

"Did you understand Shakespeare?"

---

1. The unit of thought in which the lists occur in 1 Corinthians is 1 Corinthians 11.17-14.40. For the thoughts that I will express there, I owe my thinking to Ron Ford. I first met Ron when he led two church planting initiatives that resulted in fully organized and growing congregations in Bakersfield, CA, and later in Oceanside, CA. As of this writing, he is now the Chief Marketing and Technology Officer at International Academy of Public Safety, San Diego, CA. Yes, some careers do change.

"Yes."

"How did your understanding come about?"

He told me that his teacher had spent a large amount of time talking about the background of the reading as well as helping the deciphering of some of the words within the text.

"So, what's the difference between what your literature teacher did and what I did?"

He responded, "Because you were doing that to the Bible and all we have to do with the Bible is pick it up and read it and ask the Holy Spirit to tell us what it means."

So, I pursued, "Have you ever had a discussion with someone about a Bible text who thought the same way as you do about how to understand the Bible?

"Yes," he said.

"So, was the meaning that you and he came to as you read separately the same meaning?"

"No," was the reply.

"Why?" I asked.

There was no answer. I didn't tell that story to suggest that I got the best of him. I did tell the story to demonstrate how naïve we are as we approach the reading of Scripture.

Thinking about the context of a given text in Scripture often comes as a surprise to Jesus followers who are given to seeing verses and lists presented to them ad infinitum in sermons and books. Today's church has a dualism that would not have existed in the churches in the first century. We have created churches who are not charismatic and those who are charismatic. Sermons and books have been written from both perspectives. Pick up any book on spiritual gifts and often the gifts are identified in categories, given a definition usually from experience, and then some words written about the usage of each of the gifts. As an example, I recently heard a presentation in which the speaker was talking about the word *apostolic* and he inserted many business ideas like vision and strategy into the concept as he spoke. This kind of situation was unavailable to the first hearers of the sacred text.

Chapter 6

As a further illustration of this thought, once while teaching a course on spiritual gifts, I was approached by a Jesus follower from the non-pneumatic part of the church, a well-established megachurch. He was in the course with an openness to learn from a point of view other that the one he and his church held. He wasn't argumentative. He was a learner. He came to me after the weekend course and said, "I've sat in lots of spiritual gift classes before, but this is the first time I have been offered a view of spiritual gifts that is based on the context in which the gifts are listed." So, what we would like to accomplish here in this book is to say to Paul, "what do you mean by these things you call gracelets inside the book you are writing?" and ask the same of any other author that may list one or more gracelets in their writings. We want to ask the question: what do you mean by a word of knowledge or a word of wisdom or prophecy or healings? What are your definitions, if you offer one? It seems that would be a more realistic idea than to settle for the common *experience definitions.*[2] Now we turn to the concept of what one might need to understand before tackling any text in the Bible.

Preunderstanding

It is always important to understand the context of any passage that you are trying to comprehend as you read and study Scripture. The context in which the author places his thoughts via the inspiration of the Spirit gives life to any passage we are pondering. The context then consists of the historical data that we will look at in a moment. In addition to the context, in this case we will look at the whole book of 1 Corinthians and the specific context for the passages we will observe. There are four important aspects of history that are important for a *preunderstanding* of the context for any passage of Scripture. These aspects will help you control the urge to read some twenty-first-century meaning back into the first-century language. They are:

1. who wrote the book (author),
2. to whom was it written (recipient),
3. when was it written (date), and
4. what is the aim of the book (purpose).

Author

When you read a post on Facebook from a friend that you know

---

2. This does not mean as an interpreter of the text in which the often-called gift-lists are located that the definitions that I offer are the "correct" ones. You should read the whole text surrounding a given list and wonder: What did the author of this text mean when he wrote this?

personally, you are familiar with the language s/he is using because you have most likely had a conversation with that friend at some time before reading the post. You probably don't have problems picking up when they are being cynical, or the metaphors they are using, as they write. In short, you know the author. Our problem when we read the sacred text is that we don't know the author. Yep, we've heard some things, mostly in sermons or teaching that we have heard, but we haven't investigated the material about the author ourselves. We just assume that what we have heard is correct. Often, this means that we are bringing a secondhand understanding about the author to the text. So, understanding who the author of the book or passage that is being read will help you as a reader place the book into some historical context. As an example, when we study a Second Testament book like 1 Corinthians, it is helpful to know something about the author Paul in order to better relate to why he is writing the way he does to these people.

Receiver

When you receive a message from a friend, s/he may often use words that are familiar to you within your common context. The same is true in our sacred text. When Paul wrote what we call 1 Corinthians, he had already lived and worked in Corinth for over a year. He was familiar with the folks there and their own specific culture. Knowing these circumstances of the receivers helps you as a reader solve the mystery of the text. In short, in reading the text of the Corinthian correspondence, you may have a difficult time understanding what Paul is saying to them as he stresses some thoughts.

Date

Words seem to change meaning with time. Stop reading for a moment and think about words that have changed meanings in your lifetime. When we are reading a text, the date locates the timeframe for the words being used. As an example, just because Paul uses a specific word when he wrote his first book that we call Galatians;[3] it does not follow that if he uses the same word in 2 Timothy, which was his last book, that it means the same thing. Dating the timeframe thus becomes important.

Purpose

It is commonly held that in the Second Testament that the authors are seeking to provide some solutions for specific problems in specific

3. Some Second Testament specialists believe that 1 Thessalonians was the first book that Paul wrote.

communities to whom they are writing. So, in 1 Corinthians, not knowing that Paul was writing to help the Corinthians think through the problems they were having in their church life may cause a misreading of the book and without that knowledge, a reader may not be able to make any sense of the words on the page of the sacred text.

From the helps that we listed above, discovering the occasion of a biblical book is important in your preunderstanding process. The following are suggested questions that could be asked in order to gain this information. They are only suggestive and there are many more that you might create on your own journey of discovery. You might ask:

- What were the customs of the people?
- What were the problems they faced?
- What were the needs of the people to which the book was written?
- What was going on in their community that caused the writing of this book?
- If it were a First Testament book under consideration, one might ask: What was occurring in Israel, which occasioned the writer or prophet to say what he was saying?

The process of the discovery of this information gives a new set of presuppositions through which the content of the book or passage you are reading can now pass.

This preunderstanding will augment the context of any given passage in the sacred text. As a note of clarification, the original listeners/readers of our sacred text did not have to go through this procedure because they most likely knew who the author was and may have known her/him personally. They were part of the recipients of the book. They knew when it was written, i.e., they lived in the context of where the book was written. Finally, from their reading of the book and knowing the author, recipient, and time, they were left to figure out the aim or purpose of the book. The books of the Bible were not written out of thin air but into a cultural milieu that needs to be grappled with by present readers.

You may look for material to assist you in your discovery process by looking at a Bible Dictionary,[4] an Old or Second Testament history book, or in the Introduction of a commentary, or the introduction to a

---

4. BibleStudyTools.com, "Dictionaries," BibleStudyTools.com http://www. biblestudytools.com/dictionaries/ (accessed January 30, 2015). For those who like to do basic research online, this is a list of some older and one newer Bible Dictionaries.

book in a study Bible. You can most likely find a lot of this information as close as a Google search.

However, be careful! Be aware that *all* background material is basically "interpreted history."

The reason for beginning here is for you to immerse yourself as much as possible in the culture of the recipients of the book. Remember, the message of Scripture was first given to them and the meaning is wrapped up in what the author meant when he/she was writing the material and the range of meaning and understanding the audience had.

It is now time for us to turn our attention to an overview of 1 Corinthians gleaned from asking the above questions.

First Corinthians Book Overview

To grasp the possible meaning of the two so-called gifts lists in 1 Corinthians as well as those gracelets listed separately, it is important to gain a brief amount of information about the background of the church at Corinth. Remember, the lists in Corinthians (and elsewhere) are *ad hoc* and placed in their context to support Paul's argument about diversity in the church.[5]

Here is an overview of the whole book of 1 Corinthians in two sections: the historical context and the textual context. In the next chapters, we will look at the individual gracelets in these two lists that are offered by Paul in 1 Corinthians as well as those that are possible gracelets mentioned outside of the two lists.

Historical Context

At the beginning of the letter, there are several things to observe: the author and the recipient are listed in the text: Paul, as an author and the phrase "church…in Corinth"[6] as the recipient, rather than the churches in Corinth.

Paul, called to be an apostle of Christ Jesus by the will of God, and

---

5. Russell P. Spittler Edith L. Blumhofer, and Grant A. Wacker, *Pentecostal Currents in American Protestantism* (Urbana and Chicago: University of Illinois Press, 1999), 10.

6. This is an article from the older International Standard Bible Encyclopedia on Corinth. http://www.internationalstandardbible.com/C/corinth.html

our brother Sosthenes, To the church of God in Corinth, to those sanctified in Christ Jesus and called to be his holy people, together with all those everywhere who call on the name of our Lord Jesus Christ—their Lord and ours: Grace and peace to you from God our Father and the Lord Jesus Christ (1 Cor. 1.1-3).

There may have been several different groups who met together in homes in Corinth and surrounding cities. Some of these groups could have been groups that had divided according to different teachers (1 Cor. 3). Together, all the house groups in Corinth made up the "church in Corinth." This is often a difficult concept to get our heads around because in today's Western church settings, the church is often thought about as a building on the corner of walk and don't walk and there are many such buildings in one city. To think of one church in a city made up of several groups meeting in homes causes some imaginative problems for today's readers.[7]

It is believed by most Evangelical scholars that Paul,[8] the author of several Second Testament books, was the author of 1 Corinthians. It must be noted, however, that while we call this book "first" Corinthians that it was at least the second piece of correspondence that Paul had written to the Corinthian church after being with them and leaving to go back to Jerusalem (cf. 1 Cor. 5.9).

The church at Corinth[9] was the recipient. Corinth was a Grecian city on the isthmus, which joins the Peloponnesus to the mainland of Greece. It is about forty-eight miles west of Athens. The ancient city was destroyed by the Romans in 146 BC. The Corinth mentioned in the Second Testament was really a new city having been rebuilt about a century afterwards and populated by a colony of freedmen from Rome. It was the seat of government for Southern Greece or Achaia (Acts 18.12-16) for Rome. Corinth was noted for its wealth, luxuriousness, and immoral behavior. A word was coined to speak about the citizens of Corinth: *corinthianize*. It had a large mixed population of Romans, Greeks, and Jews. When Paul first visited the city (AD 51 or 52), Gallio, the brother of Seneca, was proconsul. Paul resided in Corinth for eighteen months (Acts 18.1-18).

---

7. Robert Banks, *Going to Church in the First Century* (Beaumont, TX: Christian Books Publishing House, 1980). You can get an imaginative feel for a church gathering from Banks book. The Preface begins this way: "This brief narrative attempts to depict what it was like to attend an early church gathering in the middle of the first century."

8. This is a reasonable article on Paul from BibleStudyTools.com. http://www.biblestudytools.com/dictionaries/bakers-evangelical-dictionary/paul-the-apostle.html

9. J. E. Harry, "Corinth," Wm. B. Eerdmans Publishing Co. http://www.internationalstandardbible.com/C/corinth.html (accessed July 10, 2015).

At Corinth, he first became acquainted with Aquila and Priscilla and soon after his departure, Apollos came to Corinth from Ephesus.

The Book of Acts provides us with a summary, which helps update the history of 1 Corinthians. Even though Acts was written several years after 1 Corinthians, it records events that occurred before the writing of 1 Corinthians. Paul departed from Corinth in the fall of AD 51 and returned to Antioch traveling through Ephesus where he left Priscilla and Aquila (Acts 18.26). After some time in Antioch, he returned to Ephesus visiting Galatia and Phrygia. He arrived in Ephesus toward the end of AD 52. Luke records that Paul spent about two years in Ephesus (Acts 19.1-10; 21-22). He wrote to the Corinthians this second time (1 Corinthians) sometime during AD 54.

The main purpose of the book was to answer questions about how to deal with specific church problems, which was delivered to him by Chloe's household during their visit with him in Ephesus (1 Cor. 1.11) and by word of mouth and in a letter carried by Stephanas, Fortunatus and Achaicus (1 Cor. 16.17).

Textual Context

The book of 1 Corinthians appears to be made up of three segments. First, when Chloe's household came to Corinth, they came bearing news about some divisions within the church. There was division in the different house churches about who their ultimate leader was. These groups were probably set up not unlike the schools that gathered around some of the philosophers of the day, even though Corinth did not have a noted philosopher. Some had chosen Peter, some Apollos, some Paul, and some Christ as a possible emulation of philosophic schools. Paul answers the question about division within the church in chapters 1-4.

Second, Stephanas, Fortunatus and Achaicus (16.17) arrive with a letter asking more questions of Paul. The answers to the questions from them begin at 7.1. However, three additional problems must have surfaced after the letter had been written and before these three left for Ephesus to find Paul. Those three problems are addressed in the second segment of Corinthians in chapters 5-6. The three problems were: a specific case of immorality (5.1-13); lawsuits (6.1-11); and immorality in general (6.12-20). The final segment of this book comprises the answers to the letter, which was written and answers questions about marriage (7.1-40); and food (8.1-11.1a). Next, there were problems centering on public worship, which included the veiling of women (11.1b-15); the Lord's Supper (11.17-34); spiritual gifts (12.1-14.40); the resurrection (15.1-58); collections (16.14); and finally Apollos (16.12). This overview gives the flow of the author's material as he answered the many questions that the Corinthian church had.

Lists Context

It is within this overall context that we can now turn to the specific context of two passages, which will help readers understand Paul's thoughts on individual members of the Body of Christ owning (discover, develop, and deploy) their gracelets or if gracelets are received on an occasional basis. These two passages provide us with interpretive keys for understanding this material.

I might point out that we have moved from the historical background to an overview of the whole book and now we move to a larger section within that book and will finally move to a smaller section of the book for discussion of the specific so-called spiritual gifts. These are the "circles of context" mentioned earlier. It is important to remember that meaning comes within the context and only within the context. We can now look at the text of this section, which appears at 1 Corinthians 11.17-14.40.

The Interpretive Clue for 1 Cor. 11.17-14.40

We must remind ourselves that when we are reading the books of the Second Testament, we are reading problem-solving literature. While some focus on the letters of Paul as church problem solving, others suggest that *all* of the books of the Second Testament were written to solve problems of specific congregations. The church of the first century had problems. In order to solve these problems, God provided writers who offered his solutions for those problems. In the First Corinthian correspondence, there are at least twelve such problems, which have been identified. Three of those problems are written about in the section in 1 Corinthians 11.17-14.40. They are:

- The divisions within the body (11.18 cf. 1.10–12)
- The violation of the Lord's Supper (11.20ff.)
- The misuse of the gracelets of the Spirit (12.1-14.40)

We must note again that this section on the gracelets is presented by Paul to the Corinthians as correction. He was not writing a book sharing all his insights about gracelets. He was not writing an essay for a course project. He was not providing information or instruction about this topic. He was providing correction to the abuse of a specific gracelet: tongues. In the Corinthian church, the problem was "speaking in tongues." It was seen as a mark of being spiritual or as Russ Spittler suggests, it was the Corinthians propensity to value "spirit over matter."[10] This problem in the Corinthian church may be put to present-day churches: what problem does a present-day church have that the correction of this letter could help solve? Here's an illustration from the Vineyard[11] denomination where I spent almost thirty years. From the earliest days of the Vineyard when "clinics" for ministry were invented by John Wimber, the idea of praying based on a "word of knowledge" became a standing component in those ministry clinics and became a foundational idea within the Vineyard. One has to wonder if that might not be a problem that the "correction" of the text in 1 Corinthians could address. In the Vineyard, one might suggest then that one problem to address is speaking a "word of knowledge" as a mark of being spiritual or to have a time specifically devoted to the presentation of these so-called words as a mark of the spirituality of the local Vineyard church where this occurs. One only has to ask oneself if when a person has a so-called "word of knowledge" that the idea of the person participating is not being thought of as "spiritual?" While that thought may be denied by those within the Vineyard, it is nevertheless a question that could be asked. Other churches certainly have other problems like the disease of *topicalitis*, where a group of verses are thrown together by a teacher and presented as the Word of God.

So the point here is: the Corinthian material is corrective, not instructional nor informational. The sentence that begins the direct interaction about the problem, which is at 1 Corinthians 12.1, could be paraphrased to say, "Now about the things of the Spirit, brothers and sisters, I am not willing to allow you to be continually uninformed so here's a corrective slant on your present thinking."

It is important to remember when we visit this passage that Paul's corrective manner drives his choice of words and thoughts. Overkill can be a technique of correction. We must, in the final analysis, understand that Paul was trying to drive the self-immersed, self-taught spiritual Corinthians back toward a central point of understanding of the gracelets of the Spirit in general and tongues in particular as being part of the diversity that needed to be experienced within the Corinthian church. Most likely that would also be an idea that could be floated within any church when one idea becomes prominent and sought out for its supposed spiritual value.

---

10. Edith L. Blumhofer, *Pentecostal Currents in American Protestantism*, 10.

11. I participated with the Vineyard from its inception and have considered myself a "critical loyalist" all the years that I was associated with this group. This idea was impregnated in me by my friend and mentor, Russ Spittler. But, let me hasten to say that how that idea has worked out in my life is solely my own responsibility. I am still a critical loyalist, but with a broader canvas to work on, i.e., the whole church.

Chapter 6

The context of the passage on gracelets is set in the larger context of 11.17–14.40. In this larger setting, Paul's own language provides us with the clue for understanding the passage. The phrases are as follows:

- ...for your meetings... (11.17)
- ...when you come together as a church,... (11.19)
- When you come together,... (11.20)
- ...when you come together (11.33)
- ...when you meet together... (11.34)
- ...edifies the church. (14.4)
- ...that the church may be edified. (14.5)
- ...in the church... (14.19)
- ...the whole church comes together... (14.23)
- ...when you come together,... (14.26)
- ...keep quiet in the church... (14.28)
- ...should remain silent in the churches... (14.34)

The clue that helps us interpret Paul here is the phrase: *when the body comes together.* This helps us interpret the listings of gracelets at 1 Corinthians 12.8-10 and 12.27-31. These lists do not catalog all of the gifts of the Spirit. Within the context of problem-solving, they may have been the ones that the Corinthian church was having the most difficult time in controlling when they came together. Most likely they are given to demonstrate to the Corinthians that there are some very visible gifts, which God will send when the body comes together, and that their specially chosen one, tongues, is not the only one that God sends. The central message may have been that God is a God of diversity not a God of singularity.

This *clue* also helps us interpret the questions of 1 Corinthians 12.29-30. The questions asked by Paul in this passage should be answered *No!*, because of the way they are phrased in the original language. It is true that not everyone present at a meeting of the church will be used by God in all the gracelets of the Spirit. Thus, does everyone work a miracle? Certainly not! Does everyone heal? *No!* Does everyone speak in tongues and give an interpretation? *No!* When understood in this way, one can see that Paul is not prohibiting any of the gracelets to flow through the followers of Jesus. He is suggesting that not all followers will be used by God in the same way and that the Spirit delivers his gifts how he wills through individuals to whom he wills. It does not appear that they bring the gracelets with them, all polished, shiny, and better developed than on the last occasion of their coming together.

The actual, *charismatic* service of 1 Corinthians 14.26ff. can be seen as a realistic model where the Spirit will certainly use each one as he sees

fit to minister to another. We must note that the language of 14.26 is
...*each one has*..., not ...*all have*. We might extend this thought, though
not specifically found in the text, that how God works when they come
together is the same way that God works when they are scattered into
the community where they live.

The Body of Christ Metaphor

Within this section (11.17-14-40), Paul also presents the metaphor
of the Body of Christ. This is to persuade the Corinthians that their
individual spirituality was misplaced. That real spirituality comes
within the confines of functioning as a part of the Body of Christ, not
functioning with an independent, self-indulged spirituality. We must
redefine and reimagine in our own Western culture the idea of the
corporate identity in the church. There is the need to think clearly about
the unity of the community and diversity of individuals within the
community. Individualism is a Western cultural value not necessarily a
biblical value. Let me hasten to say that oftentimes small communities,
sometimes in our timeframe called small groups, is where individuals
attend to "show off" their individual spirituality in the presence of
others.[12] This should not be so!

The *context* of the body metaphor includes the following five items.
Paul wants the Corinthians to be completely informed:

- About how to solve their problem (12.1-3).
- That God as Trinity (although the word is not mentioned) was
  committed to the giving of gracelets (12.4-6).
- That the Spirit revealed himself in the gracelets (12.7).
- That there are many gracelets, which God does give (12.8-11).
- That while there are many gracelets, there is only one body in
  which they are used (12.12-13).

The Body Metaphor in 1 Cor. 12-14-2

Paul used a common metaphor with which his audience could
identify—a physical body. The choice of that metaphor is not bound by
time in that it is still understandable today. He told his readers that each
physical body is an organism that has many parts, which work together.
Only when the various parts perform their diverse functions does the
body become whole. Wholeness is the result of the gracelets being
used appropriately. If discord occurs, destruction and degeneration will

---

12. Randy Frazee, *The Connecting Church* (Grand Rapids, MI: Zondervan 2001), 8.

affect the vitality of the body. James D.G. Dunn believes that while *the metaphor of the body illustrates Paul's theology; it must not be allowed to dictate it.*[13] I'm in his corner. The metaphor is illustrative, not wooden or concrete in its characteristic.

We must understand that for Paul, *a member of the Body of Christ does not mean* individuals who have, in the sense of own or possess a specific gracelet. The Body of Christ for Paul is dynamic. It is never static. The Body is constantly being energized by the giving and receiving of gracelets from one member to another as the Spirit directs. The purpose of Paul in using this metaphor seems to be to further his interest in demonstrating unity and to suggest that while the Corinthians have pointed to one gracelet, tongues, as the most important, the idea of the body having many parts would mitigate against such an interpretation and lifestyle among the congregants. It seems that our Western glasses focused on individualism has been used to see this in a way that is opposite from what Paul intended.

The Traditional View of this Metaphor

The traditional view of 1 Corinthians 12.14-26 affirms that the Body has many parts. The point is that a foot can never be a mouth no matter how hard it tries. Each member has a specific function and only in that specific function can the member operate. Just like the physical body is dependent on each member, the spiritual body is dependent on each member. This view believes that *body member equals gift* and that each gift has a specific function, which is developed by its owner.

The traditional view of 1 Corinthians 12.28-29 suggests that God has appointed in the church these gracelets (apostles, prophets, teachers, miracles, healings, etc.), that each person (Body member—hand, eye, etc.) does not do the same thing. This understanding comes from the specific answers to the questions of 1 Corinthians 12.29: Are all apostles? Are all prophets? Are all teachers? Do all work miracles, heal, speak in tongues, or interpret? As we previously wrote, each of these questions must be answered *No!* The original text allows for no other answer. However, when you set the list outside of the context, one can make it mean anything that one wants to make of it.

The traditional view concludes that each believer already possesses one or more gifts of the Spirit just like a body has parts like a hand, which is always a hand, and that all that needs to occur is for the believer to

---

13. Dunn, *Jesus and the Spirit*, 430, footnote 27. Dunn is a British scholar who has written extensively on the Spirit.

discover which gift(s) (body part) he or she has and then develop(s) those gifts. This view also teaches that a believer should be content and not seek any other gift or gifts. Can a liver also be an esophagus?

Does Scripture Support the Traditional View?

The following Scriptures from 1 Corinthians provide some insight into the answer of the question above. The Scripture is referenced in part (in italics) and then a brief comment is provided.

- *...eagerly desire the greater gifts* (1 Cor. 12.31). If each member of the body is equal to a gift and God has given to each of us a specific gift or gifts, then why are we commanded to desire? The text could here be translated in a present tense sense, *keep on eagerly desiring....* In the traditional view, the stress is put on "eagerly desiring the greater gifts" and refers to the preceding gifts, which are said to be ranked, first apostles, second prophets, third teachers, etc. (12.27-28). It should be said that Paul's argument through this section has been the need for diversity within the body, not the ranking of gifts, which would cause divisions within the body. The following verses (12.29-30) demonstrate that ranking is not Paul's mindset but variety is. To demonstrate further that Paul's mindset is not ranking, we may note that prophecy is listed sixth in the first list and second in the second list in chapter 12. Paul does not include five of the nine gifts in the first list also in the latter list. From the four he does include, the first three are in reverse order in the second list. Finally, we may say that this whole idea of ranking the gifts where some are superior to others clashes head on with the metaphor of the body where Paul stressed mutual interdependence not superiority. These reasons all demonstrate that Paul has a lack of concern for ranking gifts. It is fair to say that no one gift is superior to any other gift.
- *I wish you could all speak in tongues* (1 Cor. 14.5). Paul asks the Corinthians, (12.27) do all speak with tongues? The only answer available is *No!* The context, as we have seen, is *when the church comes together*. Paul's word *wish* in this verse is also in 7.7 where Paul wishes that all were celibate. He certainly understands that not everyone will be celibate. *Wish* is something like; *it would be my greatest hope that....* The same meaning would apply at 14.5. Paul's *greatest hope* is that all could speak in tongues, but he knows that all shouldn't because it would not be orderly (14.40).
- *Therefore* (because you should build up the body), *he who speaks in tongues should pray for the power to interpret* (1 Cor. 14.13). Another question that Paul asks in 12.30 is *do all interpret?*

Again, the answer is *No!* If the gifts are already given to each member of the body, then why would Paul require these believers to pray for a specific gift as they were meeting together as a church?

It seems more likely that the traditional view of the Body of Christ is without foundation in its acceptance of *member equals gift.* Paul's point is that in the body, there is diversity within unity. He concludes that there must be a greater acceptance of a variety of gracelets in the church over against one, the gift of tongues. When the charismatic church focuses on one gracelet like tongues, healing, or prophecy, a word of knowledge, and a non-charismatic church focuses on cerebral gifts, then God's intended diversity for the Body of Christ is destroyed. On the other hand, when we find ourselves believing that others are not as important as we are in the community of believers, then God's intended unity for the Body of Christ is destroyed.

So What?

When we understand the interpretive clues that Paul provides for his readers, the passage in this section of Corinthians takes on the life its first readers would be more likely to have understood. It appears that sometimes when the church came together that the Spirit moved in what we might call spontaneity, giving each member a gracelet to share for the common good of the group. However, the Spirit is never spontaneous; he knows exactly what he is going to attempt to do when a community gets together. What looks spontaneous to us is planned by him. Our job is to become tuned to his frequency. Often when the church comes together, it is frequency deficient.

There is constant tension in charismatic churches today as to when these more visible gracelets of the Spirit should operate. Paul suggests an answer for this dilemma. There are times when the early church was more conducive for the gracelets mentioned in 1 Corinthians to occur. Remember, this material was and is corrective material. Paul refers to this in 1 Corinthians 14.26. On the other hand, there were times that Paul implied that the church came together for the purpose of instruction from Scripture as seen in 1 Timothy 4.13-14. As corrective material, this passage might suggest that the gracelets as was known in the Corinthian church needed to take second chair to the gracelet of instruction. In the fast-paced Western world, we want to cram everything into a Sunday service in about an hour, as if that is the only time when the church comes together. You would think that we are selling glasses in a mall somewhere! If we understand Paul correctly, the church comes together at different times for different reasons. There is ample opportunity for believers to benefit from this divine harmony that God provides in these specific times.

Let's Have a Conversation

- Why is it important for you to make a difference between owning a gift or being the conduit through which God sends a gracelet?
- How would being a conduit for God's gracelets for the benefit of others make your relationship with God better?

∞

GRACELETS

Chapter 7: The Gracelets in 1 Corinthians: Part 1

Check Your GPS: Where We Are Going!
- Where We Have Been
- The Gracelets in 1 Corinthians
- Supernatural?
- Celibacy (*thelō de pas anthrōpos eimi hōs kai emautou*): 1 Cor. 7.7, 25-40
- So What?

Where We Have Been

In the previous chapter, we opened a discussion on two clues to help us understand the setting of the gracelets as they appear in the sacred text. We began with context and briefly about hierarchy, which will be developed more fully in the next chapter. Then we talked about the idea of preunderstanding that a reader needs to make sense out of the text. They were author, date, historical, and textual context. We provided an overview of the book of 1 Corinthians and finally looked at the context in which the first and second lists in 1 Corinthians 12 reside. Now we turn to the specific gracelets listed in 1 Corinthians beginning with celibacy in this chapter and, then, move on to others in the next chapters.

The Gracelets in 1 Corinthians

The main purpose of 1 Corinthians was to note the problems in the Corinthian church and offer solutions to problems. Paul could do the first because of the visits and letter that he received from the church at Corinth. He could do the latter because he had spent about eighteen months in the church at Corinth, so he had a pretty good idea of how to go about offering specific ideas about how they should move forward. Remember, the letter was corrective material. We will share about the gracelets in the way that they appear in the context of 1 Corinthians. Some appear by themselves while others appear in one of the two lists. In order of mention, they are:

- celibacy (*thelō de pas anthrōpos eimi hōs kai emautou*): 1 Cor. 7.7, 24-25
- word of wisdom (*logos sopias*): 1 Cor. 12.8

- word of knowledge (*logos gnoseos*): 1 Cor. 12.8
- faith (*pistis*): 1 Cor. 12.9, 13.2
- gifts of healings (*charismata iamaton*): 1 Cor. 12.9
- miracles, Effects of (*energemata dunameon*): 1 Cor. 12.10, 29
- prophecy (*propheteia*): 1 Cor. 12.10, 28
- discernings of spirits (*diakriseis pneumaton*): 1 Cor. 12.10
- tongues, kinds of (*gene glosson*): 1 Cor. 12.10, 28
- interpretation of tongues (*hermēneia glōssa; diermēneuō*): 1 Cor. 12.10, 28
- administrations (*kuberneseis*): 1 Cor. 12.28
- philanthropy (*psōmizō pas*): 1 Cor. 13.3

Supernatural?

As we begin to look at the lists of gracelets and the individually listed gracelets, let's begin with a question: Are the gracelets natural or supernatural?

It is not easy in a worldview that espouses a split level philosophy to return to a holistic theology. A lot of words that we use today in English came into existence during the Middle Ages and contain an implicit platonic dualism.[1] One such word is "supernatural," which was first used during that timeframe.[2] This word reflects "a nonbiblical worldview universe, [and] is not found in Hebrew thought.[3] Rather, the word used for the word supernatural is the Hebrew word *bara*, a verb with God as its subject,[4] which implies "an origin in and continued dependence on God."[5]

Thus, before the Middle Ages/Enlightenment, "supernatural" basically was used to talk about the creation as a whole. The Middle Ages/ Enlightenment basically produced a worldview in which creation was split into two parts. God was up there (heaven) and humankind was down here (earth).[6] The meaning of the word supernatural was directed

1. James R. Coggins and Paul G. Hiebert. Eds., *Wonders in the World* (Hillsboro, KS: Kindred Press, 1989), 128-129.

2. Dictionary.com, "Supernatural," Dictionary.com http://dictionary.reference.com/browse/supernatural?s=t (accessed February 8, 2015).

3. James R. Coggins and Paul G. Hiebert. Eds., *Wonders in the World*, 129.

4. Winn Griffin, *God's Epic Adventure [The Reader Edition]* (Woodinville, WA: Harmon Press, 2014), 84.

5. James R. Coggins and Paul G. Hiebert. Eds., *Wonders in the World*, 129.

6, N. T. Wright, "Ask. N. T. Wright: April Q & a Response," Facebook: N.T. Wright Discussion Group https://www.facebook.com/notes/n-t-wright/ask-n-t-wright-april-q-a-response/644725545580506 (accessed November 4, 2015).

up toward the God realm and was thought of as something that from time to time would show up down here in the humankind realm. When we use the word supernatural now, it is a way of confirming that the present worldview is split. We live with this present dualism, so we are constantly misusing the idea of supernatural because we have not been exposed to the thoughts that supernatural is not a split reality but a wholeness reality. God doesn't really live upstairs but lives with us here and now where "...in him we live and move and have our being" (Acts 17.28). He does not have to be called upon to come to where we are because he is already here where we are. Thus, in the area of gracelets, from time to time the breath of the Spirit infuses our actions in this present world through word and deed and flows through us a "drop of his grace," to others because he wants to effect change in his world. The use of the word supernatural to describe those moments is usually mis-understood as God invading our world from his world, when all along he is living in his world with us.

Sometimes we have to work really hard to change a mindset that we are so impregnated with by not using a word or phrase that will be taken within the common mindset to mean something different than we intend it when we say or write it. Maybe, by the grace of God, we can find a new expression that is fully impregnated with a "whole world" concept instead of a "split world" concept and use it until such a time when it becomes corrupted with a different meaning. So, take a journey that is worth taking by helping folks understand that supernatural doesn't mean what is commonly thought when one hears the word, and help find a new expression to use.[7]

In *The International Dictionary of Pentecostal Charismatic Movements*, W. J. Hollenweger, writes:

Russ Spittler suggests that glossolalia is a human phenomenon, not limited to Christianity, not even to religious behavior...."[8]

7. N. T. Wright, *Simply Good News: Why the Gospel Is News and What Makes It Good* (San Fransciso, CA: HarperCollins, 2015), 78-79. The above paragraph is influenced by Wright's comments and were written on my Facebook page on February 4, 2015 at https://www.facebook.com/winngriffin/posts/10152972643588260 and here edited.

8. Stanley M. Burgess. *The International Dictionary of Pentecostal Charismatic Movements (Revised and Expanded Edition)*, W.J. Hollenweger. "Gifts of the Spirit: Natural and Supernatural." (Grand Rapids, MI: Zondervan, 2003), 667-668. Later in the same dictionary, in the Glossolalia article (670) Russ Spittler says: "Whatever its origin, glossolalia is a human phenomenon not limited to Christianity nor even to religious behavior among humankind."

It seems to me that Spittler is pointing out that the dualism of natural and supernatural may be untenable.[9] With that seed thought, because glossolalia is one of the so-called spiritual gifts, one wonders if that idea can be extended out to think about other gifts/gracelets in the lists of Paul and elsewhere in NT writings. Hollenweger seems to think: "The notion that glossolalia (or any other gift of the Spirit, including healing and precognition) is essentially 'supernatural' is in my view biblically and scientifically untenable."[10]

Paul does not seem to divide these gracelets in these two categories that they are often categorized into: supernatural and natural, but rather as Hollenwegner suggests, which is that they are "functional." Paul is not trying to define the gracelets as he lists them because he is much more at ease with their function than their definition. For him a gift is a "natural gift that is given for the common good, [and] operates in an ecclesiological and Christological context. This makes the gracelets open to the community for participation and for discernment."[11] I think that Spittler and Hollenwenger are on to something. This is a different reflection than the controlling thinking within the Pentecostal, Charismatic, or Third Wave movement where they are seen as openly supernatural.

In the same article, Hollenweger quotes Miroslov Volf:

Christians should not be defined so narrowly as to include only ecclesial activities. The Spirit of God is active not only in the fellowship (of the church) but also through the fellowship in the world. The Spirit who is poured out upon all flesh (Acts 2.17ff.) also imparts charisms to all flesh: they are gifts given to the community, irrespective of the existing distinctions or conditions within the community. Very frequently charismatic is taken to mean extraordinary. Ecclesiologically this restricted understanding of charisms can be found in some Pentecostal (and "charismatic") churches that identify charismatic with spectacular. A secularized form of this "supernaturalistic reduction" is found in the commonly accepted Weberian understanding of Charisma as extraordinary quality of a personality. One of the main points of the Pauline theology of charisms is to overcome this restrictive concentration on the miraculous or extraordinary.[12]

---

9. Not his words, my interpretation of his words.

10. *The International Dictionary of Pentecostal Charismatic Movements*, 667-668.

11. Ibid., 668.

12. The quote by Miroslov Volf is from the article "Human Work, Divine Spirit, and

What if, what we have accepted as supernatural was all along normal but empowered by the Holy Spirit? What if we changed our language a bit to get the theological gist of this shift? What if what we have perceived as natural is "subhuman," i.e., less than the true humanity of Genesis 1? What if what we call supernatural is true humanity, which Jesus came to restore, i.e., the second Adam metaphor? What if the gracelets are a taste of true humanity in a present evil age? Thus, gracelets that often look like they are natural talents in the fallen world take on a different thrust when the Holy Spirit moves through the truly human person in order for his purposes to be served. It is with this possible thought pattern that we write and think about the gracelets as we find them in our sacred text: natural talents infused by the Spirit.[13]

We now begin our tour of gracelets in the Corinthians passages, which appear in lists and by themselves with a summary statement by Paul at the very beginning of his letter that we refer to as 1 Corinthians.

Eagerly Waiting (1 Cor. 1.4-7)

Paul writes:

I always thank my God for you because of his grace (*charis*) given you in Christ Jesus. For in him you have been enriched in every way—with all kinds of speech and with all knowledge—God thus confirming our testimony about Christ among you. Therefore you do not lack any spiritual gift (*charisma*) as you eagerly wait for our Lord Jesus Christ to be revealed.[14]

This introduction sets up the idea that seems to be behind the concern of Paul as he writes to the Corinthians. Because of God's grace, the Corinthian congregants are enriched in all kinds of speech and knowledge (think gracelets). There is no lack of the diversity of gracelets within the Corinthian church.

New Creation: Toward a Pneumatological Understanding of Work." *Pneuma* 9 (2, Fall 1987).

13. One scholar, Dr. Matthew Croasum, in the Vineyard denomination, which sometimes has a fixation on at least one gracelet, i.e., word of knowledge, with a certain definition that is more closely aligned with Pentecostals and Charismatics than it may be with the text of 1 Corinthians, presented a paper at the 2015 Society of Vineyard Scholars conference in which he suggested that natural and supernatural are not biblical terms.

14. I have added the transliterated Greek words in italics so the reader can get connections for this topic in this text. We discussed the idea of *charismata* in Chapter 6.

It may be that Paul's first thought in his push for diversity is found in 1 Cor. 7. 7.7, 25-40. So, it is with that text that we begin.

Celibacy (*thelō de pas anthrōpos eimi hōs kai emautou*): 1 Cor. 7.7, 25-40

The spontaneous proficiency for married or single, male or female, to have one's sexual appetite lowered to a hibernation status in times of being apart. In the case of those who are married, or in close encounters with those who are not married. It is the gift, which provides the Jesus follower a way to escape sexual sins.

As one will discover, sexual activity was part of the Corinthian culture and some of the followers of Jesus were involved in such a lifestyle.

The transliterated Greek above is translated in the NIV as: "I wish that all of you were as I am." This sentence is in the discussion about marriage that begins at 7.1, which reads, "It is good for a man not to have sexual relations with a woman." While Paul wrote those words, they are not his. He is quoting the concept propagated by the Corinthian church. He is most likely referring to his gracelet of celibacy.[15] *The Good News Bible* translates this as "Actually I would prefer that all of you were as I am; but each one has (received) a special gift (*charisma*) from God, one person this gift (*charisma*) another one that gift (*charisma*)." The word "has" in the above sentence could be understood in the sense of the receiver, the end user, having received for the moment of need, rather than "has" in the sense of being given a gift that is now possessed. So, paraphrased we might read these verses as follows: "My greatest wish would be that you could be like I am. But, each of you continues to receive gracelets from God, one receiving one kind of gracelet and another receiving another kind of gracelet." What we are contending for here is that a gracelet is a momentary drop of God's grace for the occasion that it is needed.

With our continued notion that one is what they are when they are, we would say that one receives the gracelet of celibacy in the moments that celibacy is needed. It is true that a person, male or female, may

---

15. Gordon D. Fee, *The First Epistle to the Corinthians: The New International Commentary on the New Testament: Revised Edition* (Grand Rapids, MI: W.B. Eerdmans Publishing Company, 2014), 316. Fee suggests that celibacy here is "the singular gift of freedom from the desire of need of sexual fulfillment that made it possible for him to live without the need for marriage at all." It is from that thought that I constructed the possible definition above. It should be clear to the reader that this may not be what Paul had in mind when he wrote these words. It is an evaluation of his meaning because of the topic matter at hand.

choose to live a celibate life; the gracelet of celibacy is received in those moments when sexual desire is heightened and sustains a person during that period.

I have lived in a Pentecostal/Charismatic environment since nine months before I was born. I may have been in a Pentecostal church service the first Sunday after I was conceived. I've lived with Pentecostals and Charismatics in their major denominational expressions. In all those years, I have never heard a Pentecostal or Charismatic person ask for the gracelet of celibacy. Ask for tongues, yes, prophecy, yes, pray for the sick, yes, cast out demons, yes, but not celibacy. I wonder why that is?

I think celibacy is a wonderful gift to talk about with youngers who are not married so they can ask the Spirit for this gracelet while they are on a date. God can send to them this gracelet in those heightened moments of arousal and make them in that moment celibate. This may be one of those gracelets that comes directly from God without the participation of another human being such as the UPS person who delivers a package.

Over the years, I have traveled to teach. When I leave my wife on one of those occasions, I ask God to give me the gracelet of celibacy for the time that I am away from her. When I return, as I like to tell the story, as the plane is landing, I ask God to remove that gracelet. I want to make sure that I get my request in early so that by the time I arrive at home, I have been fully restored to my normal sexual appetite. I trust that this personal illustration is not too embarrassing to you as a reader.

Fee has a contrary view as he presents it in his book *God's Empowering Presence*. One should remember while talking about *charismata* at 7.7, Paul's conversation partner are the Corinthians who have decided to argue that being celibate was surely more spiritual than being married. Fee says that Paul "would never have imagined that the word means 'spiritual gift,' as thought all *charismata* were Spirit manifestations of some kind.[16] Fee's point may be valid, but then again it may not be inconceivable that Paul could have seen it the way he saw all other uses of *charismata*. The reader must decide. It should be noted that Fee seems to have changed his mind between the writing of the *God's Empowering*

---

16. Gordon D. Fee, *God's Empowering Presence: The Holy Spirit in the Letters of Paul* (Peabody, MA: Hendrickson Publishers, Inc., 1994), 138. It should be noted that Fee seems to have changed his mind between the writing of this book and his revised 1 Corinthian commentary, which is noted above. Yep, even the great ones change their mind on occasion.

Presence book and his revised 1 Corinthian commentary.[17] Yep, even the great theological minds change their mind on occasion.

So What?

One has to wonder if this is a gracelet, what might occur if it were taken seriously!

Let's Have a Conversation

- Does the gift of celibacy really make a difference? In what ways?

༄

17. Fee, *The First Epistle to the Corinthians.*

GRACELETS

Chapter 8: The Gracelets in 1 Corinthians: Part 2

Where We Have Been

In the previous chapter, we discussed the gracelets, along with the the question of whether the gracelets are supernatural or natural. In order to get at that topic, we wrote about the idea of a split level worldview that has seriously impacted the way in which we view things of the Spirit. We suggested that Spittler and Hollenwenger are on to something that can help us in our understanding of the gracelets.

What Does Two-Three-Four Mean?

Patterns are fun. I remember when I was first given a kaleidoscope. It was fascinating to see all the patterns, unlimited patterns, all made possible with reflections. So, when someone suggests a pattern in the text of Scripture, it does not necessarily follow that the author of the text had that pattern in mind when it was written. This is most likely the case for the following material.

As a reminder, we must always keep in mind that when we are reading the Second Testament or one if its books, we are reading problem-solving literature. The Corinthian church had a long list of problems. One of those problems was the misuse of the gracelets of the Spirit. Most likely, as we suggest below, it was the misuse of the gracelet of tongues. When Paul answers their question about gracelets (12.1-14.40), he begins with a short catalog of nine gracelets and gives another catalog in 12.28. The two lists here are the first such listings of gracelets in Paul's writings.

In the original language, the gracelets in 12.7-11 appear to fall into a two-three-four pattern. We will use this pattern in discussing the gifts in this first list. We must remember that this is not an exhaustive list of gifts, only a representative list of the diversities of the Spirit's manifestations. Lists in the sacred text are not inclusive of everything but ad hoc as these two lists demonstrate. The lists themselves are unimportant; what is important is that they demonstrate the diversity that Paul is driving the Corinthians toward understanding so that the Corinthians would stop focusing on only one gracelet, tongues, to the exclusion of all other possible gracelets.

We propose the following categories reminding ourselves that these are our categories not necessarily Paul's categories. The categories are:

- Gracelets that Ellucidate (wisdom and knowledge)
- Gracelets that Facilitate (faith, healings, miracles)
- Gracelets that Edify (prophecy, discerning prophecies, tongues, interpretation of tongues)

The classification of the gracelets is an attempt to suggest a pedagogical alignment by me for the nine gracelets listed in the first list in 1 Corinthians 12. Paul was probably not thinking my thoughts on this subject, but I am trying to think his thoughts after the fact, most likely an impossible task, but one worth entertaining. What can factually be said about the lists is that they are *ad hoc*. Their main purpose for Paul was Paul's way of demonstrating that there is diversity in the gracelets and that one specific gracelet should not be the only desired gracelet. The main purpose of this list for Paul seems to be a way of demonstrating that there is diversity in the gracelets given by God and that no one specific gracelet is better than another and that possible bragging about its use was counterproductive since God was making the decision through whom he sends a gracelet to another.

A question to consider is: How do we understand these gracelets when the decisive character and function of each gracelet is not made clear in the passages where they are recorded? The Corinthians must have known what Paul was talking about when he listed these gracelets. It is at this point that we often bring our own experiences to bear on the text.[1] While our experiences are our experiences, they must often be shaped by what Scripture teaches us. It is true that sometimes we are taught something and then we experience it. While other times,

---

1. Sometimes this process is called eisegesis, which is a reading of one's own agenda into a text, as the opposite of exegesis, the reading out of a text using a wide range of disciplines.

we experience something and then we view the teaching of Scripture through that new lens. It might be well for us to remember that the experience of theology came before the writing of theology. Sometimes the writing was to enlighten the understanding of a correct experience, while at other times it was to correct a malfunctioning experience. The goal of the authors who have experienced and then write theology or write theology and then experience is to bring harmony between theology and experience, not to pit them against each other making one more important than the other. The latter activity, as such, is the work of the spirit of reductionism, which is a product of the Enlightenment.

While interpretation must ultimately be grounded in the text, practice of biblical truths will often illuminate the meaning of some Scripture. Current manifestations of the so-called spiritual gifts, including their use and misuse, can aid our understanding of Paul's teaching.[2] But, while this is helpful, it seems that the better way to grasp what Paul is talking about is to look at the gracelets within their specific context.

The section in which these two lists of gracelets occur is 1 Corinthians 12.4-31. The specific problem that Paul was addressing was *inspired utterances* or *speaking in tongues*, which use was believed to set apart those spiritual ones who had been initiated into a higher mystical plane by having spoken in tongues from those who had not spoken in tongues. Sound familiar? The same idea is often present in contemporary communication about the gracelets.

Perichoresis: Diversity In Unity

Paul's discussion begins with the presentation of God's character as the ultimate model of diversity within unity. It is Paul's intention to reinforce the point that diversity, not uniformity, is essential for a church to be healthy. His interest seems to be in "the unity of source, which lies behind a diversity of phenomena."[3] Just before the gifts list, which gets most of the attention in studies about spiritual gifts, Paul wants to demonstrate the idea of unity within diversity because of the evaluation that tongues was a "higher-status" gift and that "diversity is secondary" to unity.[4] He provides his reasoning that the source is not

2. Hummel, *Fire in the Fireplace*, 131.

3. Anthony C. Thiselton, *The First Epistle to the Corinthians: A Commentary on the Greek Text (NIGTC)* (Grand Rapids, MI: William B. Eerdmans Publishing Company, 2000), 928.

4. Ibid.

just the Holy Spirit, but God who is the giver of grace through Jesus and the Spirit.[5]

In 1 Corinthians 12.4-6, we discover that there are varieties or different assignments of the gracelets. While there are different apportionings[6] of gifts, their source is the *same* Spirit (v. 4). There are also diversities of services, but the *same* Lord (v. 5). In Jesus there are innumerable ways in which the gracelets become a service to his followers. There are diversities of workings, but the *same* God (v. 6). Diversity, as we suggested above, not uniformity, is the essential character of a healthy church. God, who is one, is characterized by diversity and has decreed diversity for his church. Diversity within unity is surely a mark of the character of God.

The word apportionings "alludes to the sovereignty of the Spirit of God in apportioning of gifts to each as the Spirit wills. Although different apportionings may seem stilted or clumsy;" it brings out the idea of what is allotted by God. "One does not question what is freely given as one's portion."[7] What we have suggested through this book is that the gracelets are given to individuals who are the beneficiary of God's grace. As a beneficiary, we have received the portion that God deems fit. It's his choice for his purposes. While that runs counter to our very Enlightened understanding of God, who we see as a loving God that will give us exactly what we want in the portion that we want it, it is important to note that these are his gracelets to give as he wills. Remember, they are gracelets, God's drops of grace, which he freely and generously gives to his children individually. It is apparent that one cannot say that he or she is more important because of the gracelets that God provides occasionally. As an example, those who claim status as pastor-teacher, or prophet, or apostle, or evangelist, for which we provide details below, cannot claim prominence thereby supporting some hierarchal system, which produces an *"us and them"* system of practice that has become systemic in the ChurchWorld[8] of today. The playing field is flat. We are all priests in reality. It seems to me that what needs to occur is a revamping of the way we think about gracelets. While for the Corinthian, it was tongues as a highly valued gift, in today's church, it seems to be pastor is a very highly valued gift. Not

---

5. Ibid., 929.

6. Ibid., 928.

7. Ibid., 929.

8. ChurchWorld is the term that I use to describe the "organized/institutional" church in today's society over against the term "church" which are those gathered any time and any place without the presumption of institutional practices.

so, says Paul! Of course, this concept applies to all the gracelets that are mentioned in the sacred text.

Paul may be designing a pattern for how the dance of the Trinity (*perichoresis*)[9] occurs by suggesting that the *source* of the gracelets is the Spirit. He gives gracelets through Jesus who *services* or *ministers* through and to the individuals and God brings about the intended result or the divine effect. The word *working* (NIV) is the root word for *energy*. It is a word, which expects a result.

We must note that this passage is a clear reference to Trinity and is the earliest Second Testament text written with such implication. It has been stated that "Trinity is the name of the Christian God."[10] It is obvious that the working of the gracelets is solely by the action of the Triune God. Here is a possible way to get our heads around this idea. As each member of the Trinity is working out their parts, humankind becomes the *conduit* through whom the Trinity sends the gracelets to the fallen world as the tools of redemption in the Trinity's reconstruction project of renewing this world. In addition, humans, who are conduits of gracelets, may well be the direct *recipients* of the gracelets of the Spirit as well.

Mel Robeck, a professor at Fuller Seminary, once described the word *manifestation* in verse 7 as meaning *a festive hand* or *a dancing hand*.[11] With that mindset, one could think about God's dancing hand giving a gracelet through a Jesus follower *to* another follower or to one who is not presently following Jesus. This *giving* is done for his fame and for the benefit of others, i.e., for his name's sake. The manifestation of the gracelet is a disclosure of the activity of the Spirit in the midst of the community gathered and scattered. The manifestations are given through us to build us up so that we can participate in the renewal of God's universe from a healthy standpoint rather than an unhealthy one and this activity is all captured in the tension of the now but not yet of the kingdom.

One can see that in this concept of gracelets, individuals do not "have" or "own" a gracelet or a cluster of gracelets. The gracelets belong to the Spirit, who shares them through Jesus and God ensures that the

---

9. *Perichoresis* is the idea that theologians believe suggest the partnership of the Trinity in a kind of circular dance in which all dancers are equal and no one partner is a leader, but all three carry on specific assignments as they interact with each other.

10. Fee, *God's Empowering Presence*, 161, footnote 275.

11. Russ Spittler and Mel Robeck. "Spiritual Gifts." Sprint Quarter. 1982.

gracelet given has the results that he wishes in his renewal project. With that concept in mind, let's turn to the gracelets under discussion in this chapter.

Elucidating Gracelets

The first two gracelets in the list in 1 Corinthians 12 are gracelets that are sent by God to enlighten us with instruction. They are *Word (Message) of Wisdom* and *Word (Message) of Knowledge*. Think of the word, *word*, as a *message* of content. These two utterances bring understanding. They allow us for a brief moment to see something as God sees it. These two gracelets may be the flip side of one coin. They are transrational, that is to say, beyond our own rational thought processes. They are not learned activities, but activities that are given by the Spirit for one follower to give to others.

So, let me take a stab at seeing the text as a corrective for some possible poor practices that the Corinthian church was practicing. In current reality, we have condoned poor usage of these gifts because we have identified these gracelets from experience rather than from the corrective context in which they were found or from translations, which are unclear, such as *The Message* on 1 Corinthians 12.8, which identify the first two gracelets as "wise counsel" and "understanding." In my opinion, this could not have been Paul's mind.

Wisdom, Utterance of (*logos sopias*): 1 Cor. 12.8

The proclamation of the good news as the Spirit imparts a depth of understanding of the truth of the gospel that may not have been understood before by the recipient of the gracelet.

The Greek word *logos* can refer to *speaking* or *thinking*. When it refers to speaking, it is *word*, not in the grammatical sense of a single word, but in the sense of language, i.e., a group of words, which is spoken and contains a concept or idea. It is in that sense that it is used here.

This gracelet is not the wisdom of God but the *speaking* of the wisdom of God. Wisdom is the content of the gracelet, but the gracelet itself is the declaration. It is given through a member of the body of Christ and received by the community, by another in the body, or by others outside the community of faith.

Wisdom in 1 Corinthians

Let's try to grasp what Paul may mean when he used this phrase here for the only time in his writings. When writing to the Corinthians, Paul uses one of the favorite words (wisdom) of the Corinthians to demonstrate for them the great diversity of the gracelets of the Spirit that were available to the church at Corinth. Remember, they were fixated on one gracelet, namely tongues. Paul, on the other hand, is working on disproving their fixation by pointing to the diversity of gracelets that are at hand in the kingdom. In short, he wanted them to understand that there was more than one gracelet.

The word for *wisdom* (*sophia*) is used fifty times in the Second Testament. Twenty-eight of those times Paul uses it. From the twenty-eight times in all his writings, he used it seventeen times in 1 Corinthians. Sixteen of those times are in Chapters 1–3. The only other occurrence in 1 Corinthians is here at 12.8 (*logos sophia*). This may suggest to us as readers of 1 Corinthians that Paul's abundant use of the word *wisdom* in 1 Corinthians may have been because of the Corinthians' own misunderstanding of the concept, therefore, he had to bring correction to them.

Paul presents two kinds of wisdom: human and divine. My labored point here is that it is within the book of 1 Corinthians that one has to begin to understand this gracelet. To begin elsewhere, i.e., in someone's experience, is to be misguided or simply wrongheaded. To demonstrate how Paul presented the concept of *wisdom* to the Corinthians, the following verses are quoted from the *New Revised Standard Version* with comments and the word wisdom is **bolded** in each selection.

- *For Christ did not send me to baptize but to proclaim the gospel, and not with eloquent **wisdom**, (en sophia logou:* in wisdom of speech*), so that the cross of Christ might not be emptied of its power* (1.17). The distinct suggestion that Paul states is: the words, which he came to share with the Corinthians, were not from his own human speech, but from speech empowered by God, i.e., an utterance of wisdom.
- *For it is written,*
    *"I will destroy the **wisdom** of the wise,*
    and the discernment of the discerning I will thwart." (1.19)
  The preceding verse speaks about the message of the cross, which Paul had preached to the Corinthians. The message was foolishness to those who were perishing and the power of God to those who were being saved. The message of the cross is God's way of saying what he had already spoken about doing. Through the cross, he would set aside and destroy human wisdom. It appears that some in the Corinthian church thought themselves so spiritual, that the wisdom they had, matched the wisdom of God. The message: it is lunacy to try to outwit God.

- *Where is the one who is wise? Where is the scribe? Where is the debater of this age? Has not God made foolish the **wisdom** of the world?* (1.20)

  The wisdom to which Paul refers belongs to this present evil age. The cross has made the wisdom of the world mere foolishness.

- *For since, in the wisdom of God, the world did not know God through **wisdom**, God decided, through the foolishness of our proclamation, to save those who believe* (1.21).

  What Paul had just declared in verse 20 is now stated as true. God's wisdom is the precise opposite of humankind's wisdom. Through the proclamation of this wisdom, the message of the cross, the Corinthians found salvation.

- *For Jews demand signs and Greeks desire **wisdom**, but we proclaim Christ crucified, a stumbling block to the Jews and foolishness to the Greeks,…* (1.22-23).

  What the Corinthians desired above all else was human wisdom. This was true of some of the Corinthian Jesus followers who brought this idea into their church. God's wisdom, however, is the direct opposite of the wisdom they were seeking. The Jews were looking for miraculous signs of the coming of the Messiah. Because God had acted in power in their past, their expectations were that the Messiah would also come in power. The Greeks, on the other hand, had turned from their traditional gods to the gods of wisdom, because ultimately these gods had brought into being an enlightened culture such as the world had never experienced before. Within these two structures of belief, we still struggle today. The desire for power and wisdom are still ever present in our society and world.

- *…but to those who are called, both Jews and Greeks, Christ the power of God and the **wisdom** of God* (1.24).

  If the Jews were looking for signs and the Greeks looking for wisdom, then why not just give them what they are looking for so they could believe. Paul's point is that the foul crucifixion of a Messiah was the absolute declaration of God's power and wisdom. Paul wants his readers to view things as they really are, from God's point of view, not from their fallen point of view.

- *He is the source of your life in Christ Jesus, who became for us **wisdom** from God, and righteousness and sanctification and redemption…* (1.30).

  The Jesus followers in Corinth, in contrast to the world, owe their new existence to the activity of God and Jesus on the cross. Jesus is the wisdom of God (v. 24), but not the kind of wisdom by which the Corinthians were bewitched. The true wisdom of God can be understood in three specific metaphors: righteousness, sanctification, and redemption. These three metaphors are equal to one event: the salvation the Corinthians found in Christ.

- *When I came to you, brothers and sisters, I did not come proclaiming the mystery of God to you in lofty words of* **wisdom**... (2.1).
  Paul reminds them of his own preaching ministry when he first arrived in Corinth from Athens. He did not preach with the eloquence of a human speaker.
- *My speech and my proclamation were not with plausible words of* **wisdom**, *but with a demonstration of the Spirit and of power*... (2.4).
  Paul's words were not from human effort to influence or inspire his hearers. His words were a demonstration of the Holy Spirit. The verbalization was itself a manifestation of the power of God. One must note that Paul does not say that his preaching was accompanied *by* a demonstration of the power of God, but that his words *were* the demonstration of the power of God. Paul may be illustrating an "utterance of wisdom" in this personal illustration.
- *...so that your faith might rest not on human* **wisdom** *but on the power of God (2.5)*
  The belief of the Corinthians must finally focus not on spoken human wisdom but on God's wisdom spoken as power to bring about transformation in their lives.
- *Yet among the mature we do speak* **wisdom**, *though it is not a* **wisdom** *of this age or of the rulers of this age, who are doomed to perish* (2.6).
  The *mature* that Paul refers to are those who in their conversion have received the Spirit. Paul again contrasts the kind of wisdom that he brought to the Corinthians with the kind of wisdom with which they were so fascinated. The wisdom that he proclaimed was the cross of Christ.
- *But we speak God's* **wisdom**, *secret and hidden, which God decreed before the ages for our glory* (2.7).
  The word *mystery* in Paul means something that was in the past hidden but is now revealed through Christ and made understandable through the Spirit. This message, that there is salvation in Jesus, was hidden in God from the beginning until the period of the gospel of the kingdom was preached and lived out by Jesus.
- *And we speak of these things in words not taught by human* **wisdom** *but taught by the Spirit, interpreting spiritual things to those who are spiritual* (2.13).
  Paul's message of the cross of Christ was presented to the Corinthians, not by an utterance of human wisdom but by an *utterance of wisdom*, which came from God. This utterance of wisdom could be taught to those who had the Spirit. The

spiritual ones, then, would be the Corinthians who understood the message of the cross, which Paul had proclaimed, not the ones who believed that they were spiritual because they had spoken in tongues. Those speaking in tongues thought that the wisdom they possessed excelled them beyond the human realm, while, in fact, those supposed spiritual ones were trapped by human wisdom.

- *For the **wisdom** of this world is foolishness with God. For it is written, "He catches the wise in their craftiness,..."* (3.19).
  Paul is trying to demonstrate that the wisdom, which the so-called spiritual Corinthians had adhered to, was, in fact, folly.

- *To one is given through the Spirit the utterance of **wisdom**, and to another the utterance of knowledge according to the same Spirit* (12.8)...
  The implication of Paul's own use of the word **wisdom** *(sophia)* discloses his belief that an *utterance*, which comes from God and shares God's wisdom, is not dependent on any form of human wisdom or fluency.

It appears from these summary points that the conclusion of Paul in 1 Corinthians is that a *word of wisdom* was a gracelet used in the proclamation of the good news about Jesus. This is not the popular understanding of the gift. In the Pentecostal and Charismatic forms of the church, there are definitions that range from a revelation of God, which concerns people, things, or events in the future, to hearing God's wisdom in a difficult situation, which would resolve some problem. Some see this gracelet as the ability to give wise advice as per the previously mentioned translation of this verse in *The Message*. The common definition for the gracelet from Pentecostal circles is to understand it as a message given by the Holy Spirit to a congregation to provide wisdom at a particular time or for a particular need. The difficulty with these definitions is that they do not take into account the context of the Corinthian church in whose correspondence the gracelet was listed. It seems that for Paul, the gracelet was to help the Corinthian believers proclaim the same message of the cross that Paul had shared with them. Thus, in the proclamation of the good news, whether by preacher, teacher, or lay speaker, the Holy Spirit moves on a person as he wills to impart a depth of understanding of the truth of the gospel that may not have been understood before by the listener. As the person speaks, a *word of wisdom* is being heard and received.

An illustration of the utterance of wisdom from this perspective comes right out of the pages of the book of 1 Corinthians at 2.1-6 that we covered above where Paul writes:

And so it was with me, brothers and sisters. When I came to you, I did not come with eloquence or human wisdom as I proclaimed to you the testimony about God. For I resolved to know nothing while I was with you except Jesus Christ and him crucified. I came to you in weakness with great fear and trembling. My message and my preaching *were* not with wise and persuasive words, but [my message and my preaching *were*] with a demonstration of the Spirit's power, so that your faith might not rest on human wisdom, but on God's power. We do, however, speak a message of wisdom among the mature, but not the wisdom of this age or of the rulers of this age, who are coming to nothing.

The subject of the fifth sentence in the above quote is "my message and preaching." I have added it in brackets after the word "but," so you as a reader won't miss picking up what Paul is saying. Often and unfortunately, this passage is used to support a supposed supernatural event over against preaching, when in fact the preaching itself was the empowered event, that is, the gracelet of the utterance of wisdom, so that the faith of the followers of Jesus in Corinth rested on the power of God's declaration to them.

Remember, the context of this gracelet is the church. Remember also that the church is not just the meeting that you attend on Sunday or some other day/evening of the week at the corner of walk and don't walk. You may be the vehicle through which God sends the gracelet as you function as the church in the world. The *gracelet* is the message to the person or persons who receive/hear the gift.

Knowledge, Issuance of (*logos gnoseos*): 1 Cor. 12.8

A message of inspired teaching or instruction given by the Spirit that brings a new level of maturity in following Jesus to the receiver of the gracelet.

Again, let's remember, we are reading problem-solving literature. The Corinthian church had at least twelve problems to which Paul responded. In the first three chapters, Paul assisted the readers to understand their need for the wisdom of God instead of their worldly wisdom. In chapter 8, he worked on solving their attitude about *superior knowledge*. Gordon Fee says that Paul is freeing this gift of the Spirit from the Corinthians own fascination with knowledge.[12] I think Fee is on to something.

---

12. Gordon D. Fee, *The First Epistle to the Corinthians,* The New International Commentary on the New Testament (Grand Rapids, MI: W.B. Eerdmans Publishing Company, 1987), 592.

The Classical Pentecostal and Charismatic way of understanding this gift is that it is a supernatural ability to know factual information that could not otherwise have been known unless the Spirit supplied it. Facts such as a certain disease, something that is lost, or a person's inner life situation are often thought to be "words of knowledge." Often Peter's knowledge of Ananias and Sapphira's transgression, which is recorded in Acts 5.1-11, is understood as an illustration of this gracelet. It seems that *revelation* would be a more appropriate designation for that story. Stanley Horton, an early Assemblies of God theologian put it well:

> God did give knowledge of facts through visions and in various other ways, but there is absolutely no indication in the Bible that the gracelet of a word of knowledge is meant to bring revelation of where to find lost articles or of what disease or sin a person may be suffering with."[13]

It seems that Horton was writing to curb an experiential way of understanding this gracelet within his own tradition.

Paul uses *knowledge* ten times in 1 Corinthians. To help understand what he may mean by this gift, we must look at 1 Corinthians 2.12-13 where he wrote:

> We have not received the spirit of the world but the Spirit who is from God, that we may understand what God has freely given us. This is what we speak, not in words taught us by human wisdom but in words taught by the Spirit, expressing spiritual truths in spiritual words...,

Three things should be noted in this passage: *First*, there is a reception of the Spirit. *Second*, we received the Spirit so that we might understand what God has freely given us. *Third*, what has been freely given to us is spoken to us in words the Spirit gives. What God freely gave was salvation. Out of the knowledge of what we have been *freely given*, we speak in words taught by the Holy Spirit. James Dunn, a Second Testament specialist, writes with this background in mind when he says that a word of knowledge denotes "some charismatic insight into the things given us by God."[14] Those things given to us by God are some outworking of knowledge given by God as compared to the knowledge they were exposed to in their culture.

13. Stanley M. Horton, *What the Bible Says About the Holy Spirit* (Springfield, MO: Gospel Publishing House, 1976), 272-273.

14. Dunn, *Jesus and the Spirit*, 219.

In 1.5, the Corinthians are told by Paul that "in every way you were enriched in him with all speech and all knowledge."Their knowledge was not limited, because through the reception of the Spirit at conversion they had been enriched in Jesus with all speech and all knowledge. An *utterance of knowledge*, an insight into the things that are freely given by God through Jesus, could have been spoken at any time when the Corinthian church came together or any time that a follower of Jesus was speaking on his own to others any place.

Again, this does not fit well with the popular understanding of *word of knowledge* in which hidden facts within the human situation, some sickness that a person has is revealed, or the location of something lost is revealed. While these do fit into a First Testament seer/prophet situation, they are *not* words of knowledge from Paul's point of view. God can and does reveal facts, sicknesses, and even location of lost things, but it is a mistake to call these *words of knowledge*. They rather should be called *prophetic insights*.[15]

Why is getting the correct idea of the words so important? It's really simple. If you call something, something that it is not, then you are at risk to miss what it is because you have misidentified it. So, if one keeps calling a word of knowledge, a word about someone's sickness, etc., then that person may never have the opportunity to realize the real gracelet of "inspired teaching or instruction given by the Spirit, which brings a new level of maturity in Christ to the listener." Here's an illustration:

Years ago I taught Bible as Literature for several community colleges in the Ventura (CA) Community College system. On one of those occasions while teaching at Moorpark Community College at their extension campus in Simi Valley, CA, I was giving a final exam. For the final exam, I chose to give an oral exam. Each student was given a time during a three hour block to sit with me as I asked them questions about the course we had just finished. At the conclusion of the exam time, a female student asked if she could ask me a question. I responded positively to the request. She was a new follower of Jesus who was struggling with an issue in her former life. The question that she asked was: "What about horoscopes? Can I still read them and depend on their message?" I thought for a second not knowing how I was going to answer the question and without any prompting just began to talk. The story I told her was about the wise men

15. The story of the Samartian woman in John 4 is often seen by Pentecostal/ Charismatics as a "word of knowledge." However, it may be thought of as a *prophetic insight*, which the woman picked up on with her phrase: "I can see you are a prophet."

(astronomers) who came to visit Jesus who followed a star for nearly two years to the location where Jesus was. After the visit, they were instructed by an angel to follow a different route back to their homeland and not follow the suggestion that had been given to report back to Herod. When I finished the story, she looked puzzled and then in a moment of inspiration she observed, "So, God can use lots of different things including horoscopes to lead someone to find him, but after the encounter, he offers a new way of communicating with them."

I was unsure of what to call that encounter until later when studying this passage in Corinthians and it dawned on me that what had occurred in that episode with this new follower of Jesus may have been an authentic "word of knowledge."

The church members at Corinth believed that they possessed an *ultra*-knowledge, which made them peerless in the church. The words of 8.1-2 must have exploded in their ears: *knowledge puffs up but love builds up. The man who thinks he knows something does not yet know as he ought to know.* We have normal knowledge that is acquired as we daily live our lives. But, on occasion, God allows us to *see* a tiny part of his knowledge through the Spirit (1 Cor. 2.12). Remember, gracelets are not the possession of a person to be used at his or her will. "...it is a particular word given in a particular instance and is 'mine' only in the act and moment of uttering it."[16]

One has to wonder how much we have missed of the Spirit in the life of the church by mislabeling and then constantly using the language of this gracelet to mean something other than what it should mean. The tradition of the Vineyard where I spent about thirty years seems fixated on this idea in their ministry times. One wonders how much more robust ministry times would be if a language correction occurred that would allow for a gracelet whose identity has been lost to now be incorporated into the life and ministry of the church. I believe it is time for a new imagination to be birthed for the use of the "word of knowledge" gracelet by retiring its old definition and usage and replacing the language of what we presently call a "word of knowledge" with "prophetic insight," which seems to be more in line with the teaching of Scripture. At the same time, we begin listening for the Spirit who may want to provide "a word of inspired teaching or instruction...," which brings a new level of maturity in Christ to the listener. Wouldn't that be interesting?

16. Dunn, *Jesus and the Spirit*, 221.

Chapter 8

So What?

The two gracelets covered in this chapter are some of the most misunderstood and abused gracelets in this list. The one we call a "word of knowledge" has produced a misplaced idea of this gracelet. When "word of knowledge" takes on the qualities of being a so-called supernatural gift that is defined as the ability of one person to know what God is currently doing or intends to do in the life of another person or being able to see the secrets of another, great abuse occurs and has occurred. One wonders how big the trash heap is in the lives of people who became victims of this misappropriated definition and attributing it to special knowledge of God without any discernment. It's not that God can't communicate in any way he chooses, but if we keep playing by the same rules of the road, the same results are going to continue to happen. What if we allowed God to provide us with prophetic insights, which would carry with it the benefiting gracelet of discernment, to reveal to folks things that God wants them to know. Then, we would be freed up to actually be mentally prepared to be used by God as a conduit of a "real" word of knowledge. Surely, we need more inspired teaching in the body of Christ, don't you think?

Let's Have a Conversation

- How does the information about word of wisdom and word of knowledge differ from the conventional information you have heard? What impact does it make on you?
- Has God ever used you to speak the proclamation of the good news imparting a depth of understanding that you may not have known before? What was the result?
- Have you been used by the Spirit to instruct others in a way that brought a new level of maturity to them? What was the result?

Scripture presents God as one who acts.

His actions are accompanied by his power.

GRACELETS

Chapter 9: The Gracelets in 1 Corinthians: Part 3

➠ **Check Your GPS: Where We Are Going!**
- Where We Have Been
- What Are Facilitating Gracelets?
- Faith (*pistis*): 1 Cor. 12.9, 13.2
- Gifts of Healings (*charismata iamaton*): 1 Cor. 12.9
- Miracles, Effects of (*energemata dunameon*): 1 Cor. 12.10, 29
- So What?

Where We Have Been

Previously, we ask the question: What does two-three-four mean in relationship to the first list of gracelets in 1 Corinthians 12? Before we answered that question, we introduced the concept of diversity in unity, a problem that the Corinthian church was displaying in Paul's absence. In order to understand the concept, we introduced *perichoresis* to demonstrate that there is diversity in God while there is unity. Then, we turned to the first two gifts in the 1 Corinthians 11 list: utterance of wisdom and utterance of knowledge.

What Are Facilitating Gracelets?

The second gracelet list is those gracelets, which facilitate God's pronounced power. They are *faith, gracelets of healings,* and *effects of miracles*. Scripture presents God as one who acts. His actions are accompanied by his power. From the beginning of Scripture in Genesis to its conclusion in Revelation, the whole of the story is about God who is acting in power on behalf of his children.

Faith (*pistis*): 1 Cor. 12.9, 13.2

The confidence that is infused by the Spirit that a specific situation or need is going to be met by God.

General Background on Faith

In the Second Testament, there are a number of kinds of faith (*pistis*) mentioned:

- *Faith* can be a body of truth that we believe. It becomes a synonym for *doctrine* (Eph. 4.13; 1 Tim. 6.20-21; Jude 3).[1]
- *Faith* can be the basic trust that one has in God for his/her salvation; a *saving* faith (John 3.16; Eph. 2.8; Heb. 11.1-4, 6).
- *Faith* is a reliableness that is grown by the Spirit (Gal. 5.22).
- *Faith* can be a mountain-moving surge that is spoken about by Jesus and Paul (Matt. 17.20; 21.21; 1 Cor. 13.2).

What is the Gracelet of Faith?

Dunn believes that faith gives a person a transrational certainty and assurance that God will act through a word or action.[2] Bruce suggests that faith may be understood as "…a special endowment…for a special service."[3] The modern view of this gift is built around our concept of individualism and makes its meaning susceptible to a personal standalone gift. One has to work hard to escape the dualistic worldview that we have inherited, which places each gift in the supernatural realm. Anthony Thiselton suggests that "It seems unwise and unnecessary to impose onto Paul dual models of "natural" and "supernatural."[4]

Gordon Lindsay, a revivalist preacher in the '40s-'60s of last century, wrote, "Although the gift of faith appears to be passive…in reality it sets forces in motion that are irresistible."[5] Paul presumably has in mind that mysterious surge of confidence, which sometimes arises within a human being in a particular situation of need or challenge and which gives him/her a certainty and assurance that God is about to act through a word or through an action.[6] So it may be fair to say that the gracelet of faith is a surge of faith that God is going to act in a present circumstance.

The gracelet of faith may be the immediate background for the exercise of the two gracelets, which follow in Paul's list, *gracelets of healings* and *effects of miracles*. Faith is the atmosphere in which healings and miracles occur. Sometimes in certain church circles where healing for the sick is practiced,

---

1. If you chose to look these verses up and read them, let me remind you that they should be read in their full context not independently by themselves. We are using them here as a possible pointer to where the verses might be understood according to the proposition, i.e., doctrine, saving, reliableness, or a surge.

2. Dunn, *Jesus and the Spirit*, 211.

3. Bruce, *1 and 2 Corinthians*, 119.

4. Thiselton, *Corinthians (NIGTC)*, 946.

5. Gordon Lindsay, *Gifts of the Spirit* (Dallas, TX: Christ for the Nations, 1963), 2:43.

6. Dunn, *Jesus and the Spirit*, 211.

the idea has been created that when a person is prayed for and is not healed, it is because s/he did not have faith for the healing. Really? How would that work in the person who is being prayed for who is an infant or a person with such a debilitating disease that the person doesn't even know they are being prayed for? What if the person is dead? One might look at the resuscitation of the widow's son whose body was on a bier being carried to its resting place when Jesus and she had an encounter and the boy was raised from the dead (Luke 7.11-17). The point is that someone had faith, but we are not told who. One thing is for sure: it was not the dead boy!

The gracelet of faith may be connected, then, to the following two gifts, gracelets of healings and effects of miracles, which most likely might occur in the atmosphere of faith.

Gifts of Healings (*charismata iamaton*): 1 Cor. 12.9

The gracelets of healings are the actual outcomes of healing, which a sick person receives.

In the original language, the two words gift (gracelet) and healing are both plural. The passage should be translated "gifts of healings" or "gracelets of healings." As one can see in the Gospels, there are all kinds of healings that were performed by Jesus. There are two words used elsewhere in the Second Testament, which may help us understand what Paul was talking about, but it should be pointed out that the use of these words elsewhere would not have helped the Corinthians understand, unless they were aware of these words from hearing Luke, as Paul's companion in Corinth. What was available to the Corinthians, however, was the cultural practice of making specific clay body parts that the Corinthians presented to the gods that needed to be healed.[7]

Remember, Paul and Luke were traveling partners. Luke began his partnership with Paul as the "we" passages in Acts demonstrate (15.10-17; 20.5-15; 21.1-18; 27.1 to 28.16). It is truly possible that as traveling partners, they discussed the stuff they were thinking about and for Paul, what he was writing about. So, it is conceivable that Luke's ideas of healing were influenced by Paul or possibly the other way around. Luke, after all, was a doctor!

7. "Temple Cures," University of Indiana http://www.indiana.edu/~ancmed/curecult.htm (accessed July 20, 2015). Corinth's Asklepieion is only one of many temples to the Divine Physician. When the temple of Asklepieion, the god of healing, was excavated, clay based representations of heads, hands, and feet, arms and legs, breasts and genitals, eyes and ears. These represented the afflicted members cured by a god. They are representatives of prayer for or thanks for healing from.

The Two Words in Luke Are Often Synonyms

When Luke talks about healing in his first book, he used two different words that could be understood as synonyms. The first is often translated as *heal* or *cure* and is from the word *therapeuo* from which our English word therapeutic derives. *Heal* or *cure* is also used to translate the original word *iaomai* as well. It is *iaomai* that Paul uses three times in his writings to the Corinthians (12.9, 28, 30). While Luke used it abundantly in his books, twenty of the thirty-eight times used in the Second Testament, it seems reliable to conclude that it was a Lucian word. With that in mind, let's note again that Luke and Paul were traveling partners and were surely aware of each other's language habits.

It should be pointed out that in our present scientific worldview, in which the split worldview of the world is still accepted, it is believed that science is the "healer" because that is the stuff of "earth living." It may be also said that this is far too true of many contemporary Jesus followers who have a theology that disjoins the *then* and the *now* of the work of the kingdom of God. The root cause of this disjunction is an incoherent belief about the kingdom of God. According to the teaching of the Second Testament, the kingdom of God came in a renewed way through Jesus, who was empowered by the Spirit, who is the one that continues the work of the kingdom until its consummation occurs at the Second Coming. We must remember that the Spirit did not make his first appearance in God's EPIC Adventure on the Day of Pentecost. He's been around from the beginning of the story.

The following four stories may help the reader understand the praxis of the gracelet of healing. They are *ad hoc* occurrences and are only used to suggest how this gracelet may be in use. The first is about a healing that occurred in my wife's work place when she was a teacher in Southern California. The remaining three are healing stories that I was involved in one way or another.

Prayer in a Classroom

This first story occurs in Southern California when Donna Faith and I lived in Santa Clarita Valley, a valley just north of Los Angeles and San Fernando Valley, which was the home of Magic Mountain. Okay, so we are clear, there are no fees collected for advertisement of Magic Mountain.

While we lived in the Santa Clarita Valley, Donna Faith worked as a high school English teacher serving a school in the district. One day as she was checking in at the school office, she overheard the teacher from the classroom next door to her tell the secretary about a bad case of hemorrhoids that she was experiencing, so bad that the teacher had set up an operation date to take care of the problem.

When the lunch bell rang that day, the teacher from next door came through Donna Faith's room to go to the teacher's lounge for lunch. As she entered the room, Donna had a strong impression that she should ask her if she could pray for her hemorrhoid condition. But, the objections in her mind thwarted the occasion and the teacher passed on through on her way to enjoy her lunch. Donna stayed in her room hoping for another chance to come at the end of the lunch period. Sure enough just minutes before the bell was to ring to begin the next class, the door opened and the teacher began making her way across the room to enter her own class room. Donna told her that she had overheard her conversation in the office about the hemorrhoids and operation and then asked the teacher if she would mind if she prayed for her. Without hesitation, the teacher said, "yes, that would be great!" Realizing that touch was/is important, but not mandatory, Donna asked if she could hold the teacher's hand as she prayed. She again responded with a "yes." Donna prayed a very short prayer telling the hemorrhoids what to do. It was quick, less than a minute and as she finished, the classroom doors opened and students began to pour in for the next class.

Over the next few weeks, the teacher walked through her room each day never saying anything about the moment of prayer that had occurred. Donna later told me that she died a thousand deaths thinking that she had made a fool out of herself or that she was being seen as some kind of a religious fanatic. The silence from the teacher went on for weeks. Then one day, out of the clear blue, the teacher stopped and told Donna that she had totally forgotten to tell her that she had returned to the hospital a few days after the prayer and when she was checked out by her doctor, the hemorrhoids had completely disappeared. The doctor had no explanation. The operation was cancelled. This prayer experience emboldened Donna to pray for others when she had such an impression as she had for this teacher.

Do You Have To?

This second story happened with me after I had taught a Second Testament Overview course for many hours on a Saturday in a local church in Bakersfield, CA.

After teaching the course, Donna and I stopped at Denny's on our way back home. Yep, you read that right, Denny's. For readers outside of USAmerica, that's a roadside diner that stays open 24 hours a day. While sitting in a booth relaxing after the long day of teaching, I saw an elderly lady enter the aisle where our booth was situated. She was pulling a small oxygen cart behind her with a breathing mask over her face. It was apparent to me that she most likely had emphysema, which I knew about because a friend of mine worked daily with such folks and talked about it all the time. As she drew closer to my booth, I realized that God was asking me to pray for her.

Here are the thoughts that ran through my mind in a quick fashion. Do you mean silently as she passes? The most prevalent thought was: You must be kidding, I've been teaching all day, that's my gift and I have deployed it with great care. Neither of these thoughts got any traction. Finally, she was at my table. I spoke as she passed. "Wow that really looks uncomfortable."

Without hesitation, she stopped and responded, "it is!"

I replied, "Would you like for me to pray for you?"

She looked puzzled and asked, "you mean right here, right now? Don't you have to be in a church to do that?"

"Yes," you can do that in a church building, but I mean right here, right now."

Without hesitation, she said, "Okay!"

Next, I asked her if it would be okay if I touched her hand."

She looked at me quizzically and responded, "Do you have to?"

"No!" I quickly said.

She smiled and said, "okay" as she put her hand down on the table.

So, I reached out and laid my hand on top of hers and prayed a very direct prayer speaking to the Emphysema. When I finished, I asked her if she felt anything going on in her body.

She replied, "No! not really!"

As I looked at her, I could see that she was weeping quietly as she stood there.

"What is happening?" I inquired.

She responded with a quivering voice, "I can't believe that God cares so much about me that he would have a complete stranger stop me in Denny's to pray for this condition."

Was she healed? I have no idea since it is not my job to heal only to be the conduit through which a gracelet of healing may find its way to a person to whom God wants to heal in his own way and time.

Hemorrhoids

This story is personal to me because it is about me and my own request for healing.

I worked for John Wimber, the founder of the Vineyard Movement for five years as his research director and served as his Teaching Assistant at Fuller for the infamous MC510 course, Signs, Wonders and Church Growth.

During the time that one of the MC510 courses was being taught, I developed a case of "bleeding hemorrhoids." One evening when I was driving Wimber from Yorba Linda, CA, to Fuller Seminary in Pasadena, CA, and was sitting on my "donut" to reduce the pain, I turned to him and asked him if he would pray for me. After all, we were heading to a "Signs and Wonders" course where there would be a healing clinic after the time of instruction. There was a moment of silence before he answered. He looked across the car and politely said, "No." I have to admit, his answer was a bit distressful to say the least. I pushed back on him, "So, I am traveling with a person who teaches and prays for the sick, and he is saying "no" to my request for prayer for healing." He looked at me again, smiled, and said "that's right."

We went to class and it concluded with a "ministry time," but still no prayer for me. After class, we walked back to the van and I got in and arranged my "donut" in plain sight and began the drive back to Yorba Linda. A few miles into the trip, I asked for prayer again. John again said, "no!" Several minutes later he turned to me and said to me, "You need to forgive your sister." I asked simply, "where did that come from?" He quietly replied that it was a thought that he had and decided to share it with me. There was no fanfare. No background music. No hype. No pleading. No revivalistic accoutrements whatsoever. Just a shared thought!

When I arrived home that evening, I thought about what John had said and remembered that several months before, my sister had called me to ask about whether she should take my mom to the hospital because mom's blood pressure was slowly dropping. I suggested that she ask mom, who was conscious, what her wishes were. She said that she had and mom had told her to just let her go home to be with Jesus. I suggested that she should follow mom's desire. She didn't and took mom to the hospital. They restored her blood pressure and in a few days sent her back home.

Not too many weeks after that episode, mom developed gangrene in one of her feet that became unmanageable and they had to amputate her leg. She never felt whole after that and kept suffering "phantom pain" in her foot till the day she died.

I had become angry with my sister over this situation, but had never addressed it with her at my mom's funeral or afterwards. I realized on that evening that my anger was still there.

I sat down at my Commodore 64, yep, that dates me, and began keying in a letter asking my sister for her forgiveness. As I did, my eyes moistened and then the moisture turned into tears. When I finished, I printed the letter on my dot matrix printer, folded it, placed it in an envelope, put a stamp on it, and set it aside for the morning mail.

I went to bed still in pain from the hemorrhoids. When I awoke the next morning, the hemorrhoids were gone. No bleeding! No pain! Just gone!

A Prophetic Insight

The following story happened during the week of preparation for teaching and after a time of teaching in a Sunday evening church service.

At the conclusion of a meeting at which I had taught on something unrelated to healing, we had an open ministry time. It was a small gathering, which had about forty folks that were present. During the week while I was preparing, I had an impression that there would be someone present at the meeting that had just found out they had a troubling sickness. So, I asked the congregants present if anyone had any prophetic insights using that designation instead of what was usually called in that group of churches a "word of knowledge," We waited. When no one spoke up, I told the folks present that during the week I had an impression and stated what it was. A gentleman raised his hand and said that description might fit him. The group prayed asking God to deliver him a gracelet of healing that was perfectly designed to meet his health problem. The next week during the evening service, the person reported that he had gone back to the doctor who had taken more tests and his previous health situation that the previous tests had revealed had been reversed. He had received a gracelet of healing.

One of the important things to remember about this last illustration is that a group of Jesus followers prayed. God worked through their prayers and delivered the outcome effect of healing that God desired to deliver. No one in the group could claim to have the "gift of healing." No one was ready to "pitch a tent in an empty field and open up a healing ministry." It was just simple, straight, non-hyped prayer. It was up to God to do what he wished with the prayer.

Prophetic insights are a valuable part of our Christian experience. They often come almost unaware, but they do come, and when spoken and responded to, the result is left up to God; he does what he wants to do. Remember, the kingdom of God is now but not yet. On that occasion, the "not yet" of the kingdom slipped into the "now" and the man was healed. Yes, it is true. The kingdom is still available today.

Miracles, Effects of (*energemata dunameon*): 1 Cor. 12.10, 29

The effect of an extraordinary event in which the power of God has been displayed.

What if "effects of miracles" is a summary statement (cp., the word used in 12.6 and 12.10? "Effects" may be the results, which God produces with gracelets, i.e., human words are spoken and God produces "powerful" (*dunamis*) results. Of course, our current word *miracle* is so watered down that it is overused to describe almost anything. As an example, in the 2015 Super Bowl game between the New England Patriots and the Seattle Seahawks, there was a play in the last few minutes of the last half, which was reported by USA Today Sports as follows: "Jermaine Kearse's bobbling catch was a miracle..."[8] Too bad

8. ESPN, "Jermaine Kearse's Bobbling Catch Was a Miracle (Even Though It Didn't Matter in the End)," ESPN http://ftw.usatoday.com/2015/02/jermaine-kearse-catch (accessed June 3, 2015).

the supposed miracle was turned on its head a couple of plays later by a goal line interception. The cheers of a miracle were turned to the moans of defeat.

This effects of miracles gracelet most likely covers a broad range of events.[9] It is a continuing sign of the breaking in of the kingdom of God into this present evil age. Paul uses the same word to describe this gracelet as he used in 12.6. The word *effects* here in 12.10 is the same word as in 12.6 (the result, which God produces by the gracelets). The word here translated *miracles* is *dunamis*, which means *power*. The word *dunamis* implies the strength of someone to bring about an event. The evidence of God's *power* was the resurrection of Jesus (1 Cor. 6.14). Paul continues in 1 Corinthians 15.42-44 to say that Jesus was raised in power (*dunamis*) and he was raised in a spiritual (*pneumatikos)* body. He was the firstborn from the dead in a new, never-before-kind-of-body, a body infused with the life-giving Spirit of God.[10]

Illustrations

The following material is from the Gospel of Luke in which one can see how he uses the two words (*iaomai, therapeuo*) mentioned above.[11] Read these stories and look for the words that are *italicized* in parenthesis as you read. These words in Luke's stories appear to be what Paul called "effects of miracles." Sometimes Luke uses these words interchangeably. Remember, as we stated above, Luke and Paul were partners and surely Luke would have known about Paul's thoughts about what he wrote in 1 Corinthians. Here's a thought: as you read, let the stories possibly offer you a change in the way you think about and talk about miracles.

The Healing of a Paralytic: Luke 5.17-26

One day Jesus was teaching, and Pharisees and teachers of the law were sitting there. They had come from every village of Galilee and from Judea and Jerusalem. And the power (*dunamis*) of the Lord was with Jesus to heal (*iaomai*) the sick. Some men came carrying a paralyzed man on a mat and tried to take him into the house to lay him before Jesus. When they could not find a way to do this because

9. Fee, *Corinthians*, 659.

10. George Eldon Ladd, *A Theology of the New Testament*, Rev. ed. (Grand Rapids, MI: Eerdmans, 1993), 408.

11. This list is from research that I did for John Wimber for his series on Spiritual Gifts in 1985. In that material there was a list, I have expanded on that original material by presenting the text with the words that are under consideration in italics within parenthesis. This should help the reader see how Luke uses these words in his Gospel.

of the crowd, they went up on the roof and lowered him on his mat through the tiles into the middle of the crowd, right in front of Jesus.

When Jesus saw their faith (*pistis*), he said, Friend, your sins are forgiven."

The Pharisees and the teachers of the law began thinking to themselves, "Who is this fellow who speaks blasphemy? Who can forgive sins but God alone?"

Jesus knew what they were thinking and asked, "Why are you thinking these things in your hearts? Which is easier: to say, 'Your sins are forgiven,' or to say, 'Get up and walk'? But I want you to know that the Son of Man has authority on earth to forgive sins." So he said to the paralyzed man, I tell you, get up, take your mat and go home." Immediately he stood up in front of them, took what he had been lying on and went home praising God. Everyone was amazed and gave praise to God. They were filled with awe and said, "We have seen remarkable things today."

A Multitude: Luke 6.17-19

He went down with them and stood on a level place. A large crowd of his disciples was there and a great number of people from all over Judea, from Jerusalem, and from the coastal region around Tyre and Sidon, who had come to hear him and to be healed (*iaomai*) of their diseases. Those troubled by impure spirits were cured (*therapeuo*), and the people all tried to touch him, because power (*dunamis*) was coming from him and healing (*iaomai*) them all.

The Centurion's Slave: Luke 7.1-10

When Jesus had finished saying all this to the people who were listening, he entered Capernaum. There a centurion's servant, whom his master valued highly, was sick and about to die. The centurion heard of Jesus and sent some elders of the Jews to him, asking him to come and heal his servant. When they came to Jesus, they pleaded earnestly with him, "This man deserves to have you do this, because he loves our nation and has built our synagogue." So Jesus went with them.

He was not far from the house when the centurion sent friends to say to him: "Lord, don't trouble yourself, for I do not deserve to have you come under my roof. That is why I did not even consider myself worthy to come to you. But say the word, and my servant will be healed (*iaomai*). For I myself am a man under authority, with soldiers under me. I tell this one, 'Go,' and he goes; and that one, 'Come,' and he comes. I say to my servant, 'Do this,' and he does it."

When Jesus heard this, he was amazed at him, and turning to the crowd following him, he said, "I tell you, I have not found such great faith (*pistis*) even in Israel." Then the men who had been sent returned to the house and found the servant well.

The Woman with a Hemorrhage: Luke 8.42b-48

Then a man named Jairus, a synagogue leader, came and fell at Jesus' feet, pleading with him to come to his house because his only daughter, a girl of about twelve, was dying.

As Jesus was on his way, the crowds almost crushed him. And a woman was there who had been subject to bleeding for twelve years, but no one could heal (*therapeuo*) her. She came up behind him and touched the edge of his cloak, and immediately her bleeding stopped.

Who touched me?" Jesus asked.

When they all denied it, Peter said, "Master, the people are crowding and pressing against you."

But Jesus said, "Someone touched me; I know that power (*dunamis*) has gone out from me."

Then the woman, seeing that she could not go unnoticed, came trembling and fell at his feet. In the presence of all the people, she told why she had touched him and how she had been instantly healed (*iaomai*). Then he said to her, "Daughter, your faith (*pistis*) has healed you. Go in peace."

The Sending of the Twelve: Luke 9.1-2

When Jesus had called the Twelve together, he gave them power (*dunamis*) and authority to drive out all demons and to cure (*iaomai*) diseases, and he sent them out to proclaim the kingdom of God and to heal (*therapeuo*) the sick.

For Luke, the two healing gracelets (*iaomai*, *therapeuo*) and power gracelet (*dunamis*) seem to work hand-in-hand with the gracelet (*pistis*). All of these are mentioned in 1 Corinthians 12.8-10. We might conclude that healings (*iaomai, therapeuo*) in reality are the effects of miracles (*dunamis*) and had their accomplishment occurring in the sphere of faith (*pistis*). Let me hasten to say that this may not be Paul or Luke's conclusion, but it is worth contemplating.

We now turn to those gracelets of speech. As we will see below, when a prophecy is given to the church, discernments need to occur to protect the community from those spurious words that too often seem to occur. Or, when someone speaks in tongues, someone should be present to interpret what has been said into the common language of the listeners.

So What?

The idea of healing has also been a blessing and a bane. It is wonderful to receive healing as I did, recounted in the story above about hemorrhoids. It becomes a bane when it becomes the primary ministry of an individual who professes to have "the gift of healing" and touts how many folks have been healed as a marketing ploy to gain larger audiences to ply his/her trade. Sounds cynical, huh? That cynicism has been fed over the years by watching the dashed hopes and lives of those caught up in the intoxication of the moment of prayer. I realize that my cynicism is clouded with my mother's example of being a "faith healer groupie." I don't fault her for wanting to be healed, but she traveled to any faith healer that pitched a tent close to where we lived and then participated in buying every trinket, picture, and prayer cloth that she could lay her hands on. All of this time, energy, and money brought no healing to her but only more devastation to her because she bought the premise being delivered to her by the "faith healers" that she didn't have enough faith. And some of "having faith" was "buying" accessories to expedite faith.

After I had graduated from college and was traveling, I returned home for a visit and as I sat in her living room looking at the picture of the hands of one of the "healing evangelists" and asked her why she didn't have a picture of my hands on her walls because from time to time in my travels I prayed for the sick as well. She stopped what she was doing and said very sternly, "Don't be sacrilegious, son!"

Do folks get healed in these kinds of meetings? Yes. Does their healing authenticate the antics of the "faith healer"? No, absolutely not!

God does heal, and sometimes he doesn't heal in a way that we expect. But, don't put your faith in the one who is praying but in the one who has the power to bring you healing.

Let's Have a Conversation

- Has God ever flowed through you a "surge" of faith to believe for something beyond what you were seeing? What was the result?
- Have you ever prayed for the sick and watched God deliver a "gracelet of healing" to the one you were praying for? What was the result?
- How does the understanding that a gracelet is given to the one who needs the gift (the end person) rather than you possessing the gift to administer it at will affect your theology? Does it free you or bind you?

∞

Chapter 10: The Gracelets in 1 Corinthians: Part 4

➠ Check Your GPS: Where You Are Going
- Where We Have Been
- What Are Edifying Gracelets
- Prophecy (*propheteia*): 1 Cor. 12.10, 28
- Discernings of Spirits (*diakriseis pneumaton*): 1 Cor. 12.10
- Tongues, Kinds of (*gene glosson*): 1 Cor. 12.10, 28
- Interpretation of Tongues (*hermēneia glōssa; diermēneuō*): 1 Cor. 12.10
- Administrations (*kuberneseis*): 1 Cor. 12.28
- Philanthropy (*psōmizō pas*): 1 Cor. 13.3
- So What?

Where We Have Been

In the preceding chapter, we looked at what we titled facilitating gracelets: faith, gifts of healings, and effects of miracles. We noted that faith appears to be around when the gracelets are flowing through believers. We also demonstrated that the gracelet of healing was rather the gracelets of healings, many kinds of healings for many kinds of situations. While we often use the word miracle in almost any fashion, most likely it is a word that covers a broad range of events.

What Are Edifying Gracelets

The final four gracelets: *prophecy, discernments of spirits, tongues,* and *interpretation of tongues* are all gracelets of speech that seem to edify a listener. We begin with prophecy.

Prophecy (*propheteia*): 1 Cor. 12.10, 28

Communicating the pulse of God's heart for the purpose of edifying.

The British scholar James D. G. Dunn says that prophecy is declaring the heart throb of God to his Church for the purpose of edification. It is not a skill or aptitude or talent. It is the actual speaking forth of words given by the Spirit in a particular situation and ceases when the words cease.[1] This idea indicates that one may be a prophet when s/he is prophesying but is not a prophet as a specific gift retained by an individual. I realize that this idea is a difficult one to get one's head around, when, for years, prophet has been thought of as an office gift.

The only consistent gracelet in all the so-called lists of gifts in Paul is *prophet* or *prophecy*. Historically, during the life of Paul, the concept of prophecy suggested something, which was spoken only under inspiration. Plato had taught that there were two kinds of prophecy. The *first* was called mantic (divination) or inspired prophecy. The speaker's speech was believed to be directed by a god and was enchanted by and became the spokesperson for a specific god. The *second* was prophecy, which was a skill that was taught and could be learned and called for explanation. A prophet was understood as one who had the capability to analyze the signs by reasonable insight. The Oracle of Delphi, near Corinth, where the Pythia or the oracle, who was a woman, spoke in a state of ecstasy and the prophet analyzed the signs by reasonable insight.[2]

In today's ChurchWorld, we still make the same Platonic distinction. However, ChurchWorld is usually only open to the latter Platonic understanding, which we call preaching, which is an acquired skill that requires the interpretation of Scripture. This theological point of view gives visible attention to preaching as the meaning, presuming that prophecy means preaching. While preaching may be a valuable asset to the church, it seems clear that Paul's view of prophecy is that of the Hebraic tradition of inspired speech.[3]

First Corinthians 14 gives the clearest instruction on prophecy. Again, let's remind ourselves that this material is problem-solving literature. The following is a summary of the material presented by Paul in chapter 14.

- First Corinthians 14 records that prophecy consisted of Spirit-inspired messages, which were intelligible and delivered orally when the church met together, and by extension, it could be considered that what happened in the gathered community could also happen in the scattered community. It was intended to bring strengthening, encouragement, and comfort. The

---

1. Dunn, *Jesus and the Spirit*, 229.

2. Ibid., 228. See also: Gerhard Kittel, Geoffrey William Bromiley, and Gerhard Friedrich, *Theological Dictionary of the New Testament* (Grand Rapids, MI: Eerdmans Publishing Company, 1964), 6:786, 788.

3. Dunn, *Jesus and the Spirit*, 228.

individual who was so moved to deliver a prophetic message was understood to be in control (14.29-33a). Individuals who spoke these messages more frequently were often called prophets (we will discuss this gracelet later).

- For Paul, the result of prophecy was to strengthen, encourage, and comfort (14.3, 31). These three words may set the parameters of the divine intent of prophecy. They probably indicate that in Paul's view, the primary focus of a prophetic utterance is not the future, but the present situations of the people of God. The aim of prophecy is the growth of the church corporately, which also involves the growth of its individual members.[4]
- Prophecy serves as a signal for the followers of Jesus (14.22). When the church comes together, understanding of a prophetic word draws attention to the message being given by God.
- When one prophesies, the secrets of those who do not believe can be exposed. Dunn suggests that prophecy in this vein prevents a man from pretending to be something or someone that he is not.[5]
- Testing of prophetical words by those present is a must and keeps the ones listening from being led astray. Discernments of spirits, as a gracelet, is given for this purpose.[6]
- The gracelet of prophecy is desirable (14.1, 39-40). The desirability is presented because it edifies the whole body when gathered and listening. It does not seem to mean in these passages that it is superior to any other gracelet, as is often held.

When you open to the first pages of the Bible to the First Testament, you can observe that Genesis presents God as a speaking God (Gen. 1). He came to the garden on a daily basis to *talk* to Adam and Eve (Gen. 2-3). Noah built an ark because God *spoke* to him (Gen. 6). Abram moved from his country and his people because God *spoke* to him (Gen. 12). God *talked* to Moses through a bush (Ex. 3). Through prophecy by Eldad and Medad, God *spoke* to the children of Israel (Num. 11.26-30). Joel prophesied that the potential to prophesy would be given to all. While in the First Testament story only a select few presented the prophetic word of God, it was going to be different in the Second Testament part of the story.

---

4. Fee, *Corinthians*, 657-658. One must give consideration that when church is used in the modern sense of its usage, it misses the point of a gathered group of folks who meet for interaction and who are prepared for interjection into the world in which they live. The church is gathered and sent. Our present culture has often focused on one without the other. We should beware of such a dichotomy.

5. Dunn, *Jesus and the Spirit*, 229-233.

6. See below: Discernings of Spirits.

GRACELETS

The prophets of the First Testament were the covenant *spokespersons* of God to Israel. The First Testament demonstrates that God began speaking at the beginning of the First Testament story and continued through the whole of that part of the story.

As one turns to the first pages of the Second Testament (although not written first), the reader is captured by the same story of a speaking God. God *speaks* to Joseph about Mary through an angel in a dream. From God and Mary came Jesus the ultimate spokesperson, the *logos* of God. The prophetic gracelet seems to be widespread among the churches in the first century (1 Thess. 5.19-22; Rom 12.6). As it appears in 1 Corinthians 14, it looks like the gracelet was available to all, which was a direct fulfillment of the prophecy of Joel.[7]

The Second Testament, no different from the First Testament, presents God throughout, as a speaking God. A part of his character is to seek out his children and speak to them. The whole composition of Scripture, written by many authors over many years, is, in fact, demonstrating that God expects to talk to his children.

God is not a quiet God, but one who continues to communicate through the prophetic word. While this is the means, he also provides some truly human help to make sure his followers are not led down a path that will be harmful to them. It's called the *discernings of Spirits* and to that gracelet we now turn.

Discernings of Spirits (*diakriseis pneumaton*): 1 Cor. 12.10

Perception empowered by the Spirit to judge the source of prophetic words, whether divine, human, or demonic.

We should note that when Paul wrote this small list of gracelets in 1 Corinthians 12.8-20, *discernings of spirits* was listed between prophecy and tongues. In his book, *Jesus and the Spirit*, Dunn suggests that this gracelet should be coupled with prophecy, that it should *not* be considered as an independent gracelet, but rather seen as a test for any prophecy, which would control the abuse of the gracelet of prophecy.[8] If this idea were adhered to, there would be far less abuse of prophetic words taken with authority than there presently are.

---

7. I first ran into this litany of a speaking God in a course that I took from Russ Spittler at Fuller Seminary in 1982. I have added the Second Testament material to round the thought process out.

8. Dunn, *Jesus and the Spirit*, 233.

Scripture does indeed teach the church to test any prophetic utterance and give an approval or disapproval to its content (1 Cor. 14.29; 1 Thess. 5.21; 1 John 4.1-6). The church would do well to heed these admonitions and, in so doing, would not find herself often abusing the gracelet, the giver, and the recipient of the gracelet.

The word *discernings* is only found three times in the Second Testament (Rom. 14.1; 1 Cor. 12.10; Heb. 5.14). In the Hebrews 5.14 context, it means to judge between what is evil and what is good. Discerning prophetic words is a lost art in the ChurchWorld. It seems that almost anything can be said and listeners tacitly approve it by the words "this is what the Lord says, are applied to the end of the speaker's words. This is not the suggestion of 1 Thessalonians 5.21 and 1 John 4.1-6.

In 1 Corinthians 14.29, the verb form of the word appears. The Corinthians are advised to discern what is being said. The command indicates that this should be the habit of life for the community as they come together. In the original language, the word is a present imperative, which suggests that the command should be a habit of life for the church gathered. The usage in 14.29 indicates that when discerning occurs, it should be done by more than one individual (it is a third person plural verb). If we apply our beginning definition from above to this, we could say that discernment is a truly human insight, which indicates the source of the speech. When we attend a church service where prophetic words occur, both preaching and spontaneous standalone words, we should insist on this gracelet. It offers divine protection so that we are not easily deceived by every word that proceeds from someone's mouth. By the way, I think that this gracelet is useful to a congregation who is listening to the "preaching/ prophecy" as well. Lord knows that we would be in a better place if there was a bit more discernment in the pew about the sermonic presentations being offered week after week in local churches at the corner of walk and don't walk.

Remember, usage of gracelets in 1 Corinthians is in the context of church gathered and scattered and is corrective. It is in this very arena that the Jesus follower within his/her community of faith should be asking God to help him or her discern so as not to be deceived. As an example, at the time of this writing, there is an exodus of folks from the organized church. Some of these turn to online environments to hear preaching or they turn to Facebook in a closed community of folks. In these environments, one can hear almost every conceivable proclamation presented as a certain fact. Wouldn't it be great if we allowed the Spirit to caution us as we listen to TV preachers, prophets, and teachers as well as when we read Facebook feeds?

While loyal to the church, I am often critical of the ChurchWorld. There are so many things that simply pass as legitimate because the senior pastor, worship leader, or prophetical voice says them with no appropriate time to discern if the message being given is actually from God. It is no wonder that folks get confused, perplexed, and frustrated because this gracelet is not allowed to be received by the congregation so as to secure its own safety.

The last two gracelets, tongues and interpretation of tongues, are a further demonstration that God loves communication.

Tongues, Kinds of (*gene glosson*): 1 Cor. 12.10, 28

The human phenomena of speech infused by the Spirit that is sometimes a known language, sometimes an unknown language that is spoken and should be accompanied by the gracelet of interpretation so that the community can be edified as well as the individual.

Interpretation of Tongues (*hermēneia glōssa; diermēneuō*) 1 Cor. 12.10

Human speech in the listener's language that brings edification to the group that interprets what has been spoken with the gracelet of tongues.

Paul and Luke's Take on Tongues

Remember, Paul and Luke were partners on their church planting missions. Both of these Second Testament authors write about tongues. First Corinthians comes from the pen of Paul and was written before Acts that comes from the pen of Luke. Here is some basic information about these two writers.

Luke was a Gentile physician whose writings are an excellent illustration of Hellenistic historiography.[9] This was a kind of history writing, which flourished from 300 BC–AD 200. This style of history writing was not just a chronicle of past accounts, written as most of Western history is written, which simply offers facts about the past. It was history written to entertain (to be good reading) as well as to inform, or offer an apologetic. The two volumes, which Luke wrote, i.e., Luke-Acts, fit into this category of writing very well. Luke is often

---

9. Gordon D. Fee and Douglas Stuart, *How to Read the Bible for All Its Worth (3rd Edition)* (Grand Rapids, MI: Zondervan, 2003), 109. The Hellenistic Age is defined roughly as the period between the death of Alexander the Great and the Rise of the Roman Empire. Historiography is a body of literature dealing with historical matters and often written in a narrative presentation.

called the *theologian of the Holy Spirit*.[10] Part two of Luke's writings, the Book of Acts, is a theological history, a history with a theological purpose in which not everything that happened to the early church is recorded, but those that were recorded had theological significance.

Paul, a converted Jew, was a missionary[11] church planter who wrote theological letters to help his churches solve problems as they encountered them after he left to plant other churches. He wrote to a historical situation concerning tongues in 1 Corinthians. He wrote 1 Corinthians before Luke wrote Acts, and, therefore, it has priority. It is very probable that Luke was influenced by Paul in his own view of this subject.

The following lists are gathered from a Spiritual Gifts course that I took at Fuller Seminary in 1982.[12]

There are some similarities between Luke and Paul:

- Tongues has a Spirit dimension (1 Cor. 12.8, 14.2; Acts 2.4)
- The same term (*latein glossai*) is used by both authors for speaking in tongues (1 Cor. 12-14; Acts 10.46; 19.1-6).
- When one speaks in tongues before unbelievers, the result may lead to accusations (1 Cor. 14.23ff.; Acts 2.5ff.).
- Speaking in tongues is directed toward God (1 Cor. 14.2; 14-17; Acts 2.11; 10.46).
- Prophecy and tongues are different (1 Cor. 12; Acts 19.6).
- Unity and diversity can be seen (1 Cor. 12.14-26; Acts 2.2-4).
- Both Paul and Luke see the Spirit as the source of power to equip the saints for the work of the ministry (1 Cor. 12-14; Eph. 4.11; Acts 1.8).

There are some ideas, which belong only to Luke:

- The first occurrence of speaking in tongues occurs in Acts at the birth of the church (Acts 2.4).[13]
- Tongues occur surrounded by symbolic language (Acts 2.2-3: sound like wind; tongues like fire).

---

10. Ben Witherington, *The Indelible Image: The Theological and Ethical Thought World of the New Testament* (Grand Rapids, MI: InterVarsity, 2010), 278.

11. Missionary is another way of translating apostle.

12. These lists are gathered from my notes from a course on Spiritual Gifts (NT576) taught by Dr. Russ Spittler and Dr. Mel Robeck that I took in the spring of 1982.

13. There is a story in the Gospels where Jesus may have spoken in tongues. See below in the section called Tongues.

There are some ideas, which only belong to Paul:

- These gifts are temporary; when Jesus returns they will cease to operate (1 Cor. 13.8).
- Tongues need to be lubricated with love[14] (1 Cor. 13).

According to 1 Corinthians, the purposes of tongues are:

- A means of truly human inspired communication to God (14.2).
- An edification of the speaker, even if others are not edified (14.4).
- To bring edification to the Body. When tongues are properly interpreted, edification is the result. (Tongues plus interpretation equals prophecy in edification value: 14.5).
- To serve as a sign to the unbeliever (14.22). In this passage, Paul used a first-century hermeneutic (a way to interpret) to say that tongues improperly used (i.e., without interpretation) could be understood as a judgment for the unbeliever who would leave the meeting of the church and possibly never return because s/he believed that those practicing such activities were mad (v. 23). By leaving and never returning, the unbeliever judges him/herself by not receiving the life of the Spirit to bring them into the new humanity of God. For a full discussion of this difficult passage.[15]

Tongues

Paul is clear that tongues can be utilized in private to pray and sing to God. In this case, there is no need for interpretation, because no one is there to hear except the speaker (14.14-15).

Praying in tongues is sometimes called *praying in the Spirit* in today's church. The curious question to ask is: Did Jesus pray in the Spirit, i.e., pray in tongues? There is no clear evidence in the Gospels to support the theorization that Jesus spoke in tongues. However, there are some places, which suggest the possibility.

14. This is a phrase used by Dr. Russ Spittler in a lecture in his Corinthians course, which was delivered at Fuller Seminary in Spring of 1982.

15. Fee, *God's Empowering Presence*, 235-247. See also: Ronald F. Youngblood. General Editor, *Nelson's New Illustrated Bible Dictionary* (Nashville, TN: Thomas Nelson Publishers 1986), 754-757.

In the story in Mark 7.34,[16] Jesus is working a miracle. The text declares that Jesus gave a *deep sigh*. In 8.12, Mark records that *he sighed deeply*. The word, which translates *sigh*, is the same word as *groan* in Romans 8.22-23, 26. The word was a technical term in the Hellenistic world of prayer that did not involve the mind, but was caused by a spirit.

In the first reference, the term *sighing (stenazein)* is used along with the word *ephata*. *Ephata* was an expression in a strange language, which, according to numerous parallels in the Hellenistic world, was often used in connection with healing the sick and casting out demons. These are inconclusive to say that Jesus spoke in tongues, but should give our thinking some out-of-the-box elasticity.

Singing in Tongues

Paul seems to make it clear in 1 Corinthians 14.15 that there is a kind of charismatic music, which includes singing in tongues, which he calls *with the spirit* and singing with intelligible words, which he calls *with the mind*. The singing, which is referred to, happened spontaneously when the church came together. This spontaneous singing mentioned is found in public use in 14.26. This passage may have a parallel from Paul's writings in Colossians 3.16 and Ephesians 5.19. In these passages, Paul wrote about three forms of singing: psalms, hymns, and spiritual songs. In those passages, he may have had in mind what today is called *singing in the Spirit*. The kind of singing that Paul is referring to, while including what we might call singing in the Spirit, goes beyond this simplistic belief. What we have settled for in our churches are hymns and choruses that have been prewritten and are sang over and over again, especially modern choruses, which may be the emphasis of Marva J. Dawn's book: *A Royal Waste of Time: The Splendor of Worshiping God and Being Church for the World*.[17]

This conclusion may be drawn from two factors:

1. Being continually filled with the Spirit is the context of this passage. Paul contrasts the impulse of the Spirit to what occurs when the stimulus is wine.
2. Both passages use the word *spiritual* to characterize that the music is prompted by the Spirit. The text is unclear and may not be referring to three different kinds of music mentioned. The

---

16. Remember, Mark was a traveling partner with Paul and it is very likely that each was familiar with the other's language, just like the partnership with Luke and Paul mentioned above.

17. Marva J. Dawn, *A Royal Waste of Time: The Splendor of Worshiping God and Being Church for the World* (Grand Rapids, MI: Wm. B. Eerdmans Publishing Co, 1999).

word *spiritual* is an adjective and could probably be translated as *psalms, hymns, and songs, which the Spirit inspires.* Dunn points out that even if the word *spiritual* belongs to songs, the distinction between psalms and hymns and spiritual songs is not between established liturgical forms and spontaneous songs. It would be a contrast between spontaneous singing of intelligible words and spontaneous singing in tongues.[18]

Interpretation of Tongues

Every coin has two sides. The last four gifts (prophecy, discernings of spirits, tongues, interpretation of tongues) in this small list have two sides. Prophecy should be accompanied with discernings of spirits and tongues must be accompanied with interpretation of tongues. So closely are they connected in the mind of Paul that one is not thought about without the other when the church is together (1 Cor. 14.5, 23, 27ff.). As with all of the gracelets, these two gifts are for the common good of the church when it is together (1 Cor. 12.7). When *glossolalia* is a gracelet, it is a service to the church and is completed by its companion gracelet, interpretation.

The following information should be noted about this gracelet:

- It is not an independent gift; it is used as the completion of the gracelet of tongues (1 Cor. 12.10).
- It provides edification for the believer when the church is together and the gracelet of tongues is spoken. It causes the unlearned to understand (1 Cor. 14.5).
- When the gracelet of tongues is spoken in a public service of the church gathered, believers should pray to interpret (1 Cor. 14.13). Here is an overlooked stipulation of the use of these gracelets: if there is no one present to interpret and the one speaking in tongues has not interpreted, s/he should keep silent and speak to him/herself and to God (1 Cor. 14.28).
- Together both of these gifts should be operative in an orderly manner (1 Cor. 14.37-40).

Remember, the God that the story of the Bible presents is a speaking God. He loves to speak to us and through us. Don't resist the opportunity to let the God of the universe speak through you.

The following two gracelets also appear in 1 Corinthians.

18. Dunn, *Jesus and the Spirit*, 238-289.

Chapter 10

Administrations (*kuberneseis*): 1 Cor. 12.28

To steer or direct the affairs of the church by giving direction, which results in the effective accomplishment of spreading the gospel, i.e., the message of the kingdom of God.

The word used here translated in most translations as "administrations" was well-known in the Second Testament era. It could be defined as *steering, directing,* or *governing.* These are all words, which are metaphors drawn from the art of being a helmsman who steers a ship. The meaning of the word indicates some activity, which gives direction. Dunn says that perhaps we should strive for nothing more precise than *giving guidance....*[19] We must not forget that the First Testament church did not have the administrative structures that we have created in the twenty-first-century church. These more modern phenomena have on occasion tinted our understanding of Scripture. The gift is the activity and not the person. It doesn't have anything to do with "administration" as we have come to understand that word. Really!

Philanthropy (*psōmizō pas*): 1 Cor. 13.3

Acquiring wealth and freely giving it away for the proclamation of the kingdom.

In the society in which we live, gaining money is often looked at as something that is sinful. The lack of money is something that is seen as the lack of faith, *a la* the Faith and Prosperity doctrine. However, in keeping with our thought that the gracelet is for the end user, what if philanthropy was understood as a sacred reason for acquiring wealth so that it would then be used to proclaim the kingdom. Giving generously is a benefit that comes with the responsibility of having acquired, in this case, money!

So What?

The list of gracelets in this section has had thousands of pages written about them. These gracelets often form the crux of a Pentecostal understanding of the so-called spiritual gifts. One of these, speaking in tongues, may have been the whole reason that Paul constructed this section of his letter to the Corinthians. It appears that the purpose of the gracelet of tongues was as misunderstood then as it may be now. Only recently, I heard about a conclusion in a church, which is part of the so-

---

19. Ibid., 252.

called Third Wave, which does not profess to be a Pentecostal church, that in order to be in an intercessory prayer group that one must have already spoken in tongues. You were excluded from that group without that gracelet. One has to wonder if they have seriously given much time to Paul's writings about tongues as being the central problem, which generated such a problem within the Corinthian congregation.

The institutionalized form of modern Christianity has often used the idea of administration as a qualifier with the same qualities as an administrator in a business. I am sure that this has led to many who took a Spiritual Gifts Inventory and discovered that the inventory identified their gift as "administration." They were then hired to administer the business of a local church becasue of the results of the inventory. This concept only demonstrates how completely syncretism has invaded the modern church much as it had the ancient Corinthian church and completely misses the point of the wording that Paul chose to use when mentioning this gracelet.

In the Western world, acquiring wealth has been for the sake of consuming more goods and products to make life easier, rather than acquiring wealth with the primary purpose of helping others. In some Christian circles, wealth has become a barometer of success and it is also seen as a lack of faith if one is not wealthy. This kind of pervasive thinking is a bane on the followers of Jesus.

Let's Have a Conversation

- Which if any of these gracelets has God sent through you to others? What happened?
- How does understanding that the "gift of tongues" and "praying in tongues" are two different things free up your theology or make you more confused?
- How does the administrations gracelet differ from the modern concept of administration? Who can be used by God in this way? How would that affect the direction and governance of your church?

∞

GRACELETS

Chapter 11: The Gracelets Listed in Romans 12.6-8

Where We Have Been

In Chapter 10, we discussed the last three gracelets in the first list of 1 Corinthians 12 and closed out the chapter with two gracelets that standalone in the text: administrations and philanthropy. The object of all the gracelets in 1 Corinthians 12 is the final reciepent, not the one who the gracelet is passing through. This concept usually sounds foreign to the ear of folks today. It's an adjustment to think about healing as something that I receive versus a gift that I have ownership of as in "I have the gift of healing." We can now move to the next selection of gracelets found in the book of Romans.

Romans: An Overview

After writing the Corinthian correspondence, Paul left Ephesus to return to Corinth via Macedonia. There he met Titus who shared that the Corinthian church had finally taken care of the discipline problem within the church. He continued his trip to Corinth and from there in a more peaceful time of his ministry, he wrote the book of Romans.

The following introduction to the book of Romans is from my book *God's EPIC Adventure*.[1]

---

1. Winn Griffin, *God's Epic Adventure* (Woodinville, WA: Harmon Press, 2007), 248-250.

Till this moment in Paul's writing career, he had written to churches that he had planted. Now, he was going to write to a church that he had not founded nor had he ever visited. In the moments of peace after solving the Corinthian problems, Paul wrote his view of the Christian faith and how to live within its Story as he had come to understand it at this point in his life.

The book of Romans has had tremendous influence through the years having influenced significant figures like Augustine, Martin Luther, John Wesley, and Karl Barth as well as all those who have been blessed because of them.[2] It has been suggested that the book has multiple purposes: first, a missionary and public relations purpose. Every place Paul had gone to minister, unrest had broken out because of what he preached. It would be insane for him to go to the seat of the Roman government and cause unrest for the believers in Rome. After all, it had been less than a decade since the emperor Claudius had issued an edict, which expelled Jews including Jewish Christians, though later they were allowed to return.[3] So he wrote to assure the Roman church that his intentions were to bring them the gospel and to move on from their midst to minister in Spain (Rom. 15.24).

Second, Romans can be understood as having an apologetic purpose. Therein, Paul wanted to defend the gospel he had come to understand. Finally, Romans has a pastoral purpose, which shares Paul's thinking about how God has broken the barriers between Gentiles and Jews so that a full on rupture between Jewish and Gentile Christians could be avoided.[4]

The following is a brief outline of Romans:

Introduction 1.1-17
Slave to Sin 1.18-3.20

God has created a worldwide family of Jews and Gentiles as the fulfillment of the promise to Abraham. This is marked out by the covenant sign of faith.

2. I. Howard Marshall, Stephen Travis, Ian Paul, *Exploring the New Testament: A Guide to the Letters & Revelation*, vol. 1 (Downers Grove, IL: InterVarsity Press, 2002), 105.

3. Ben Witherington, *New Testament History: A Narrative Account* (Grand Rapids, MI: Baker Academic, 2001), 242, 292.

4. Robert H. Gundry, *A Survey of the New Testament*, 4th ed. (Grand Rapids, MI: Zondervan, 2003), 395.

Slave to God 3.21-8.39

Slavery to sin, because of Adam, is to be exchanged with slavery to God because of his faithfulness to his Covenant. The power to live a newly human life in Christ comes only through the Holy Spirit who works in every area of our life to make us just like Jesus.

Salvation of Israel 9.1-11.36

It turns out that the failure of Israel to follow God's Covenant is used by God through Jesus to bring about salvation for the whole world. Israel, too, must be saved, not as a nationalistic salvation but an individual one. Every Jew must come to God the same way as every Gentile. While enjoying the benefits of relationship with God, Gentiles are not to become anti-Jewish.

Service to God 12.1-16.24

God has created a new humanity by the death of Jesus. Life, as a newly created human, includes the coming together of races, heretofore separated, to worship the Creator God. The greetings of the final chapter may be a way of putting this picture together in the Roman church.

Conclusion 16.25-27[5]

What Are the Gracelets of Romans 12?

There are surely many gracelets salt and peppered through the story found in Scripture, which are not given in a list in which other gracelets are found. In the previous chapter on the gracelets in 1 Corinthians, we looked at the ones that were listed and in the next chapter we will look at the ones Paul places in a small list in Ephesians. Our job is to look at the ones that are listed and not express our opinion about others that may appear elsewhere.

The list of gracelets appears in the last of the four sections that I have outlined above (Romans 12.6-8). Paul turns the corner on the bountiful theology of the book of Romans and turns to the praxis. An apparent observation is that some of the gracelets that are in other lists appear here. Thus, when Paul wrote to the Roman church, he was trying to solve his own personal relationship problem as well as establish a new base for his continued church planting trips with his eye toward Spain. In chapter 12, he provides the Roman church with a list of what has been called service gifts. That designation is most likely read *into* the list rather than being read *from* the list. Remember, we are reading problem-solving literature. However, with the exception of prophecy, the gifts listed were ways of

---

5. Griffin, *God's Epic Adventure (The Reader Edition)*, 297.

serving, but so are others in other places. The gracelets are actions whose divine prompting is evidenced not by inspired speech or displays of power, but precisely by their character of service: that which serves the needs of fellow believers or the life of the community.[6]

The Spirit gives the gracelets of Romans 12.6-8 as he desires. Everyone should be rendering service, teaching, exhorting, and giving all the time in his or her daily life. These activities characterize the expected lifestyle of a Jesus follower.

Here's the list.

Prophecy (*propheteia*): Rom. 12.6; 1 Cor. 12.10, 12.28

Prophecy is communicating the pulse of God's heart for the purpose of edifying.

It should be noted that prophecy and prophet are the only consistent gracelets, which appear in all of the lists of Paul (Rom. 12.6-8; 1 Cor. 12.8-10, 28ff.; 13.1-3, 8ff.; 14.1–5, 6ff., 26-32; Eph. 4.11; 1 Thess. 5.19-22). We have already explained these gifts previously (see above).

Service (*diakonian*): Rom. 12.7

The divine recognition and response to specific needs in the Body of Christ.

On Paul and Barnabas' first church planting trip, they took along Mark. Luke records that Mark was their helper. That does not mean that Mark was a gofer. The word translated *helper* (service) indicates that he played an active part in the ministry of Paul and Barnabas. Paul understood Stephanas (1 Cor. 16.15) as functioning with this gracelet as well as Phoebe did in the church of Rome itself (Rom. 16.1). Paul could have had these real life illustrations in mind when he listed this gracelet for the Roman church.

Teachers (*didaskalous*): Rom. 12.7; 1 Cor. 12.28

The natural function of communicating spiritual truth and information that is infused by the Spirit, which benefits the ministry and health of the body of Christ.

Teaching is included in the list mentioned in 1 Cor. 14.6 and 26. We should note that the companion gracelets in verse 6 were: revelation, knowledge, prophecy. First Corinthians 14.26 lists teaching alongside a

6. Dunn, *Jesus and the Spirit*, 249.

psalm/hymn, a revelation, a tongue, and an interpretation. It appears that a charismatic "insight" is to be understood here. Teaching (or a word of instruction) may be considered a spontaneous utterance as knowledge, revelation, prophecy, psalm, tongue, and interpretation certainly are. According to Dunn, ...the particular insights of teaching are probably to be distinguished from the particular utterances of prophecy in that prophecy would suggest a new word from God as such, whereas teaching would tend to denote more *a new insight into an old word from God*, into the traditions already accepted by the community as authoritative in some degree, i.e., Old Testament writings, tradition of Jesus' sayings, the gospel they initially received (cf. 1 Cor. 11.2, 23, 15.3; 2 Thess. 2.15, 3.6). Thus, in Colossians 3.16 the "teaching" arises out of "the word (logos – *logos*) of Christ dwelling in you...." [7]

The following passages are an illustration of the possibility of *a word of instruction* (teaching). Charismatic exegesis might be found in Paul's use of the Old Testament (Romans 11.25–32; 1 Cor. 9.7–18; Gal. 3.8; 1 Thessalonians 4.2). These are possible examples of charismatic instruction. Paul is referring to instructions given under inspiration. The translation should read *through the Lord* (NAS margin).

Paul may understand teaching to include both recognition of traditional material as authoritative and an appreciation of the need for it to be interpreted and applied charismatically to the ever-changing needs and situations of the believing communities. [8]

Exhortation (*parakaion*): Rom. 12.8

The sensitivity to draw close to others in their time of need in order to encourage and motivate them to conquer the experiences of life.

The gracelets of prophecy and exhortation are linked together in 1 Corinthians 14.3. Paul says that a prophetic utterance should edify, exhort, and console. A prophetic word builds up the body of Christ because it speaks to a need or situation, which the body presently has.

Some Illustrations from Scripture

The following passages are illustrations where the word exhortation is used as translated by the New American Standard Version of the Bible where indicated.

7. Ibid., 237.
8. Ibid., 238.

- Paul's word to the synagogue attenders in Antioch of Pisidia: Acts 13.15
- *Urge*: NAS = exhort: Romans 12.1f.
- *Urge*: NAS = exhort: Romans 15.30
- *Exhort*: NAS: 1 Corinthians. 1.10
- *Urge*: NAS = exhort: 2 Corinthians 10.1
- *Urge*: NAS = exhort: Philippians 4.2
- *Urge*: NAS = exhort: 1 Thessalonians 4.10f.
- The whole letter to the Hebrews is a *word of exhortation*: Hebrews 13.22. It is altogether possible that Hebrews was a first-century sermonic presentation. On more than one occasion over the years, I have read the complete letter to the Corinthians as a Sunday teaching presentation. One report from those times has stuck with me over the years. A wife reported that after that experience on a Sunday morning that she found her husband, not known for his reading, sitting in his easy chair in the early hours of the morning reading Scripture. When asked by his wife what he was doing, he shared with her that he had never heard Scripture read in public before as a whole, but had only heard a verse here and there in sermons. He told her that he just had this strong urge to read a book in the Bible from the beginning to the end. When I heard the story, I was delighted to hear a firsthand illustration of how the Scripture text itself had served as a "word of exhortation," functioning as a gracelet to a person who was not much for reading.

Giving *(metadidous)* | Aiding *(proistamenos)* | Showing Mercy *(eleon)*: Rom. 12.8

The following gracelets are most often misunderstood because of the English words that have been chosen to be in the translations we read. We have read them so many times that we are conditioned to think of their English definition instead of the word definition that is within the language behind the English.

Giving *(metadidous)*: Rom. 12.8

This is the act of sharing food or possessions within the community with generosity (aploteti). It is giving, but it is not necessarily currency/money that is in the definition of this word.

Aiding *(proistamenos)*: Rom. 12.8

To care for others in the community such as widows, orphans, slaves, and strangers, i.e., those vulnerable within the community.

Chapter 11

Showing Mercy (eleon): Rom. 12.8

The giving of financial assistance to the "poor" in the church.[9]

The NIV has taken the easier road in translating this passage. RSV has taken a more exegetical road while the NRSV moved back toward the NIV. I think the RSV has the more accurate translation: *...he who contributes, in liberality; he who gives aid, with zeal; he who does acts of mercy, with cheerfulness.*

While these definitions run contrary to the popular ideas about these three gifts, I believe that this presents a more biblical view of them within their charismatic environment and biblical context. These three gracelets cover the whole range of what could be called the *community's welfare service.* In 1 Corinthians 12.28, the word *helps* is used as a gracelet. I believe that this one word covers all three of the words, which Paul has used in the Romans passage.

Thus:

Giving is to be understood as *sharing or giving a share of.* For Paul, the Spirit is shared experience. Ephesians 4.28 (written from Rome) teaches the basis for this giving. *Giving* is charismatic in that it is the sharing of what is of value to both. Paul's exhortation here is to give *with generosity.* The gracelet of giving may be seen in Acts 2.45; 4.32–37.

Aiding is usually translated by the word *lead* (NAS) or *gives aid* (RSV) or *leadership* (NIV). It seems best to understand the word as *he who cares for others* (i.e., widows, orphans, strangers, etc.). The word *aid* is set between two forms of aid-giving (giving and mercy) and would probably bear a similar meaning. Paul may have this in mind in 1 Thessalonians 4.12 where the word translated have charge over you (NAS) is also the same word, which Paul uses as a gracelet. The verse should be translated "...who diligently labor among you and give aid in the Lord to those in need...."

Mercy could refer to general acts of mercy, but Paul probably has in mind the giving of financial aid.[10] This gracelet may possibly be seen in the giving to the Jerusalem Church (2 Cor. 8–9).

---

9. Ibid., 251.
10. Ibid., 250.

149

Over the years, the church has forfeited its duty to take care of those in the community of faith opting out for government welfare programs in many cases. Sometimes the church contributes food for the under privileged in the community, but stops short of providing aid for the widows and orphans. Sometimes financial help is secured by those who are in need, but oftentimes there are so many hoops to get through, folks just give up. What if we taught Jesus followers to take care of other Jesus followers without hype or red tape. In your community, listen for the needs of the widows and the orphans, pull out your checkbook or cash and give generously to them. Really, you don't need to get a tax receipt to function as Paul most likely had in mind here.

The exhortation at 1 Corinthians 12.8 is to show mercy with cheerfulness or hilarity. Second Corinthians 9.7 exhorts the giver to be cheerful (the same word). Relief for the poor was an important part of early Christian piety. Mercy outside of Romans 12.8 always refers to the mercy of God. We may infer, therefore, that, for Paul, giving to the poor is a gracelet only in so far as it reflects God's unmerited generosity to us in Christ.

So What?

It is easy to see how this list of gracelets has been called "service gifts." But, that is not Paul's designation. Falling as they do in the last part of the letter to the Romans, it is much more likely that these gracelets are as charismatic as those found in 1 Corinthians, which get all the attention from those in Pentecostal or Charismatic churches. It is like Paul is saying: Hey guys and gals, here's the stuff you should be doing in your community of faith to make it a strong witness to the communities in Rome where these little ecclesial groups were living day to day.

Let's Have a Conversation

- While all of us should be continually serving, which of the preceding gracelets has God sent more often through you? What happened?
- How does the gracelet of *teaching* fit into the proposed theological scheme of this grouping of gracelets?
- How will the understanding of giving, aid, and mercy change you and your churches as you observe what God is doing and become the conduit through which he does it?

GRACELETS

Chapter 12: The Hierarchical Clue

➠ **Check Your GPS: Where You Are Going**
- Where We Have Been
- Hierarchical Clue
- Primitivism
- Restorationism
- Hierarchical Clue: Who Is In Charge?
- Overview of First and Second Testament
- So What?

Where We Have Been

In order to comprehend the place of the gracelets in Romans, we provided an overview of the book, pointing out where in the overall book the list appeared. Then we shared the list comprised of the following gracelets: prophecy, service, teachers, exhortation, giving, aiding, and showing mercy, suggesting that these gracelets, like those in 1 Corinthians 12, are all ad hoc and are given through the followers of Jesus to others at the discretion of the Trinity.

Hierarchical Clue

We now come to the second clue to help us understand the idea of gracelets in the writings of Paul. We will examine the long-lasting hypothesis where a lot of ink has been spilled that suggests that the church has a hierarchical structure created by the Bible.

In relationship to this subject, Howard Snyder suggests the following:

The Second Testament does not speak in terms of two classes of Christians—"minister" and "laymen"—as we do today.... The clergy-laity dichotomy is unbiblical and therefore invalid. It grew up as an accident of church history and actually marked a drifting away from biblical faithfulness.... The Second Testament doctrine of ministry rests therefore not on the clergy-laity distinction but on the twin and complementary pillars of the priesthood of all believers and the gifts of the Spirit. Today, four centuries after the Reformation, the full implications of this Protestant affirmation have yet to be worked out. The clergy-laity dichotomy is a direct carry-over from pre-Reformation Roman Catholicism and a throwback to the First Testament priesthood. It is one of the principal obstacles to the church effectively being God's agent of the Kingdom today because it creates a false idea that only "holy men," namely, ordained ministers, are really qualified and responsible for leadership and significant ministry. In the Second Testament, there are functional distinctions between various kinds of ministries but no hierarchical division between clergy and laity.[1]

Snyder covers a lot of territory in those brief words and pinpoints the issue that the present church in the twenty-first century still deals with. Of course, those within the cocooned system of the church have a difficult time with this concept. Some leaders therein are unaware of the data of the Second Testament; some are aware but ignore it, while others simply have a different interpretation of the data. Therefore, the focus of this chapter is on an interpretative key that may help one understand the splitlevel operation of the present church in its institutional form. We begin with a brief discussion of primitivism, which is sometimes used to discredit the kind of material that is presented below. While I present a point of view, my hope is that the reader will feel that they can agree or disagree with the conclusions.

Primitivism

In philosophy, there is a designation that is often used as an argument that is sometimes used as a category to disparage ideas that are found in the modern/postmodern world. It is called primitivism. The word is defined as "a belief in the value of what is simple and unsophisticated, expressed as a philosophy of life or through art or literature," or "the notion that the value of primitive cultures is superior to that of the modern world." In the history of ideas, it is a relatively new word, as words go, coming into existence in 1860-1865 that described beliefs stretching back to the Greek philosophers. *The Dictionary of the History of Ideas* suggests the following:

> *Primitivism is a name for a cluster of ideas arising from meditations on the course of human history and the value of human institutions and accomplishments. It is found in two forms, chronological and cultural, each of which may exist as "soft" or "hard" primitivism.[2]*

1. Howard Snyder, *The Community of the King* (Grand Rapids, MI: InterVarsity Press, 1977), 94-95.

2. George Boas, "Primitivism," University of Virginia Library http://xtf.lib.virginia.edu/xtf/view?docId=DicHist/uvaBook/tei/DicHist3.xml;chunk.id=dv3-72;toc.depth=1;toc.id=dv3-72;brand=default (accessed July 30, 2015).

As a nonspecialist in philosophy, it seems to me that the category is used when it is convenient for an argument as per James K. A. Smith in his book on Postmodernism[3] where he is arguing that a return to premodern liturgies might be the best way forward for a postmodern church.[4]

Since Smith's penchant is for the theology of Calvin, he seems to think that form of primitivism is okay, but those in the Plymouth Brethren, Baptist, and Pentecostal Christianity are pointed out as operating in this tradition.[5]

If the basic primitive stuff from Scripture is not normative for the church, then:

- What purpose does the Scripture have?
- Why do the traditions from the centuries in which the shape and size of Scripture was being determined become normative?

Restorationism

Roger E. Olson writes in a recent article: "Can 'Authentic Christianity' Be Found Today?"[6] This present series of articles on leadership are not suggesting that a return to the Second Testament church is a goal. While their culture may have had some similarities, it was not the same culture that faces the church today in many parts of the world. Culture is not monolithic. As Olson points out, most restoration movements look for symbols like buildings with a preference for no buildings, the mode of baptism that is used, signs and wonders, displays of the so-called spiritual gifts, and in some churches the non-presence of musical instruments. Rather, Olson suggests in his article that some marks of authenticity that one can look for are:

1. how much the church reflects the culture around it.
2. to what extent the church values being "respectable" over being authentically Christian.
3. doctrinally sound preaching and teaching that appeals to the heart as well as to the head.

---

3. James K. A. Smith, *Who's Afraid of Postmodernism?: Taking Derrida, Lyotard, and Foucault to Church* (Grand Rapids, MI: Baker Academic, 2006).

4. Ibid., 127-135.

5. Ibid.

6. Roger E. Olson, "Can 'Authentic Christianity' Be Found Today?", Patheos.com http://www.patheos.com/blogs/rogereolson/2015/03/can-authentic-christianity-be-found-today/ (accessed July 30, 2015).

4. true community manifested by sharing lives and property.
5. passionate commitment to Christ, the gospel, and the church.
6. unity in Spirit and in truth as opposed to non-spiritual similarity.
7. clear evidence that God is there busy changing lives for the better in super-normal ways.

It seems to me that if one wants to have a mooring in a conversation that Scripture would be the place to begin, not the traditions as well-meaning as they may be. These are surely issues for conversation, not certitudes. So, it is with conversation in mind that I present the following thoughts.

Hierarchical Clue: Who Is In Charge?

Here's the question: Was the system of leadership in the Pauline churches around the Mediterranean world in the first century a hierarchical one? To provide a beginning answer, we must start with the concept of what is often called spiritual gifts. To understand that idea, I have used the word gracelets[7] in the writings of Paul throughout this book as a substitute for spiritual gifts to help understand his view of leadership in his letters. Thus, we will examine the long-lasting hypothesis, on which a lot of ink has been spilled, that suggests that the church has a hierarchical structure. Here are some questions we could consider.

- How did this idea originate?
- Did it come from the writings of Paul?
- Was early catholic theology attributed to the books of 1 and 2 Timothy?
- Was it a Hebrew thought form or was it a Greek thought form in its origin?
- Is it possible that the Western mindset, with its need for specificity and reductionism, has taken what the early church saw as function and turned it into specific categories or offices?

The following is a synopsis of Scripture on this subject of hierarchical structure in Scripture. We begin with a short survey of the First Testament.

Overview of First and Second Testament

The First Testament: A Short Survey

By the time we get to the story of Exodus in the First Testament, it seems to point to the notion that God deliberately wanted his people to

---

7. Gracelets is the word that I am using for the so-called spiritual gifts.

be a "kingdom of priests." Moses was instructed by God to tell the people of Israel as recorded in Exodus 19.4-6:

> "'You yourselves have seen what I did to Egypt, and how I carried you on eagles' wings and brought you to myself. Now if you obey me fully and keep my covenant, then out of all nations you will be my treasured possession. Although the whole earth is mine, you will be for me a kingdom of priests and a holy nation.' These are the words you are to speak to the Israelites."

The idea suggested by "a kingdom of priests and a holy nation," is that all the citizens of Israel were to be regarded with dignity and power.[8]

The family of Aaron, the older brother of Moses, was a family of high priests in which the oldest representative of the family functioned as high priest. Consecrated in the same way as all the other priests, the high priest shared in the usual daily duties. The major difference was that when the Day of Atonement arrived, the serving high priest became the representative of the people before God.[9]

The priests functioned as manual laborers in the care of the Tabernacle (Num. 3.5ff). Their service timeframe was about twenty-five years from the age of twenty-five to fifty (Num. 35.1). Each city in Israel had dedicated a section of land that was for their use.[10]

What could this mean? It could be that The First Testament does not appear to have what one might call an office in which ministry occurred because the intention was that all would be priests. It could also be said that the priests functioned as laborers on land set apart for them on which to work. That is to say, they were not "paid wages" for their service of being a priest.

The Second Testament

To summarize this idea, the Levitical priesthood and the sacrificial system in which the First Testament operated was replaced by the life and ministry of Jesus. Jesus is seen as the high priest (Romans 3.25,

---

8. Carl Friedrich Keil and Franz Delitzsch, *Biblical Commentary on the Old Testament* (Peabody, MA: Hendrickson Publishers, 1996), 2:97.

9. D. R. Wood and others, *The New Bible Dictionary*, 1st ed. (Grand Rapids, MI: InterVarsity Press, 1996), 1029.

10. Ibid., 1028-1029.

Hebrews). The incarnation identified Jesus with humankind (Heb. 2.14-18; 4.15; 5.1, 7-10). He mediates the new covenant (Heb. 7.23-28; 8.6-13; 9.5). A community gathering, as the continued people of God, continue to fulfill and echo Exodus 19.4-6. Peter says the church is a *royal priesthood* (1 Pet. 2.9).

As with the First Testament, it appears that the Second Testament does not support any form of hierarchical structure of the people of God when they gathered. It is not possible to determine in the sacred text how often they met. In the early part of Acts, they met daily. At one point in Acts, they were meeting on the first day of the week, which could have been either early Sunday morning because folks had to work on Sunday just like every other day of the week. Or, it could have been Saturday night depending on whether Luke was using a Roman accounting of a day or a Jewish accounting of the day. In the story of Acts 20, it seems to be more of an ad hoc meeting because Paul was traveling through Troas and the followers of Jesus gathered to hear what he had to say.

The Ruler of the Synagogue

A survey of Paul's own language would suggest that he eluded using words that might have been used in a Jewish setting, about the idea of a priestly office. The synagogues had an *archisynagogus*, the leader or president of the synagogue,[11] who was the presiding officer of the synagogue. An *archisynagogus* was elected for a specific timeframe, most likely a year. However, it was possible for an *archisynagogus* to be elected for life.[12] The job description of the "ruler of the synagogue" included the responsibility for maintaining the order of the service, the selecting of who the readers of the Torah and Prophets would be and the speakers. It appears that individual leaders who were the equivalent of the leader of the synagogue were not part of any church that Paul planted.[13]

The First Testament mentions several who functioned as an *archisynagogus:* Jairus (Mark 5.22, 35), Unnamed (Luke 13.10-17), Unnamed (allowed Paul and Barnabas to speak, Antioch of Pisidia – Acts 13.15), Crispus (Corinth – Acts 18.8), Sosthenes (Corinth – Acts 18.17). Both Crispus and Sosthenes became Jesus followers (Acts 18.8;

---

11. Dunn, *Jesus and the Spirit*, 285.

12. Merrill Chapin Tenney and J. D. Douglas, *The New International Dictionary of the Bible*, Pictorial ed. (Grand Rapids, MI, U.S.A.: Regency Reference Library, Zondervan Pub. House, 1987), 489.

13. Dunn, *Jesus and the Spirit*, 285.

1 Cor. 1.1). It should be noted that none of them served within the fledging community of Jesus followers. The support of the synagogue was by offerings that were given voluntarily. Years later, it appears that the model of the synagogue organization was kept by the Catholic Church and used by the Protestant Reformation.[14]

Servants, Elders

In the section of 1 Corinthians, 1 Cor. 4.1ff., where Paul is addressing the problem the Corinthians had developed of choosing who to follow, he shares with the Corinthians that they should regard Apollos, Peter, and him as "servants." The word used there and in Luke 4.20 is *hyperetes*. It is a non-technical word, i.e., these men did not have a position in the church at Corinth; rather they were like an under-oarsman, a rower on a ship's crew, or assistant.

Jewish congregations were governed by elders (*presbuteroi*, pres-bu-ter-oi). The church in Jerusalem was most likely formed after the Jewish model.[15] Remember, the Jerusalem church was made up of Jews, so it would be natural for them to continue their pattern even though they were now followers of Jesus. Elders do not occur in any of Paul's writings before the so-called Pastoral letters of 1, 2, Timothy and Titus.[16]

One wonders how the Jewish synagogue system survived as the predominant form for operating as a community of faith moving forward from the first century. Here's my perspective: The Catholic Church, beginning in the third century, took their model of operation from Acts 15 and what is often called the Pastoral Epistles, and simply overlooked the charismatic function of the Pauline churches that was created in the earliest years of his missions to create Jesus followers in the Mediterranean world.

It is often argued that if the church in Jerusalem was patterned like the Jewish synagogue, then there is a clear line that aids the argument with continuity for a hierarchical structure for the church governance. Anyone can arrive at this result if the presupposition of "unity means uniformity" is held closely. Unity and uniformity are not necessarily the same thing. Scripture reveals both unity and diversity. It is likely that there were two systems of government in the church moving into the second century.

14. Merrill Chapin Tenney, *The Zondervan Pictorial Encyclopedia of the Bible* (Grand Rapids, MI: Zondervan Publishing House, 1975), 5:566.

15. Dunn, *Jesus and the Spirit*, 285; 180-182. See also: W. M. F. Scott, "Priesthood in the New Testament," *Scottish Journal of Theology* 10, no. 4 (1957): 413.

16. Dunn, *Jesus and the Spirit*, 285.

These two forms could be called: Pauline and institutional or what I have come to designate as ChurchWorld. The Pauline form was functional and charismatic. The ChurchWorld moved from function to form and is revealed in the so-called Pastoral letters. Some First Testament specialists have suggested that the authorship of these letters was an edited version of Paul and leaned toward the institutional approach to govern the church. But, what is more important than authorship for these letters is the content that they offer for solving problems in the churches in the Ephesian and Cyprus area.

It is sometimes posited that the Pastorals are the first illustrations of a progressive form of institutionalization. It may be possible to come to this conclusion by reading back into the text of these letters the concept that all modern renewal projects find institutionalization in the second or third generation. The reasoning would be: if institutional church is true now, it must have been true then. That backward reasoning seems wrongheaded to me.

By the time of Timothy and Titus, the freshness of the renewal experiences, which brought the communities of faith about, was beginning to harden into rigid set forms. The second and third generation leaders may have been less creative and sensitive toward the Spirit. They began to treat the experiences of the founding fathers as *the faith*. The teaching and experience of the founders become the sacred words, hallowed heritage, which are to be preserved, guarded, and handed on, but never revisited or reinterpreted. The present becomes only a channel whereby the religion of the past can be transmitted in good order for the next generation. The vitality of the founders usually disappears and the second generation tries what is impossible, to live out the past experience in the present. This has not fully happened in the letters to Timothy and Titus, but the processes are well-advanced and possibly irreversible.[17] This movement toward what has been called "early Catholicism" has three features:

First, the fading of the Second Coming of Jesus in the present life of the early church is observable in the writings of Paul. In First Thessalonians, he suggested that he would be around when this event occurred when he wrote "we who are alive and remain." A little over a decade later, he has changed his opinion, not about the coming of Jesus again, but about being alive when Jesus returns. In 2 Timothy 4.6-8, he writes that he is ready to die:

For I am already being poured out like a drink offering, and the

---

17. Ibid., 349-350.

time for my departure is near. I have fought the good fight, I have finished the race, I have kept the faith. Now there is in store for me the crown of righteousness, which the Lord, the righteous Judge, will award to me on that day—and not only to me, but also to all who have longed for his appearing.

Second, there was the increase of institutionalization with its beginning concept of office, a distinction between the clergy and laity and a priestly hierarchy. This can be seen in 1 and 2 Timothy and Titus.

Third, the formalization of the faith into set forms was a way to ward off false teaching. This punctilious idea was because the founding era of the founders had not passed and the next generation has the responsibility to concretely preserve the faith for the future generations. Prophetic words were now suspiciously marked as heretical rather than acceptable in the communities of faith. It was a complete reversal of what had been created by the Spirit.[18]

Service

The Septuagint (LXX) uses the word service (*leitourgia*, LA-toor-gee-a) to converse about ceremonial service that was offered by a priest. Paul only used this word once at Romans 15.16 in relationship to his own ministry. The other uses of the word center on the ministry of the whole congregation.[19] Paul shuns this word when he writes about individuals or other ministry peers within the church.[20]

There is one exception to the above and it is found in Philippians 1.1 (see below). Therein, Paul does address what seems to be a single group of leaders who are responsible to organize or provide for the spiritual well-being of others over whom they provide oversight. It is interesting that the book of 1 Corinthians would have been a splendid place to have addressed a specific leader to handle all the problems in which the Corinthian church was involved. The reading of the opening sentences of that letter makes it apparent that Paul did not do so. The brusque implication there was if problems in the Corinthian church were going to be solved, the Spirit was going to have to do it.[21]

18. James D. G. Dunn, *Unity and Diversity in the New Testament: An Inquiry into the Character of Earliest Christianity* (Philadelphia, PA: The Westminster Press, 1977), 344.

19. Eduard Schweizer, *Church Order in the New Testament* (Norwich, UK: SCM Press, 2011: Revised Edition), 171-173.

20. Dunn, *Jesus and the Spirit*, 285.

21. Ibid.

It is fair to conclude then that a hierarchical system of church government was not created by Paul for the churches he planted, rather his was a charismatic form. While Paul was the *ad hoc* leader of the church at Corinth as its founder, the instructions that he provided to the congregants were given by the Spirit to help correct the problems at hand. This may serve the present generation of churches a model of solving church problems.

Selected Illustrations

The following illustrations suggest that there was not a hierarchical structure in the church of the first century when Paul was writing his letters.

Stephanas: 1 Corinthians 16.15

Paul's first converts in Achaia were Stephanas and his household. He records in 1 Corinthians 16.15 that *they had devoted themselves to the service of the saints*. Paul's meaning is clear. Stephanas and his family became aware of needs and directed their lives to meet the needs they encountered. This man and his household were not appointed by Paul or the church for this ministry. When they saw a need, they reached out to meet it. It would be more accurate to say that they were appointed to this ministry by God who would show them the service needed and then supply the supplies to fulfill it.[22] It was *ad hoc*, impermanent. It appears that there were no committees, no offices, and no organization as we find in the institutionalized ChurchWorld today. There was functionality based on need. The service was voluntary and Paul urges others to follow in like steps in verse 16.[23] This pattern is surely more functional than the highly structured (catholic) way of ministering used by the church at the beginning of the twenty-first century.

1 Thessalonians 5.12-15

Now we ask you, brothers and sisters, to acknowledge those who work hard among you, who care for you in the Lord and who admonish you. Hold them in the highest regard in love because of their work. Live in peace with each other. And we urge you, brothers and sisters, warn those who are idle and disruptive, encourage the

---

22. C. K. Barrett, *The First Epistle to Corinthians* (Peabody, MA: Hendrickson Publishers, Inc, 1993), 393-394.

23. Hans Conzelmann, *1 Corinthians : A Commentary on the First Epistle to the Corinthians*, Hermeneia--a Critical and Historical Commentary on the Bible (Minneapolis, MN: Fortress Press, 1975), 298.

disheartened, help the weak, be patient with everyone. Make sure that nobody pays back wrong for wrong, but always strive to do what is good for each other and for everyone else.

There are two thoughts to consider in this text in terms of hierarchy:

- The use of the words *urge you* in verse 14 is something the whole body does.
- The word *proistemi* that Paul uses in verse 12 is translated in the New American Standard Version as "have charge over you." Paul uses the same word in Romans 12.8 where NAS translates it as "gives aid" (in the margin). It is possible that the word, as used in Romans and 1 Thessalonians, means "the act of giving assistance to those who are most in need." It is altogether possible that Paul is talking about a gracelet in this passage. This text leads us to the conclusion that the ones Paul wrote to in the church at Thessalonica were the ones who were most energetic in the life of the community. When the Spirit initiated, they served. Their only authority came by the manifestation of some particular gracelet, which operated through them during the serving.[24] What if the institutional church adopted this concept of gracelets rather than the more vociferous view of "those who are in charge bless the idea of this gift is yours, walk ye in it!"

Philippians 1.1

Philippians 1.1 may be understood in the following two ways:

- Paul and Timothy are designated as servants. This is uncharacteristic of Paul's usual designation of himself as apostle[25] (see Rom 1.1; 1 Cor. 1.1; 2 Cor. 1.1). Connected with the reality that Paul spoke to a plurality of bishops and deacons has led some interpreters to conclude that Paul's address was correcting *the first case of the desire for ecclesiastical position...* and with a touch of irony at that![26] The reason Paul relinquishes his

---

24. Dunn, *Jesus and the Spirit*, 287. See also: Colin Brown. *The New International Dictionary of New Testament Theology* (Grand Rapids, MI: Zondervan, 1975), s.v. W. Link Bauder: "Engys."

25. When we hear the word "apostle," it comes with all the "office" baggage that 2000 years of church history has bestowed on it. However, it just means "messenger" as it is translated in the J. B. Phillips translation: "Paul, commissioned by the will of God as a messenger of Jesus Christ...." Or, as Eugene Peterson translates in *The Message*: "I, Paul, have been called and sent by Jesus, the Messiah...."

26. Dunn, *Jesus and the Spirit*, 439, fn. 160.

usual designation of *messenger* and settles for the term *servant* may be because he is sending a message of correction to these upstarts in the Philippian church. Remember, these letters are problem-solving literature.

- There is no indication that the bishops and deacons mentioned in the opening statements were officials of ecclesiastical offices within the church at Philippi. They were like the group mentioned in 1 Thessalonians who had taken responsibility to serve as they saw a need arise. From a grammatical point of view, there is no definite article. It is not *the* bishops and elders but simply bishops and elders. The duty of a bishop, which could also be translated guardian, was stated in Acts 20.28 (cf. 20.17), and simply means *to feed*. An Ephesian guardian was to nourish the flock (the gracelet of pastor-teacher). The deacons functioned with other gifts like helps, (1 Cor. 12.28) and service, like Stephanas in 1 Corinthians 16.15. We will discuss these gifts anon. The two supposed leadership groups are not given any prominence in the body of the letter. On the contrary, Paul writes to the whole church. There is not one suggestion that a specific ecclesiastical office was held by any person or group in the church at Philippi.[27] Most likely when it is read that way, it is the our reading back into the material (*eisegesis*) our own present baggage about church governance.

A question that is sometimes asked is: What about Paul's appointment of elders to the churches at Galatia? How does this fit with the bishop and elder interpretation above of Philippians 1.1? It could very well be that Paul appointed elders in the churches in Galatia on his first mission because he was influenced by Barnabas, so that both would be in agreement with the Jerusalem church's Jewish form of government. He saw the flaw of this procedure and did not pursue this activity as a habitual practice in his ongoing ministry in the Mediterranean world.

These appointed elders in the Galatian mission may have functioned charismatically for a time. No suggestion is given that these elders remained elders in the faith communities in Galatia. When Paul wrote to the Jesus followers in Galatia, he did not address a group of leaders or elders to help solve the problems faced by those followers of Jesus, which occurred after he left them. Paul is requested by the Jesus followers at Jerusalem to deliver a report about the ministry of their mission among the Gentiles. The letter of Acts 15.23 could have opened

27. Ralph P. Martin, *The Epistle of Paul to the Philippians : An Introduction and Commentary*, Rev. ed., The Tyndale New Testament Commentaries (Grand Rapids, MI: Wm. B. Eerdmans Publishing Company, 1987), 57-58.

with, "the brethren, both the missionaries and the leaders to the Gentile believers in Antioch, Syria, and Cilicia..." One could conclude that no ecclesiastical leaders were addressed here because there was not such an ecclesiastical group within these churches. Or, one could argue that the ecclesiastical order in the Jerusalem church was built on the Jewish synagogue since most of the followers of Jesus were converted Jews and that would be a familiar form of governance to them.

1 Corinthians 12.28

In 1 Corinthians 12.27, Paul wrote: "Now you are the body of Christ, and each one of you is a part of it." He places an emphasis on the quality of the existence of the church. The church gathered together is the general reference. In 12.28, he moves to a specific example.

The first three gifts are so-called office gifts. The next five are often called ministries. This is not an exhaustive list or even a representative list. It is an *ad hoc* list to demonstrate that there is a variety of gracelets rather than only the one, tongues, that the Corinthians were fixated on. Paul uses the word appointed, which can mean to set in their proper place. When he uses the word "first," it is not used in the sense of more importance than the others. The first ones listed were the founders of the church at Corinth, i.e., Paul and Barnabas.[28] The word *first* does not mean hierarchical authority. For Paul, ministry and charisma work together. Paul's theory of order is not a static one, resting on offices, institutions, but acts of ministry as they occur.[29] If there were a hierarchy intended, Paul would be going against what he had just taught in the preceding section about the body of Christ and its unity and diversity in which no part has a priority over any other part, but all parts work equally together.

Some Objections to this Position

The Twelve Apostles Were Unique

Why is this important? It appears that this teaching is set forth with a desire to ensure a safe ground within the history of the church for these twelve individuals who participated in things that no others have or will have access for participation. It is true that there is symbolism in the replacement of Jacob's twelve sons with twelve disciples, which

28. Wikipedia, "Paul the Apostle," Wikipedia http://en.wikipedia.org/wiki/Paul_the_Apostle (accessed January 5, 2015).

29. Dunn, *Jesus and the Spirit*, 272.

formed the new Israel of God, the church. In this sense they are unique. One must not forget, however, that there were disciple missionaries that were not a part of the original twelve. Judas faltered, and was replaced. Paul functioned as a missionary along with others (1 Cor. 15.3-7), who formed a wider group. Paul's idea of apostleship, or missionaryship, was formed by his concept of mission (1 Cor. 9.1ff. 15.10; Gal. 1.15ff. 2.9). The Synoptic Gospels suggest that the primitive sense of apostle was missionary (Matt. 10.5; Mark 6.37). It appears that it is only in the work of mission that these disciples were called apostles/missionaries.

Paul did not have a unique ministry in the churches he planted. He was personally commissioned by Christ in a post resurrection appearance (1 Cor. 9.1; 15.7; Gal. 1.1, 15ff.). He became a successful church planter (1 Cor. 3.5ff. 20; 9.2; 15.9ff.). As a founder of specific churches, he had a continuing responsibility to provide guidance and solve problems. This is the primary reason for his letters to the churches. We should take note that he did not consider himself an apostle (think authority figure) to the universal church, where his authority would be recognized by all churches. The authority he carried was confined to his sphere of influence and mission (Gal. 2.7-9, 2 Cor. 10.13-16), to the churches he planted or were planted from the churches he planted. Another possible translation of 1 Corinthians 12.28 is *God set in the local church....* Paul challenged passionately the claims that in the churches he planted that other apostles could exercise any authority (2 Cor. 10-13). Not during his lifetime is it recorded that he attempted to exercise any authority over the church at Jerusalem (Acts 15). He saw himself as a functional and situational appointee by God for the business at hand.

The Use of Nouns

The original language presents the gracelets in the form of nouns. A noun is defined as a name of a person, place, or thing. When one uses this argument to denote that the noun *apostle* means a specific person, which is concrete, the gracelet cannot be a function.[30] The other alternative is that it must be an office. In the real world of language, a noun can be a word, which has through usage found a concrete manifestation, but that does not subtract from its dynamic characteristic. That is to say that there was function before there was form and we might press that only in the function is form generated for the moment of the function. That is to say, an apostle is an apostle when s/he is apostling. As far back as 1794, William Vincent wrote: It

---

30. Unless, behind the use of the noun, the functioning in the moment of the noun being used is understood.

appears, "that in the external appearance of the Greek language, nouns appear to be derived from verbs."[31]

The issue is that noun as a description is often read with specific rigidity of possession rather than the idea of description. In light of the old question: which came first the chicken or the egg, the question might be: which came first the verbing of an action or the descriptive noun?

That leaves us with the age-old question: Which came first, the chicken or the egg? This is a timeless question around which much ink has been spilt. This riddle has a long history going back as far as Aristotle (384–322 BC) and maybe even before.

Jack Katz, in an article in 2008, suggests the following: "Somewhere in the historical organizing of contemporary understandings, the noun, 'the cook,' took on a life separate from the verb, cooking.... When research goes from noun to verb, or from 'what' to 'how,' the result almost always is a description of process. Moreover, because power insists on the importance of nouns—status is rewarded, rights are regulated, and stratification is studied by occupational titles—it is always a political economic revelation to show how nouns are socially imposed on what are essentially processes."[32]

What, one might ask, has this to do with anything? Here's a possible answer.

We have spent an inordinate amount of time in the church that uses an English Bibles to give prominence to one word found in Ephesians 4.11: "pastor" (*poimēn*). The original word appears eighteen times and is translated by the English word "shepherd" fifteen times, as Shepherd two times, and only once with the English word "pastor."

That doesn't make the word unimportant, because the amount of times a word is used does not carry any particular weight. Having said that, one would not necessarily know that when preacher and teacher alike bring out the data of a text with something like: "this word appears (fill in the number) in our Bible, their implicit meaning is that because it has frequency, it must be important. If that line of reasoning were true,

---

31. William Vincent, *The Origination of the Greek Verb: An Hypothesis* (London: 1794), A4.

32. Jack Katz, "Cooks Cooking up Recipes: The Cash Value of Nouns, Verbs and Grammar," *The American Sociologist* 43, no. 1 (2008): 127.

then the word "virgin" as in "virgin birth" would not have any priority since it only occurs a couple of times in the Second Testament.

When we use words, we get a mental picture of what we are thinking. Words are only symbols. So, on any given Sunday at a church at the corner of walk and don't walk, folks attend with the word "pastor" in their mindset, usually with that designated person standing behind some kind of podium delivering something called a sermon, while everyone looks at the back of the heads in the pews in front of them. During the week when one becomes ill, that person may call a pastor to come pray for them and in smaller congregations there is an expectation that the individual will show up at home or hospital, etc., to offer comfort and prayer. It is further believed that a "pastor" is the top leader of a local church, with the word embellished with descriptive adjectives, usually "senior" added to the noun, pastor.

This has been a growing system of belief, sometimes challenged but often with no one listening, especially those "called" pastors, because it threatens their position and, in a lot of places, their livelihood.

In reality, Scripture does not have a plan for a "pastor" being the "head" of a local church. That idea is nonexistent. That idea has taken about 2,000 years to develop and is part of the problem of why we see so many folks leaving the church in today's culture.

As we suggested above, the noun "pastor" came into existence in the Greek language after the verb that demonstrated its action. Someone was pastoring/shepherding and then the word "pastor" was used to describe what s/he was doing. Whatever that was, it is not the same as what is happening in ChurchWorld today. What if, there really are no professional pastors in God's plan for the church?

The question that often arrives at this juncture is: How would ministry get accomplished in today's church? The simple and most assuredly biblical answer is by all the congregants. Most of the stuff that professional pastors do today have little to do with the biblical concept of shepherding. It has much more to do with administration. I read in a FB post once by a "self-acclaimed pastor" as he listed his duties that he performs in a congregation of 150. The vast majority of the things that were being accomplished were administrative. One "pastor" in the same thread asked, "What would I do if I wasn't a pastor?" Someone replied, "Get a job," with a possible implication of "just like everyone else in the congregation."

The system is broken. But even in some fixes, the idea of pastor remains. That is a systemic problem because as soon as a new congregation comes into existence, folks mentally think of having a pastor. Here's the scoop, one is a pastor when s/he is pastoring. When s/he is not actively pastoring, s/he is not a pastor. There is no position of pastor in the *ecclesia*.

It seems that the "pastor" idea has become the controlling metaphor of life of the ChurchWorld. Pastors assume that they are the head of the local community of faith. What that causes is a system that is cockeyed with itself. The head leader of this out-of-whack system thinks and acts with supposed power that really doesn't exist. The ludicrous system of a local community of faith is often blinded to its own system's dysfunction. One wonders if the story of Jonah doesn't give us a clue. Jonah, thinking he was in control, decided to go with his own frail ideas of who was in charge. The results: folks on a ship that had nothing to do with his decision were affected. Jonah's response to the calamity of what he had caused was that his shipmates should throw him overboard and then the sea would calm. They did. It did.

System thinking in ChurchWorld is corrupt. Decisions made years before are now coming home to roost. The system developed by pastors over the years is dysfunctional. One of my friends on Facebook suggested: "the professionalization of ministry is disastrous." I think he was spot one. The life of the church does not come from a leader, except when the leader is Jesus. One metaphor that may be functional to relearn is that Jesus is the vine, we are the branches. Life that comes through the vine bears fruit through the branches. The branches are not the fruit and there is not "one" branch singled out as "the branch leader."

As long as ChurchWorld continues down the preposterous road of a cross-eyed system, it will remain in the same situation. No amount of changing the programs that support the structure will create a solution. Moving the deck chairs on the Titanic did not prevent the ship from sinking. Change the system and change the results. Maybe congregations should rise up and "throw Jonah" overboard so the raging waters of ChurchWorld can become calm.

Think of "Jonah" as the "pastor corrupt system" not necessarily as the individual who is designated "pastor" that perpetuates the system. Of course, sometimes the system controlled by a single pastor has to have pruning if the branches are going to continue to produce fruit. It's when the "single branch" starts pruning other branches that the system suffers. It is when the "single branch" starts telling the other branches that the folks leaving ChurchWorld are being pruned by God so the local community of faith can grow again that the problem may actually be that the "single branch" (read pastor) is actually the problem. The "single branch" line of thinking is seriously misguided and narcissistic. The corrupt system and its pruning becomes crazy making and the whole system falters and sometimes cannot be redeemed and a tear drops from the eye of Jesus.

The Pastoral Epistles

One has to wait for the writings of 1 and 2 Timothy and Titus to discover that there are folks called elders, etc. The argument goes that by the time of these writings, the so-called "office gifts" were stable in the church. It is true that the more formal structures of Jewish congregations following the structure of the Jewish synagogues seem to have taken over the more charismatic and dynamic expression of the church. However, it does not necessarily follow that the structure of the church found in Timothy and Titus was the ideal form. Rather, it was one form. Yes, the letters demonstrate a movement from function to form. This is a sociological situation that does not "have" to occur. Other writers of books found in the Second Testament have also hinted at this movement. Peter's first letter reflects the charismatic reality of Pauline churches writing about the idea of continuing gracelets (4.10), but he also writes about elders (5.1). What we may be witnessing in the first letter by Peter is a Pauline church that is beginning to adopt the model of the Jewish Christian church and Peter's exhortation is to stay free and flexible within the Pauline charismatic expression of the church.

Matthew appears to be trying to develop a form of Pauline churchmanship. John, Hebrews, and Revelation are books, which also resisted the idea of the institutionalization of the church.[33]

Church History: Luther

Martin Luther wrote about this issue in 1520 in one of the most significant documents of the period of the Reformation, a tract called *To the Christian Nobility*. This tract demonstrates that he has a firm belief in the *priesthood of all believers*. Here is a summary: Three sections comprise the tract. Therein, Luther writes a host of ideas from which the Western world had been following for nearly a millennium. He wrote about legal, political, social, and religious thought. In Section One, Part One, Luther lays down the axe and cuts into the root of the clergy and laity idea. "It is pure invention that pope, bishop, priest, and

33. James D. G. Dunn, *Unity and Diversity in the New Testament: An Inquiry into the Character of Earliest Christianity* (Norwich, UK: SCM Press, 2006: Third Edition), 101-123.

monks are called the spiritual estate while princes, lords, artisans, and farmers are called temporal estate. This is indeed a piece of deceit and hypocrisy...all Christians are truly of the spiritual estate, there is no difference among them..."[34]

Luther also wrote *Concerning the Ministry* about three years after *To the Christian Nobility*. This document was addressed to the Bohemian Christian. They were quarreling with the Pope about ordination. He gave them some advice to help them along in their quarreling match. Here are some selected excerpts:

> But let us go on and show from the priestly offices (as they call them) that all Christians are priests in equal degree. For such passages as "You are a royal priesthood" (1 Pet. 2.9) and, "Thou has made them a kingdom of priests (Rev. 5.10), I have sufficiently treated in other books (*To The Christian Nobility*). Mostly the functions of a priest are these: to teach, to preach and proclaim the word of God, to baptize, to consecrate or administer the Eucharist, to bind and loose sins, to pray for others, to sacrifice, and to judge of all doctrine and spirits. Certainly these are splendid and royal duties.[35]

On yet another occasion (1544) in a sermon for a church dedication, Luther makes this point again.

> But we, who are in the kingdom of our Lord Christ, are not thus bound to a tribe or place, so that we must adhere to one place alone and have only one race or one particular, separate kind of persons. Rather, we are all priests, as is written in 1 Peter 2.9; so that all of us should proclaim God's Word and works at every time and in every place, and persons from all ranks, races, and stations be specially called to the ministry.[36]

Luther did argue that in 1 Peter (2.5, 9) that Peter was thinking about a "general priesthood of all believers" in juxtaposition to any kind of episcopacy, which the Roman Catholic church rendered sacred. It is fair to say that Peter did not mean what Luther thought he meant. More than likely, Peter's intention was that a Christian community would be seen as a true continuation and consummation of the chosen people of

---

34. Martin Luther, *Luther's Works* (St Louis, MO: Concordia Publishing House, 1958), 44:127.

35. Ibid., 40:21.

36. Ibid., 51:335.

God. It was Peter's intent to honor the church with the honorary titles that were first bestowed upon Israel. The context of the language in both books (Exodus and 1 Peter) is missionary. The church as a "royal priesthood" carries with it the distinct privilege of being the story of Jesus to the world.

So What?

Paul's writings reflect his belief that the church was a charismatic community. His concept of church was that of continued ministry at the direction of the Spirit to serve each other by being available to God for him to send gracelets for the common good of the community. It does not appear that Paul had a concept of a hierarchy of offices.[37] He conceives of authority in dynamic terms, not in terms of an office or a fixed form. The whole of the community had authority to order its worship and affairs. First Corinthians 14.26 may give us the guidelines for both worship and community affairs.

The issue to solve is *gift-function* or *office-hierarchy*. It is clear to me that there should not be a hierarchical structure in the church. Even the Trinity is a dance without a leader. The life of the church is carried to the church by the Spirit. It is true that corruption came through the institutionalization of the church. However, the church has to have some form in which to exist. What we could do is examine again the form of the Pauline charismatic church and see if it offers us any practices that we could use in today's church. There will always be friction between freedom and form, but according to Genesis 1, real freedom only comes within the boundaries of form. There are certainly no clear or easy answers to this ongoing problem.

Let's Have a Conversation

- What are your initial thoughts about the material presented in this chapter?
- What value do you see in an organization pursuing a hierarchical position of leadership for its participants to follow?
- What harm do you find in a hierarchical structure?

⌒∞⌒

GRACELETS

Chapter 13: The Gracelets of Ephesians 4.11 – Introduction

➟ **Check Your GPS: Where You Are Going**
- Where We Have Been
- What are the Ephesians 4 Gracelets?
- Ephesians: An Overview
- The Context for Ephesians
- So What?

Where We Have Been

In Chapter 12, we looked at the Hierarchical Clue. Now we can turn our attention to the background of Ephesians 4.11. In order for us to understand the gracelets listed in Ephesians 4, we must understand how the church was shaped in the first century when Paul writes about these gracelets in the book of Ephesians.

What Are the Ephesians 4 Gracelets?

The list of gracelets in Ephesians 4.11 are often understood as the "five-fold" gifting of certain men in the church. We must say from the outset that there are only four (4) gifts listed here: apostle, prophet, evangelist, and pastor-teacher. We shall look at each in turn. But first let's take a look at the background of Ephesians in which book this list is located.

Ephesians: An Overview

In my book, *God's EPIC Adventure*,[1] I wrote the following overview of Ephesians.

The next book Paul wrote while in Rome was Ephesians, which is one of the greatest books that he wrote.[2] Some suggestion

---

1. Griffin, *God's Epic Adventure*, 258-259.

2. Markus Barth, *Ephesians: Introduction, Translation, and Commentary on Chapters 1-3 (Anchor Bible, Vol. 34)*, 1st ed. (Garden City, NY: Doubleday, 1974), 3. There is

has been made that the recipients of this letter were Gentile converts who had found their way into the church after Paul's departure.[3]

It is a tremendous document that gives a theology of the church and is closely aligned with Colossians.[4] It was likely a circular letter that began at the church in Ephesus and made a round-trip to other churches, forming a circle beginning and ending with Ephesus.[5] The primary purpose of Paul was to instruct these believers about what was involved in their commitment to Christ and his church. Christianity was not something that one could achieve; it was something that God had done on one's behalf.

The following is a brief outline of Ephesians

Introduction 1.1-3

Purpose and Plan of God 1.4-23

The purpose of God (to create a new humanity) is accomplished by the Son and applied by the Spirit. Paul prayed for the churches.

Purpose Demonstrated in the Church 2.1-22

The church is shown from a theological and historical position with a portrait of before and after God's decisive act in Jesus.

Purpose Demonstrated in Paul 3.1-21

Paul used himself to demonstrate how God creates new humanity.

Purpose Lived Out in Community 4.1-6.20

The new humanity—the church—is the focal point for where the purpose of God is lived out. Paul gave household instruction about marriage, parents, slaves, and masters. In addition, he talked about warfare and the armor the community and believer have to use in defense, as well as in taking an offensive stand against the enemy.

Conclusion 6.21.24

The Context for Ephesians

As we begin to look at the four gifts of Ephesians 4.11, we pause

---

ongoing debate among NT specialists about Paul's authorship of Ephesians. For a discussion see: Witherington, *New Testament History: A Narrative Account*, 538-539.

3. Barth, *Ephesians*, 3-4.

4. Marshall, *Letters & Revelation*, 165.

5. Gundry, *A Survey of the New Testament*, 421-423.

to offer some context for the writing of Ephesians. The first thing to say is that the beginning sentences of Ephesians offer a dilemma. The beginning of the letter says:

> *Paul, an apostle of Christ Jesus by the will of God,*
>
> *To God's holy people in Ephesus, the faithful in Christ Jesus:*
>
> *May God our Father and the Lord Jesus Christ give you grace and peace.*

In the NIV, there is a small footnote labeled (a) which says: "Ephesians 1.1. Some early manuscripts do not have *in Ephesus:...*" Second Testament specialists have different opinions about what this means. Those specialists that think that the word *Ephesus* should not be in the text have provided a reasonable explanation of who the recipient was. One of those explanations is that Ephesians was a circular letter written to the churches of Asia minor that are mentioned in Revelation 2-3 of which Ephesus was the beginning and end of the mail route, a hub if you please. It is possible that these seven churches were the result of the two year plus ministry of Paul in Ephesus as recorded in Acts 19 (see v. 10).[6]

Historical Context

It may be that what we call the book of Ephesians is a letter to all the churches that were started during Paul's stay in Ephesus. Ephesians was like the mother church from which short mission journeys were launched and those who visited Ephesus may have returned home to bring the good news they have found in Ephesus in the hall of Tyrannus. The following material is a quick look at the background of each of the churches and possibly serves as the context for the book of Ephesians where the Ephesians 4.11 passage is located. Let's start with the origination point of these churches.

Paul Teaching In the Hall of Tyrannus (Acts 19.810)

Luke shares about Paul functioning as a teacher. The custom of Paul when entering a city was to first go to the synagogue and proclaim his

6. Craig S. Keener, "The IVP Bible Background Commentary: New Testament," InterVarsity Press. Logos Bible Software Edition: 19.8-12, Word Spreads in Ephesus. See also: Trent C. Butler, "Tyrannus," Broadman & Holman Publishers http://www.studylight.org/dic/hbd/view.cgi?number=T6335 (accessed September 11, 2013). Fausset Jamieson, Brown,, "Commentary Critical and Explanatory on the Whole Bible," Christian Classics Ethereal Library http://www.ccel.org/ccel/jamieson/jfb.xi.v.xx.html#xi.v.xx-p2.1 (accessed September 9, 2013).

message about Jesus. In each community, he found a readymade group of hearers who were looking for the Messiah (Acts 13.5, 15; 14.1; 17.1; 18.4, 19). He did not stay in these surroundings too long because his message was too radical for the Jewish hearers (Acts 17.5; 18.6).

The message that Paul delivered at each place he stopped is summarized by Luke in Acts 13. Paul divided his discourses to the synagogues into two parts.

1. A historical review (13.16b–35)
2. An exhortation (13.36–41)

When he arrived at Ephesus in his second journey, he received a warm welcome.

There were at least fourteen persons within the church at Ephesus (Acts 18.19; 19.7), although there could have been more (Acts 18.27). Paul spent three months debating with the Jews about the kingdom of God (19.8). That would have been a conversation that I would have liked to have heard. When his efforts failed to reach his kinsman, he withdrew to the hall of Tyrannus.

This hall was available to him for instruction. This was not something new for Paul. He had used other buildings for meetings—the most notable was in Corinth where he moved next door to the synagogue and set up church in a house. One must realize that "next door" was only a wall away. The hall of Tyrannus is only mentioned here in Scripture. There are four possibilities as to the usage of the hall.

- A school of the law conducted by Tyrannus.
- A private synagogue maintained by Tyrannus.
- A regular Greek school for boys.
- A lecture hall for teaching rhetoric and philosophy or even medicine.[7]

The last of the four options is usually favored. The Western text indicates that Paul had use of the building between 11 AM and 4 PM daily.[8] The custom of the area was to work in the cooler part of the

---

7. H. C. G. Moule, *The Epistle to the Ephesians: With Introduction and Notes* (Cambridge: The University Press, 1902, 1886), 12. See also: israeljerusalem.com, "Ephesus - School of Tyrannus," israeljerusalem.com http://www.israeljerusalem.com/school-of-tyrannus.htm (accessed September 2, 2015).

8. Trent C. Butler, "Tyrannus," Broadman & Holman Publishers http://www.

day—from dawn to 11 AM and then take a respite during the afternoon during the hotter part of the day. There is disagreement among scholars at this point.

Luke instructs us that Paul taught for a period of two years (Acts 19.10). The result: all of the residents of Asia heard the word of the Lord, both Jews and Greeks. It was during this time that the churches, which we read about in Revelation 23, came into existence. Paul was contacted by some of his followers from the Corinthian church during this stay in Ephesus and the result was the writing of First Corinthians.

William Barclay records it this way in his commentary on Acts

When work in the synagogue became impossible because of the embittered opposition, Paul changed his quarters to the hall of a philosopher called Tyrannus. One Greek manuscript adds a touch which sounds like the additional detail an eye-witness might bring. It says that Paul taught in that hall from 11 a.m. to 4 p.m. Almost certainly that is when Paul would teach. Until 11 a.m. and after 4 p.m. Tyrannus would need the hall himself. In the Ionian cities all work stopped at 11 a.m. and did not begin again until the late afternoon because of the heat. We are told that there would actually be more people sound asleep in Ephesus at 1 p.m. than at 1 a.m. What Paul must have done was to work all morning and all evening at his trade and teach in the midday hours. It shows us two things--the eagerness of Paul to teach and the eagerness of the Christians to learn. The only time they had was when others rested in the heat of the day and they seized that time. It may well shame many of us for our talk of inconvenient times.

Throughout this time wonderful deeds were being done. The sweat-band was what a workman wore round his head to absorb the sweat as he worked. The apron was the girdle with which a workman or servant girded himself. It is very significant that the narrative does not say that Paul did these extraordinary deeds; it says that God did them through Paul's hands. God, said someone, is everywhere looking for hands to use. We may not be able to work miracles with our hands but without doubt we can give them to God so that he may work through them.[9]

studylight.org/dic/hbd/view.cgi?n=6335 (accessed September 11, 2013).

9. William Barclay, *The Acts of the Apostles (The New Daily Study) 3 Edition (November 30, 2003)* (Louisville, KY: Westminster John Knox Press, 1975, 2003), 167-168.

Seven Churches in Asia Minor

The city of Ephesus was the capital and gateway to the province of Asia. It was located on the Western coast of today's Asia Minor. Ephesus was strategically located at the mouth of the Cayster River where shipping from all Western ports had its entrance. It also formed a point of departure for caravans between the Ionian Coast and the East Roman highways that led from Ephesus through Central Asia Minor to Antioch in Syria through the Cilician Gates. This was a rather convenient way of travel for Paul and his followers during the first century. It was important as a commercial center and had a large number of diaspora Jews living there. It was a religious tourist site because of the Temple of Artemis. Out of all the seven cities in this part of Asia Minor, it was probably the best known.[10]

Smyrna was about fifty miles north of Ephesus and was also a harbor city. It was the home of a temple in honor of the Roman Emperor Tiberius, which was a leading site for emperor worship. It was an old city founded in 1,000 BC but destroyed in 600 BC and lay fallow for about 400 years. Strabo, a Greek geographer (64/63 BC – AD 24), wrote about the cities of the ancient world and describes Smyrna as having a "street of Gold that started at the Temple of Zeus and ended at the Temple of Cybele." Barclay adds in his commentary:

Here we have an interesting and a significant thing, which shows the care and knowledge with which John set down his letters from the Risen Christ. The Risen Christ is called, "He who died and came to life. That was an echo of the experience of Smyrna itself.[11]

Pergamum was a city of substantial importance for almost four centuries before Paul. It was set atop a considerable acropolis twelve miles inland from the Aegean Sea. It too was a center of emperor worship, one of which was the Temple of Asclepius, the "god of healing," and vied with the importance with the Ascelpion in Corinth. The city thought of itself as "the custodian of the Greek way of life and of the Greek worship."[12]

10. Ibid., 164-165. On these pages, Barclay provides a good historical overview of the city of Ephesus.

11. William Barclay, *The Revelation of John, Vol. 1 (New Daily Study Bible) 3rd Edition (April 1, 2004)* (Louisville, KY: Westminster John Knox Press), 80-85.

12. Ibid., 95.

Thyatira was most likely the most insignificant of the seven cities. Of all the seven cities mentioned in Revelation, it was the least important. It was founded as a military outpost and was about fifty miles southeast of Pergamum and was seen in military terms as a place that could slow down any aggressive move toward Pergamum, but not defend its own self. It was a town of traders and crafts and was especially well known for its purple dye industry and fine bronze. It had many work-related guilds, the forerunners of today's unions. To not be a part of a work-related guild meant to lose your ability to exercise commerce. Jesus followers in this climate would be expected to attend the common meals that were often held in the local temples and began with a sacrifice to the local god and the meat that would be eaten would be meat that had been offered to the local idol. Paul had his say about this very problem in the book of 1 Corinthians. In addition, these common meals were often events that were impregnated with drunkenness and immorality.

The problem in Thyatira was inside the church with a strong leadership coming from a woman who is called Jezebel who pushed for compromise with the standards of the business trades for those who were followers of Jesus and that the Holy Spirit would protect them from any harm. Sound familiar?[13]

Sardis was well known for its location, climate, economy, wealth, and culture. With all that seemly going for it, it was noted as a city that was degenerate. The city had been destroyed and rebuilt at least two times. Sardis had been rebuilt by donation from Tiberius and grew lazy and soft and unwatchful. The lack luster attitude of Sardis bled into the church that became like a corpse instead of a living entity.[14]

Philadelphia was the youngest of the seven cities. It was about thirty miles east southeast of Sardis. It was strategically located for travel north and south and was set on a large lava deposit, which was perfect for vineyards. It was located atop of an earthquake fault, which caused it to have difficult economic times. The city was known as a dispenser of Greek culture and language, thus the words of Jesus that it was an open door to its world of the message of the gospel.[15]

Laodicea sat at the crossroad for east and west. It was an extremely wealthy city. It was famous for three reasons: First, it was wealthy. Second, it was famous for a breed of sheep that produced an extremely

13. Ibid., 111-113.
14. Ibid., 123-126.
15. Ibid., 136-138.

soft black wool. Third, its proximity to a hot springs made it a kind of ancient medical center, which was famous for a specially mixed eye salve. Laodicea receives the strongest condemnation of all the seven churches in Revelation.[16]

One can see from this brief overview that the "church" within a half century had almost lost its footing and surely needed some reminding of the gracelets available for it to regain its vigor and vitality to work out the ministry of Jesus in its time and space.

Pastor-Teacher and Eldership Acts 20.17-35

It might be possible to see in this passage by Luke about Paul's contact with the Ephesian church, how he thinks about the functionality of the gracelets that are listed in his book to the seven churches of which Ephesus was the mother with six children.

A part of being a missionary/ambassador/messenger of the gospel of Jesus, he had evangelized the area, prophetically speaking into their midst as he was teaching and pastoring the group of churches in Ephesus and beyond. He wanted those practicing elders to know that they needed to remember his example of serving the Lord among them (v. 19). He wanted them to remember that their function included teaching in public and from house to house (v. 20), a clear reference to the public teaching in the hall of Tyrannus and the many house gatherings. He wanted them to know that as Jesus followers, they must continue to declare to everyone that repentance and faith were important. Their function was to spread the good news of Jesus.

Beginning with verse 28, Paul tells the functioning elders to take care of themselves and in so doing, they would be better prepared to function as care takers of the flock. Remember, when you read a word like "overseer" (NIV), you could think of this word as one who guards, and a guard is one who guards when s/he is guarding. Action led to description, not the other way around. The same with the word "shepherd" in verse 28. The act of shepherding came before the descriptive word shepherd. It is interesting that the word *poimainō* is translated here as shepherd and *poimēn* is translated pastor in Ephesians 4.11. These words are related to each other. In John's Gospel, he demonstrates what *poimēn* means. This passage is a gage for what pastoring is like and it carries no idea of authority in a local church at the corner of walk and

---

16. Ibid., 149-152. See also: Gordon D. Fee, *Revelation* (Eugene, OR: Cascade Books, 2011), 22-63.

don't walk in today's society. In addition, 1 Peter 5.1-3 validates that the idea of shepherding is not one of authority over a local group of sheep with some self-appointed authority but rather the function of caring and feeding, and when one is "doing" that they are pastoring. Everyone has the potential to be a *poimēn* in the *ecclesia*.

Finally, in this brief passage, one must recognize that Paul's concern for those eldering was that they must understand that they make their living with their own hands as Paul had done as a tentmaker.

Paul's Last Encounter with the Ephesian Church

Paul last encountered the church at Ephesus through his friend and colleague, Timothy (1 Tim. 1.3). As his emissary to this church (Tim was about thirty-eight years old at this point), Paul wanted Timothy to provide guidance to help solve problems that the church faced. Paul also wanted him to be sure that he would help the church withstand false teaching and help the teachers themselves.

To help us get a full view of the church at Ephesus, we must understand John's words in Revelation given to the church at Ephesus (Rev. 2.17). The Ephesians had taken the words about false teachers and their teaching to heart. They had developed the ability to distinguish between true and false teachers. The church was outstanding in their purity of doctrine. They even hated what Jesus hated, the works of the Nicolaitans (Rev. 2.6). But, in their total rigor for sound doctrine, they had lost their first love. This *first love* must be understood in light of Paul's ministry in Ephesus when all Asia heard the word of the Lord. They were strong in pure doctrine, but weak in their first love—evangelism. This is one of those places where we have extracted a verse and made it mean something quite different from what the original hearers who were presently in the Ephesian church heard when they received this message and story that the church passed down from those who had been around when the church came into being.

As a review, there are eight segments to the emergence of the church at Ephesus:

- The church begins with Priscilla and Aquila with Paul: 18.18–19.7
- The church was taught by Paul: 19.8–10
- The church had miracles through Paul: 19.11–20
- The church had conflict with the City: 19.21–41
- The church received final instructions from Paul: 20.17–36
- The church learned who she is and how to live: The book of Ephesians

- The church learned how to organize and fight false teachers: The books of 1 & 2 Timothy
- The church was confronted by Jesus: Revelation 2.17

What the Ephesian church had forgotten was their first love of reaching out to their neighbors and neighboring cities and sharing the message of the kingdom of God. The forgetting of their first love was not some sentimental feeling that an individual had at the beginning of their walk with Jesus. This was not a message to individuals, but a message to the church at Ephesus. What is your local church doing to reach out to its community and proclaim the gospel of the kingdom? Has it forgotten its first love? Or even more to the point, did it ever have a love for the least, last, and lost?

Ephesians is Paul's attempt to tell the story of the purpose of the church living in the midst of a world where disharmony rules, set up by the choices of humankind at the beginning to bring harmony. Harmony between each human and harmony between each human and God is the work of the followers of Jesus.

So What?

It is my opinion that one will have a difficult time in understanding the gracelets listed in Ephesians 4 to which we turn next, without having somewhat of a grasp of the church(es) to which this letter is purported to be written. The book we call Ephesians may have been written to all the churches that were created during Paul's stay in Ephesus. The grouping of these gracelets that are listed in Ephesians 4 are suggestive that they should abound in every church for the reason of building up the saints for the work of ministry. I think this may go a long way toward the central thesis of this book that gracelets are ad hoc, and do not have permanent residence in a person.

Let's Have a Conversation

- How does historical background help you discover a different level of learning and experiencing Scripture?
- What places in the story found in Scripture do you wish you had some historical insights?

⤫

GRACELETS

Chapter 14: The Gracelets of Ephesians 4.11 – Apostles

➠ **Check Your GPS: Where You Are Going**
- Where We Have Been
- The Context in Ephesians 4
- Apostles (*apostolos*): Eph. 4.11; 1 Cor. 12.28
- So What?

Where We Have Been

Chapter 13 took us through the background of Ephesians to get a feel for the the list of gracelets in Ephesians 4. Thus, we now find our way to the gracelets that are listed in the Ephesian 4.11 passage, which are often presented as office gifts and then in the structure of the church are turned into being hierarchical positions. We will first analyze the material concerning the gracelet of apostle.

The Context in Ephesians 4

It is in the third section of Ephesians that we find a gifts list of four gifts (4.11). In this section, Paul is busy helping the Ephesians and the churches surrounding the Ephesians (Rev. 2-3) to understand the new humanity lifestyle that was theirs as followers of Jesus. Paul writes the following beginning at Ephesians 4.7:

> But to each one of us grace has been given as Christ apportioned it. This is why it says:

> "When he ascended on high,
> he took many captives
> and gave gifts to his people."

> (What does "he ascended" mean except that he also descended to the lower, earthly regions? He who descended is the very one who ascended higher than all the heavens, in order to fill the whole universe.) So Christ himself gave the apostles, the prophets, the evangelists, the pastors and teachers, to equip his people for works of service, so that the body of Christ may be built up until we all reach unity in the faith and in the knowledge of the Son of

God and become mature, attaining to the whole measure of the fullness of Christ.

He wrote that each follower receives the grace that Jesus has apportioned as a gracelet. He then provides a list of four gracelets that we now turn to.

The list in Ephesian 4, as with all lists, was ad hoc and only understandable within the context of this book and its purpose. It appears that the giving of this list of gracelets mentioned here in this text was to curb the immaturity of all the followers of Jesus in all the churches along the mail run. These gracelets were given to build up the body. One might say that if the body was not in shambles, there would have been no need for the "building gifts." Tom Wright suggests that what Paul wanted to tell these young followers of Jesus was "not to be babies."[1] It might be prudent to ask of your own community of faith, where do they need to grow and how are these four gracelets applicable for growth to occur.

Apostles (*apostolos*): Eph. 4.11; 1 Cor. 12.28

One who is commissioned by God to bring the gospel to new places and provides spiritual care for the new humanity gatherings that he/she has birthed.

The word *apostle* can be defined as *sent out* or to be an *ambassador, missionary,* or *messenger*. It has been a problem that the early translators of our English Bibles simply transliterated the word *apostolos* to "apostle." That has given rise to a long and arduous debate about the role of apostle, the ministry of apostle, and even if apostles exist in today's version of the church.

We can read in Luke 9.1-2 that Jesus called messengers and equipped them to minister in three ways. They were sent out with God's authority to expel demons, be conduits of healing for the sick, and proclaim the kingdom of God. We must remember that these first disciples of Jesus were only his messengers in the context of the ministry they were called to do. An *apostle/messenger* was not a title bestowed on him/her in the sense of an office, only in the sense of a function. When Paul opens his letters and refers to himself as an apostle, it is not a position that he has in mind but a function, and in those cases, it is the function of bringing

1. N. T. Wright, *Paul for Everyone: The Prison Letters : Ephesians, Philippians, Colossians, Philemon (New Testament for Everyone)* (Louisville, KY: Westminster John Knox Press), 46.

a message that deals with solutions to the local church problems of the churches that he had started.

Like all other gracelets, the gracelet of apostle flowed through these men and women[2] to others. At the earliest moments of the Second Testament's expression of the church, folks devoted themselves to the teaching of this first group of "sent-out-ones" by Jesus (Acts 2.42). In addition, the Jews and Greeks together who were being swept into the church were told:

> Consequently, you are no longer foreigners and strangers, but fellow citizens with God's people and also members of his household, built on the foundation of the apostles and prophets, with Christ Jesus himself as the chief cornerstone. In him the whole building is joined together and rises to become a holy temple in the Lord. And in him you too are being built together to become a dwelling in which God lives by his Spirit (Eph. 2.19-22).

Being built on the foundation of the "messengers and proclaimers" simply means, built of the messages/teaching that had been provided by those who were functioning as messengers or proclaimers. It is fair to stress again, these were not positions. Jesus was himself the capstone who held the whole building together. His life and ministry is the apex of the Story of God and the narrative that make us part of his building. There is a lot of ink about who these specific apostles were that Paul mentions here. The text simply does not say. However, the history within the narrative of the Second Testament and the narrative of Church History suggest that there were many apostles.

Church history has named numerous others as apostles. Among them are Ansgar (801-865) who was the Apostle of the North (Scandinavia) (Douglas, *NIDCC*, 46);[3] Cyril (826-869) and his brother Methodius (815-885) were Apostles of the Southern Slavs; Otto Von Banberg

---

2. William Barclay, *The Letter to the Romans*, [2d ed., The Daily Study Bible Series (Philadelphia, PA: Westminster Press, 1957), 323. Remember, there were more apostles than the twelve listed in Mark 3.13-19 and Acts 1.12-26. Scripture mentions others such as Paul (Gal. 1.1), Barnabas (Acts 14.14), James (Gal. 1.19), Silas and Timothy (1 Thess. 1.1, cf. 2.6), Epaphroditus (Phil. 2.25), Andronicus and Junias (Rom. 16.7). We should pause and notice that Junias was a female name (see margin of NAS). What we have here is a husband-wife team or a brother-sister team. They both, male and female, were considered to be well-known apostles (16.7). The obvious conclusion was that there was at least one woman who was a functioning apostle in the early church.

3. J. D. Douglas, *The New International Dictionary of the Christian Church* (Grand Rapids, MI: Zondervan Publishing Company, 1974), 46.

(1060-1139) was the Apostle of Pomerania;[4] Hans Egede (1686-1758) was the Apostle of Greenland or Eskimos (Douglas, 335);[5] and Robert Morrison (1782-1839) was the Apostle to Berma.[6]

Paul warned the Corinthians about false messengers in their own present timeframe (2 Cor. 11.13) and John also mentions the possibility in Revelation 2.2. When Scripture provides a caution, it usually is set in the context of possibility. It could be concluded that it would be useless to caution a congregation if there were only the twelve original apostles. We should note for timeline purposes that Revelation was written in the middle of the '90s in the first century.

Why is the gracelet of apostle/messenger still available to the church today? Paul gives us a clue in Ephesians 4.13. This text is part of the framework of the 4.11 passage. Paul suggests rather pictorially that folks who are becoming truly human in Jesus were living in a story; in this case the metaphor is moving along a road toward a certain destination. The text of the original language is phrased in a way that leaves no doubt that someday in the future; the intended destination would be reached.[7] M. R. Vincent's book *Word Studies in the Second Testament* enlightens us to how long this journey will last. He suggests that the word *until* specifies the duration that these ministries of 4.11 will last.[8]

Luke, in the story of Barnabas in Acts, gives us some insights how this gracelet works. In the personal life of Barnabas, Luke tells us that he, along with others, was a generous man (Act 4.32-37). Luke further shares that he was a good person who was full of the Holy Spirit and faith (Acts 11.22-24). In the letter of James that was created after the meeting in Jerusalem (Act 15), he is commended for risking his life for the name of Jesus.

Second, his life in ministry was expanded beyond Jerusalem (Gal. 2.6-10; Acts 11.22-24; 11.27-30); 15.22-34). His ministry revolved around encouraging others along their journey (Acts 11.22-24). After the first church planting journey with Paul, he is mentioned as one who functions in teaching and prophesying (Acts 13.1ff.). He was commissioned by the church at Antioch and "sent out" (apostle/messenger) along with Paul (Acts 13.1-3).

4. Kurt Koch, *Charismatic Gifts* (Grand Rapids, MI: Kregel Publications, 1975), 126.

5. Douglas, *NIDCC*, 335.

6. Koch, *Charismatic Gifts*, 126.

7. Barth, *Ephesians*, 484-496.

8. M. R. Vincent, *Vincent's Word Studies in the New Testament* (Peabody, MA: Hendrickson Publishers, 1985), 3.390.

Chapter 14

This short survey, while not including everything that Barnabas did in his function as a functioning apostle, gives some flavor of some of the activities that the gracelet of apostle included. Not all, just a glimpse.

For Paul, there appears to be limited ministry within the confines of the churches that he was called to help plant or train. The text would not consider him or any other person in this early stage of the church a capital "A" Apostle, as a position to be filled in the church.

Of course, one doesn't have to look far in the charismatic arm of the church to find that this idea is pretty much totally absent. A search of Google for the words "apostolic network" provided 30,000 plus hits.[9] Most of the organizations in the Google list are parachurch organizations. This is not meant as a slam on any of them. But, it seems clear from the sacred text that the gracelet is a part of a local church in whatever way that local community is formed. A friend of mine once told me a story that one of the latest renewal movements, all, which center on these gifts, offered him the gift if he would just join their network. For just a mere twenty-five bucks, he could be an apostle. I shudder to think how much of this goes on unnoticed and unchecked and is accepted by certain branches of the organized church.

On one occasion while I was teaching a First Testament Survey course on the East coast (I live on the West coast), I entered the classroom and within a few moments an older very friendly gentleman came up to me and inquired if I was the teacher for the course. When I told him, yes, he reached into his billfold and pulled out a card and handed it to me. His card designated him by the name Apostle. Let's just call him Apostle Ned Smith (no offense to any Ned Smiths out there that might be reading this) and formally introduced himself to me as Apostle Ned Smith. He was beaming and eager for a conversation. So I began, so you are an apostle? May I ask you a couple of questions? He nodded his head. Have you ever been sent out to plant a church? "No!" he responded. Have you ever been on a mission trip anywhere with church planters? "No!" he responded. Have you ever led a Bible study here in this church or anywhere else? "No!" he responded. Do you attend this church? "No!" he responded. "God did not call me to attend a local church but to have a worldwide ministry," he informed me. So, let me get this straight, you have never planted a church, gone on a missionary trip to help plant a church, never taught a Bible study here or anywhere else, you don't attend this church or any other church, not even a home group or anything like that? Does that about cover it? He shook his head in the affirmative. So, one final question, if you don't mind: Who designated you as an apostle?

9. Searched google for "apostolic network" on September 9, 2015.

He gave me a short story about a brief encounter he had with God and came away from that encounter with a firm belief that he was now an apostle. Really? I handed him back his card and said, "Sir, I'm sorry, but you are not an apostle. Why do I say that, because there are no apostles except when apostling occurs and from our short time together, it doesn't look like any apostling has occurred in your life. He was stunned!"[10]

I have often reflected on the above ad hoc story to illustrate how wrongheaded theology sets folks up for some pretty strange ideas, not to mention the lives that are wrecked along the way. Of course, not all the blame can be laid on the charismatic movement in the church, those who outright reject any charismatic gifts rake havoc on Jesus followers as well.

Next, we look at the gracelet of prophet.

So What?

The English word "apostle," which according to Merriam-Webster came into existence somewhere before the twelfth century[11] is unfortunate and seems to be an English word that is created from the original Greek word. Transliterations have no meaning. But, that hasn't stopped the word from appearing with a capital letter, i.e., Apostle, which gives it more emphasis than it is due. In the pre-Christian era, the use of the term is rare. In the Second Testament, Luke and Paul are the primary users of the word and it is identified as being an individual who was appointed for a special function. One has to wonder how things would be today if the first English translations were something like, "I am Paul, who was sent by God, to function as…."

For a thought, we may not know who took the gospel message of Paul from Ephesus to Thyatira, but whoever did was functioning as a missionary (apostle) to that city. But, whoever it was, male or female, h/she was an apostle (missionary) while s/he was functioning as such in Thyatira and ceased to be such when that person was not apostling.

Let's Have a Conversation

- How have you functioned as an apostle?
- Where were you sent from?
- What were you sent to do?
- When did the function stop?

186

GRACELETS

Chapter 15: The Gracelets of Ephesians 4.11 – Prophets

➠ Check Your GPS: Where You Are Going
- Where We Have Been
- Prophets (*prophetas*): Eph. 4.11, 1 Cor. 12.28
- So What?

Where We Have Been

Chapter 14 concerned itself with the gracelet of apostle. We suggested that an apostle is better understood as a missionary, not exactly in the modern sense of missionary but an emissary sent on a specific mission. Prophet is the second gracelet mentioned in the Ephesians 4.11 passage to which we now turn.

Prophets (prophetas): Eph. 4.11, 1 Cor. 12.28

One who functions as a frequent spokesperson of prophecies and is a prophet when s/he is prophesying..

The word "prophets" often causes a stir among folks when they hear the word applied to individuals. From the Second Testament forward, there are plenty of occasions when the word is applied to individuals. Just google the idea and you will get the breadth and width of the concept. However, this does not seem to be the appetite of the authors of the Second Testament. The word "prophet" appears in several passages (Acts 13.1; 15.32; 1 Cor. 12.28; Eph. 4.11). These individuals did give authoritative instruction, but the authority of the person prophesying did not extend beyond the inspiration of that person to speak.[1] The church was to receive the message offered and then discern (judge) (1 Cor. 14.3) what each person said. It is this last function that is often overlooked in communities of faith. Folks hearing a prophecy often go away being more impressed that something was spontaneously said than discerning whether what was said was actually from the Spirit.

---

1. Dunn, *Jesus and the Spirit*, 281.

The Gift of Prophecy in Acts and Paul

The material that follows comes from an article written by Mel Robeck, a professor at Fuller Seminary.[2] I read this article from which the following information is a digest after taking the Spiritual Gifts course at Fuller Seminary in Pasadena, CA, offered by Dr. Spittler and Dr. Robeck.[3] In the article, Dr. Robeck offered five passages to help understand the idea of prophet/prophecy in Acts and the writings of Paul. They are as follows:

Acts 2.1-21

The flow of this story in this passage is as follows: It was the Day of Pentecost (2.1). The disciples received the empowering of the Holy Spirit (2.3-4), which left the multitudes perplexed (2.5-13).

To possibly quieten the perplexity of the gathered audience, Peter stood to speak and told them that what they were hearing and seeing was a fulfillment of a prophecy given by Joel.[4] A new phase of God's rule on earth had commenced and the event they had witnessed had come from the Spirit of God. What seemed like only a special relationship with selected individuals in the First Testament had now become the possibility of all. Because everyone possessed the Spirit, everyone had the potential to be a spokesperson for God through prophecy (2.17-18).

The backstory begins with the phrase *the spirit of God* (Gen. 1.2), i.e., which was for the Hebrew audience "an extension of the power of God in the work of creation."[5] The very next sentence in the Genesis story tells us that God spoke. From that point in the story, he continues to speak throughout the whole narrative of Scripture. From the speaking God in the story of Genesis, we move forward in the storyline and look at the speaking God in Number 11.24-30 in which the author tells a story about prophecy. In the midst of a prophetic outbreak, a young man

2. Cecil M. Robeck, Jr., B.S. Bethany Bible College; M.Div., Ph.D. Fuller Theological Seminary. Director of the David du Plessis Center for Christian Spirituality and Professor of Church History and Ecumenics.

3. Mel Robeck, "The Gift of Prophecy in Acts and Paul," *Studia Biblica et Theologica, Part 1 and 2* Vol 4 and 5, (1974 and 1975).

4. Griffin, *God's Epic Adventure (The Reader Edition)*, 170. The prophets come from a very narrow timeframe in Jewish history: Amos from about 760 BC to Malachi about 460 BC. This approximate 300 year period was characterized by political, economic, social, and military agitation, covenant unfaithfulness, and shifts in population. The book of Joel is a prophecy of judgment.

5. Ibid., 86. See pages 85-86 for a discussion of "spirit of God" in Genesis 1.2.

came to Moses and complained that there were two men prophesying in their camp. Joshua wanted Moses to stop them. Moses replied, "I wish that all the LORD's people were prophets and that the LORD would put his Spirit on them!" At this moment in the overall narrative, it is only a wish that a lot of God's people would speak for God.

From the wilderness, we skip ahead in the storyline to the book of Joel where the reader is told that still future to Joel's time, there would be a time when God would pour out his Spirit on his people and they would all prophesy (Joel 2.28-31). Finally, Luke shares in the Acts of the Spirit that Peter announces in the event described in Acts 2 that what Joel so many years before had foretold (Acts 2) had now occurred: The speaking God of Genesis to the wish of Moses to the prophetic word of Joel to the actual fulfillment told by Luke. What had been a relationship during the Covenant Act of the story was now the privilege of all in the church act of the story. At this moment in the storyline, all who possessed the initiation act of the Spirit were potentially prophets who could prophesy. One has to wonder if this is not a key to understand that "all" are also used as the conduits of God for all the other special gracelets that God sends to others.

Acts 11.27-30

This next passage points us to a specific conclusion, i.e., there was more than a single prophet. You should notice that the word *prophets* is plural in this passage. Luke does not reveal how many, only by the use of the plural word that there was more than one. It appears that the residence of these prophets was Jerusalem and they moved around the growing church willingly (11.27; cf. Acts 15.32; 21.10). In this account, the spokesperson was either Agabus or he was the one to whom the Spirit gave the message to be delivered (cf. 13.1-3). Luke seems to lean toward the latter of these two possibilities. If the first one is favored, then one could have a difficult time explaining why the rest of the prophets accompanied Agabus to Antioch. What is illustrated here, then, is that Agabus was the conduit through whom the prophetic word came to the listeners. This band of prophets was designated as such because they also could prophesy. Kenner suggests that "...few if any movements ever claimed to have many prophets acting together,..."[6]

One could ask: "Why did the prophets come to Antioch?" No real motive is given by Luke in the text. He is silent. The message offered

---

6. Craig S. Keener, *The IVP Bible Background Commentary (New Testament). Second Edition* (Downers Grove, IL: IVP Academic, 2014), 354.

by Agabus came through the Spirit. The text is clear, the message originated with the Spirit (*dia tou pneumatics*) as presented in the original language; (bear with me), *dia* with a genitive case refers to origination, application, and realization. The message was future in orientation. The exact words of his message are not recorded for us by Luke. He spoke and called for the church to act (cf. v. 29). Luke's record of this account would correspond to the understanding of prophecy given by Paul to the Corinthian church (1 Cor. 14.3-4). The word from Agabus was a directly inspired Spirit utterance. F. F. Bruce suggests, "...the gift of prophecy was like the gift of tongues in that it was exercised under the immediate inspiration of God."[7] While the text does not say this decisively, the "through the Spirit" could be construed in this way.

What the prophet gave was a message to help the church in Antioch to accomplish her service to Antioch.

There are some specific features of Luke's story that should be kept in mind. The prophecy spoke to a specific time, a specific place, and called for an action by the church. The words used by the disciples imply that the message from Agabus was presented to the gathered community at Antioch. It was the disciples in Antioch who responded as each one was able. This may provide us some indication about how to hear prophecy.

On many occasions, more than it should be in my opinion, what passes for prophecy is a bit fuzzy. Here is a prophecy from late Bob Jones who passed away in 2014. It was delivered in 2008:

> Right now God is harvesting harvesters for the great harvest. By 2012 we will see a genuine apostolic government in place. From there we will see others come alongside and do what they are called to do.[8]

One can see that by comparing the prophetic in the Acts story, the Jones message leaves a bit to be desired. But in many Pentecostal and charismatic gatherings, this kind of spoken word is often given and praised as a prophecy. One might ask: where is the "great apostolic government" that was to be in place in 2012? I once met and sat with Bob Jones for three hours. Here's a brief summary of what occurred with some comments.

---

7. F. F. Bruce, *The Book of the Acts*, Rev. ed., The New International Commentary on the New Testament (Grand Rapids, MI: Eerdmans Publishing Company, 1988), 242.

8. Bob Jones, "New Apostolic Government in Place by 2012," bobjones.org http://bobjonesnew.unionactive.com/Docs/Words%20of%202008/2008-11-Apostolic_Govt_By_2012.htm (accessed February 17, 2014).

Three of us sat in a small office of the church where I was on staff. Bob Jones began to talk. He talked almost continually for three hours. Most of what I heard was similar in content to what is posted above. It was full of visionary language, which was never explained, just spoken.

At the conclusion of the time, he turned to me and said, "Winn, you would make a great poker player."

Why is that, Bob? I asked

He responded, "I can't read by your facial expression what your thoughts are about what I am saying."

I smiled and replied. "Well, Bob, let me set your mind at ease. What I have encountered for the last three hours is not vaguely similar to what prophecy was like in Scripture, therefore I don't believe anything you have said."

To say the least, he was taken back that I was so direct with him.

Apparently, I was placed in the "don't touch God's anointed" category. Several months later, I was prophetically removed from the staff of that church. I never saw Bob again.

By way of personal reflection, I wondered when I heard he had died what he thought about all the stuff he said while he was alive. I wonder what he thinks now. I wondered what I will think at that point of life after death. Alas, I have wandered off the path!

Luke told his readers that the prophecy given in Antioch was true because it had been fulfilled (11.28). This was one of the prominent factors in the First Testament for deciding if a prophet was true or false (Deut. 18.20, 22; Jer. 28.9). The intention of Luke may be that the same test is valid for those giving prophecies in the Second Testament, as well as when he used the phrase "...and this took place" (v. 28).

We may draw some tentative conclusions at this juncture. Since all Jesus followers now have the Spirit, prophecy belongs to the whole community of faith. Therefore, everyone is potentially a person who can prophesy. When one gave a prophecy, the thoughts translated into words were not originated by the person speaking, but by the Spirit. In the early church, functioning prophets seemed to move in clusters *from church to church as God* directed them to deliver a message. Prophecy can be directed to a specific time, a specific place, and can involve a request for action. To determine if the prophecy is valid, the church should ask, *did what was said in the prophecy happen?*

Acts 13.1-3

As Luke's story of the Acts of the Spirit progresses, we discover that all prophets were not itinerants. Some functioned in a local city church and were known.[9] For those who believe that there are "prophets" as a vested gift, this becomes a prooftext for them beyond their own reading of Ephesians 4.11. The word "prophet" should not be thought of in a narrow sense in the Second Testament.[10] The word could well be understood as to prophetic functioning.[11]

In his story of the church at Antioch, Luke presents those who taught and prophesied on an equal plane. This is an often forgotten fact in our drive to categorize list with numerical properties, so one item becomes more important than another item in a list. Luke's point here may simply be: no one functioning gracelet is more important than another. The root problem in the Corinthian church was that they had chosen tongues above all other gracelets, as we suggested above. Those prophesying in the church at Antioch were known by name to the local church in Antioch. In this story told by Luke, God gave a message, which was spoken to the church (presumably by one of the named functioning prophets) while they were worshiping and fasting (13.2). When the prophetic voice spoke, it was a command (12.2). It was specific and direct to the including of names. What did the church do? They acted on this utterance only after they fasted and prayed (12.3). In his commentary on Acts,[12] the late F. F. Bruce suggested that Christians become especially sensitive to the communication of the Spirit during times of prayer and fasting (cf. 14.23).

Acts 15.30-35

In the fourth passage, Luke tells his readers that two men, Judas and Silas, in the meeting of Acts 15.32, were prophesying. He summarizes their prophetic function as:

---

9. As a note of explanation, in the Mediterranean world where Paul was creating new communities of new humanity, there was one church per city, most likely with house churches scattered throughout the community. This idea of functioning prophets in a local church seems to be the same idea that Paul talks about in Ephesians 4.11.

10. Berding, *What Are Spiritual Gifts?*, 89.

11. See section on Use of Nouns above.

12. Bruce, *Acts*, 261.

- **Encouragers:** They exhorted the church folks to pursue a specific way of conducting their lives. The exact prophetic word is not shared. The word here in this text is the same word that Paul used in 1 Corinthians 14.3 and 31 to explain prophecy. Because Luke and Paul were traveling companions and Luke had heard Paul teach on more than one occasion, it is likely that the word has a similar, if not the same, meaning in both places.
- **Strengtheners:** These two men aided the brothers and sisters in their formation as believers. Their prophetic words brought stability to the hearers. It would have been nice to know, but we are not told how they accomplished their ministry.

What if the prophetic words themselves delivered challenge and stability? What if Judas and Silas were the delivery guys delivering the words that the Spirit provided and the Spirit-given words provided an opportunity for the Jesus followers to act upon the word given and in doing so they found stability in their lives.

Acts 21.7-14

In the final passage, we must take note that Luke shows a high regard for women in his writings (21.9 compare 2.18). We might also take note here that the NIV translates verse 9 as "He had four unmarried daughters who prophesied." The word "prophesied" can mean to exercise the function of a "prophet," i.e., one is a prophet or prophetess when one is prophesying. Also, in this passage, Agabus came from Jerusalem to give a prophecy (21.10). His message was delivered with two communication patterns:

- **Visual:** He demonstrated his prophetic word in a visual way (21.11). Some of the prophets of the First Testament used this style of delivery of their message (1 Kings 11.29-40; Isa. 20.2-6; Jer. 13.1-11; 28.10-11; Ezek. 4.1-3). This appears to be a lost art in the Western church. What Agabus did was just as important as what he said. We must remember that God is a God who acts and speaks. His actions are to be understood on an equal plane with his words. One is not more important than the other.
- **Words:** Agabus also presented his message verbally (21.11). In the First Testament, the prophets used the saying *this is what the Lord says* to authenticate his message. Luke demonstrates that the formula had changed among the Second Testament prophets to *this is what the Spirit says*.

The message of Agabus was specific: Paul would be captured by the Jews on his next visit to Jerusalem. The Jews would deliver him to the

Romans. While Luke does not use the formula of 11.28, the reader of Acts finds out that this prophecy was fulfilled. What Agabus spoke was informative and pointed toward what was going to happen. The prophecy did not request an action. He did not comment on what he said. There was no additional information or elaboration.

The question is often posed, did Paul disobey the Spirit? We must note that the prophetic word did not tell Paul to stop his journey to Jerusalem. It told him what he could expect when he arrived in Jerusalem. This story should not be posited as a prooftext for so-called personal prophecy. It is not! The message was given to Paul and the church. It was purely informational. The church realized the potential of it and responded, the will of the Lord be done (21.14). We might assume from this story that prophecy may be understood by different people in different ways, but it most likely has only one meaning. I understand that such runs counter cultural to the postmodern idea of many meanings. C'est la vie!

We may form some additional conclusions now with the added information that we have. A prophetic word may be a command (Acts 13.1-3) or it may only contain information (Acts 21.11-12). Whatever the case, the church should consider fasting and prayer before taking any decisive action (Acts 13.3). Prophetic words should result in exhortation and establishment of believers (Acts 15.32-35). Finally, there should be room in the church for both visual and verbal prophecies (Acts 21.11).

The following is a story of my own experience with a visual prophecy with a call to action.

I was teaching a four-part mid-week study on Prophecy in a church. At the beginning of the series, I suggested that we wait till we were through with the instruction sections before we functioned with the gracelet. Four weeks later with information in toe, not unlike the summary above, we opened up the floor for prophecy from the community of faith. The room in which we were teaching seated about a thousand people. For the three weeks before, the room was almost full as it was on the fourth evening. I summarized the previous three weeks and we set up two microphones in the aisles so that anyone speaking could be heard.

The first individual came to the microphone and began by asking the congregants to take off their shoes. For a moment, no one moved, and then little by little you could hear the chairs rattling as folks bent down to take off their shoes. A large number of folks followed the suggestion. Then, the prophetic speaker told each of the shoeless followers to put the shoe to their nose and take a long deep breath to smell the inside of the shoe. For a moment folks were frozen, but little by little you could hear folks deeply breathing in, some coughing at the smell of their own foot odor. Then, the speaker asked the ladies to reach into their purse and take out any perfume they had and spray it into their shoe and into the shoes of those next to them who did not have perfume. Next, he told everyone to smell their shoes again. Finally, he said, "what you smelled when you took your shoe off is like what God smells when he sniffs your unrighteous behavior; the second smell, with perfume is like what God smells when you repent and become reconciled to your neighbors." With that he sat down. The room was quiet. Everyone got the point. Some began weeping around the room.

We waited a few moments and a second person, a young lady, got up and came to a microphone and God treated us to a second visual prophecy in story form. She said something like the following: "I was up in the mountains and had to use an outhouse." (I held my breath as she continued.). As I was preparing to do business, I accidently dropped my pocketbook into the outhouse receptacle. I panicked and wondered how I would get my pocketbook back. I went outside and found a tree branch lying on the ground nearby. I brought it back inside and began to probe for my pocketbook. It took several tries until I hooked it. It was a mess. I took it outside and threw it in the snow and kept washing it until it was clean." Then she paused and said, "Though your sins smell like shit, I will wash and clean them to be white as snow." The audience was first stunned and then roared with applause and laughter. They were a younger group and the use of the probable offending word was common communication currency to them. They immediately got the point.

After the service, folks gathered to pray with each other; some sat quietly in their chairs or knelt by their chairs to pray. It was a beautiful sight. God had demonstrated visually and through vivid current symbols and his children heard him.

Lord, let it be so, over and over again!

Now, let's turn to the gracelet of Evangelists, Pastors and Teachers, to offer a review.

So What?

The gracelet of prophecy is also a troubling one, which does have benefits, but also many perils as well. Just because anyone standing or sitting in a congregation says "Thus saith the Lord," or "This is what the Lord says," it does not follow that the words that escape from the speaker's lips are in fact prophetic. The whole idea of being a prophet is possibly a creation of making more out of nouns than out of the verbs of doing. What is being said is what is important. Who says it is incidental. When words are spoken, we must remember that the gracelet of discernment by others is the safety guard to keep Jesus followers from being abused with toxic words delivered in a personal way to an individual or congregation.

Let's Have a Conversation

- Are you aware of any time that you have functioned as a prophet?
- How did you know that what you were saying or drawing, or writing, or visually dramatizing were concepts from the Spirit?

Chapter 16: The Gracelets of Ephesians 4.11 – Evangelists | Pastors-Teachers

Where We Have Been

In chapter 15, we examined the gracelet of prophecy. As with the other gracelets of Ephesians 4, they are not positions within the church that are fixed in a person, but flow through a Jesus follower to others as the Trinity determines. So, as we have said, one is a prophet when one is prophesying. We now turn to the last two: gracelets evangelist and pastor-teacher. The latter one has been long severed and has been argued to be two standalone gifts. The one that is dominant in ChurchWorld is pastor, which has risen to the top of the pile as the ultimate gracelet lived out by an individual in a hierarchical framework.

Evangelists (*evangelistas*): Eph. 4.11

The function of sharing the good news about Jesus and the kingdom and trains others to do the same.

My friend Jim Henderson wrote a book entitled *Evangelism Without Additives: What If Sharing Your Faith Meant Just Being Yourself?*[1] The idea was to put this gracelet back into the hands of the folks in the pews.

---

1. Jim Henderson, *Evangelism without Additives: What If Sharing Your Faith Meant Just Being Yourself?* (Colorado Springs, CO: WaterBrook Press, 2007). The first edition of this book was titled a.k.a "Lost" (2005). If you haven't read this book, you might consider doing so.

It had long since become the domain of small tent meetings, church revivals, and large arenas as we will see below. No doubt, many found their way to Jesus in all these circumstances, but in doing so, the church and parachurch organizations may have taken the idea of the gracelet away from those who are the intended receivers.

Only three times do we find the word *evangelist* in the Second Testament (Acts 21.8; Eph. 4.11; 2 Tim. 4.5). Those occurrences provide very little information about this gracelet that is mentioned in Ephesians. However, what we think about doing is to look at the story of Philip, not unlike we did with Barnabas, to see if we can discern any information about how this gracelet might work.

It is fair to say that this was a gracelet, which was practiced in the church in Ephesus plus six, or Paul would not have been writing about it. The church in the Western world seems to have focused on the word evangelist to the exclusion of the other three. When the word *evangelist* is used, especially in the last fifty plus years, attention is centered on names like Billy Sunday, Billy Graham, or Marjoe. In the world of entertainment, a Billy or a Marjoe crusade was a place where folks could go to see a "free" show and then pay a "fee" when the offering plates were passed. While the evangelistic teams may have worked with churches, they were not a local expression in a church. Crusades simply imported folks to run the crusade. It can be said that God uses what he uses even though it might not be the way he prefers things to be.

These large crusades gave way to an electronic version of evangelism where one could be redeemed by remote control[2] by praying a "sinner's prayer." One has to wonder if in a local church, if folks found themselves evangelizing and training, there might have been more success or maybe more lasting success than the model of moving from city to city with a machine in place to draw big crowds.

Philip as a Model

Most likely, we have all had an up close view of an *evangelist* in our modern church culture, probably not Billy Sunday but maybe Billy Graham or Marjoe (all mentioned above) or anyone of thousands who travel from town to town holding evangelistic meetings. I grew up in a denomination that had "revival" meetings every other month

---

2. Robert M. Price, "Evangelism as Entertainment," religion-online.org http://www.religion-online.org/showarticle.asp?title=1714 (accessed February 18, 2014).

that usually lasted two weeks. When the so-called evangelist left, the church simply returned to its settled pattern and things became "abnormal" again. This never made any sense to me. The question is: did what we see fit the pattern that is provided in Scripture?

Let's look at that question. The only person called an evangelist in the Second Testament is Philip (Acts 21.8). He proclaimed the message of Jesus in Samaria (Acts 8.6a). He performed signs and produced results in lives (Acts 8.6b, 7, 12, 13). The content of his message was the kingdom of God (Acts 8.5, 12, 35), not I might say, "accept Jesus so you can go to heaven when you die." He ministered to whole cities (Acts 8.5) as well as individuals (Acts 8.26). His ministry was natural (Acts 8.4ff., 26, 29). He was constantly proclaiming the good news of the kingdom everywhere he went (Acts 8.40). He was an itinerant in the beginning of his ministry (Acts 8.1-40), but became a functioning evangelist at the church in Caesarea (Acts 21.8ff.).

His ministry was linked to the local city church (21.7ff.) where he provided instruction for new converts to the faith. In Acts 8, Philip established his converts through baptism (vs. 12, 38). He was protective of them and did not abandon them to anything or anyone that could be harmful, like Simon the Magician. It is recorded that his converts rejoiced (8.8).

To think historically about these stories often puts some perspective on them. The events, which Luke recorded in Acts 21.7, occurred before Paul wrote the Ephesian passage where he names evangelist as a gracelet. It appears to me that Paul observed in the life experience of Philip the gracelet of God at work. What he observed became written theology (Eph. 4.11). He, later in life, encouraged Timothy to *do the work of an evangelist* (2 Tim 4.5) and may have had Philip's model in mind. The action of the word "do" in this verse is a command to Timothy, while "discharge" means to fully carry out the service of evangelizing. What we might say is that Paul's experience with Philip gave him the content from which his theology arose.

So What?

What appears in the story of Philip has very little to do with what has grown up in the Western culture that has been labeled evangelistic crusades. The job of the evangelist as recorded by Luke was not preaching fiery sermons to produce converts to Jesus with altar calls. Rather, Acts seems to provide a broader criteria of "proclamation," which, at minimum, included the "words and works" of the kingdom of God. In the Ephesian passage, Paul suggested that the work of the evangelist was to equip the followers of Jesus to do the work of the ministry. That equipment could have been the art of relaying information about Jesus to convert, but we are left to speculate on that issue. So, who's the "training" evangelizer in your community of faith?

We now can finally look at the gracelet of pastor-teacher.

Pastors-Teachers (*poimenas kai didaskalous*): Eph. 4.11

The function of caring for the needs of others by tending, feeding, and teaching.

We have spent an inordinate amount of time in the church that uses English Bibles to give prominence to one word found in Ephesians 4.11: "pastor," which appears only one time in the text with "pastor" as the English translation (The original word appears translated eighteen times: fifteen times as shepherd, two times as Shepherd, and one time as pastors where it appears as a plural word not a singular word). It appears as a verb (action) eleven times in the Second Testament (Matt. 2.6; Luke 17.7; John 21.16; Acts 20.28; 1 Cor. 9.7; 1 Pet. 5.2; Jude 12; Rev. 2.27, 7.17, 12.5, 19.15) where it is translated by various words like tending, feeding, or leading. One wonders why the translators would change to the word "pastor" in the Ephesians passage. This should give the reader some fodder to think about how we have forced this one occasion into the sole leader of the local church. Why is that, I wonder?

However, only appearing once doesn't make it unimportant, nor does it make it important, because the amount of times a word is used does not carry any particular weight. Having said that, one would not necessarily know that when preachers and teachers alike bring out the data saying things like: "this word appears (fill in the number) in our Bible," with the implicit meaning that because it has frequency, it must be important. If that line of reasoning were true, then, as we suggested above, the word "virgin" as in virgin birth would not have any priority since it only occurs a couple of times in the Second Testament.

Additional Descriptive Words

The idea of pastor/shepherd has very little ink in the Second Testament to try and judge what the action of the word really is. The model we see in the church today has developed over the centuries. The idea of a "pastor" has turned into the concept of "chief church leader," in our day and time. In addition, other words have been added for description purposes like "senior pastor," "lead pastor," "associate pastor," assistant pastor," and this one always brings a smile to my face, a "senior associate

Chapter 16

pastor." The additional descriptive words concept simply does not have any biblical warrant. One has to wonder why this is the activity that resides around the word "pastor." Why not "senior apostle," or "senior prophet," or "senior evangelist," or "senior teacher?"

In the passage in Ephesians (4.11), it is coupled with the word "teacher." There is a long on-going debate over whether there are four or five gifts listed there and whether these are "office" gifts, meaning permanent gifts to a local church. There is no such thing as a denomination or an association of churches, which we find in the Modern sense, which has given rise to the use of those descriptive words. So, where do we go to understand this gracelet that Paul mentions in Ephesians 4.11?

The Use of the Word Shepherd

The noun and verb form of "shepherd" appears twenty-nine times in the Second Testament and usually points to Jesus. From those twenty-nine times, five of them seem to relate to workers in the church. Paul uses the word two times (1 Corinthians 9.7 and Ephesians 4.11). Luke uses it once at Acts 20.28. Peter uses it once at 1 Peter 5.1-2. Finally, John uses it once at 21.16. The usages are listed for you in chronological order versus canonical order. This is important to notice because words change their meaning over time.

The root word is *poimaino* and is defined as tending a shepherd does for a flock of sheep. Figuratively, one could say "care taker." We have a differently abled daughter in our home. My wife and I are her care takers. Donna pulls most of the load and she has many varied duties that she performs. Here is the idea of function stated again; Donna is a care taker when she is in the act of care taking. When we talk about this, we think about what she does, not the word description that defines what she does, so we do use the words care taker, not as a title but to identify what she does.

Here are some of the places that the word "shepherd" is used. The information is a bit technical with some Greek phrases in the footnotes, which demonstrates the kind of action that these perform as they are used in the Second Testament.

1 Corinthians 9.7

Paul is the first to use the word[3] when it refers to workers. The context

3. To act as a shepherd (*poimaínei*) Verb: Present Active Indicative 3rd Singular from

is in a group of questions in his argument about receiving compensation for his ministry. The question in the text is: "Who tends a flock and does not drink the milk?" It could be read, "Who continues to 'shepherd/ feed' the flock without receiving compensation?" The mood of the verb suggests certainty in its assertion. The verb is singular and means it refers to one shepherd in this illustration.

On compensation for shepherding: Paul had exhorted the Corinthians to give up rights in Chapter 8; now he is telling them in Chapter 9 that he has also given up rights, i.e., the right to be compensated. It may be that some of the more wealthy Corinthians were put off by Paul working as a tent maker, which was different from the more regular teachers who had patrons for their teaching service. What if Paul's apologetic in this chapter is set against the elite wanting to pay Paul to gain social status with their own social peers rather than Paul asking to be paid for services, which is more normal in today's church. While he thinks he has a right to material substance, he refuses it. One must remember this was a mission that lasted some eighteen months before he moved on. In that time, Paul supported himself. This whole passage should give rise to at least examine how and why folks are paid to do ministry. If pastoring is ad hoc, then maybe the pay should be ad hoc. Different streams of income for different ministries. Or maybe, some should just do what Paul did and deny payment and work in the marketplace.[4]

Ephesians 4.11

The word[5] in this passage by Paul is plural, meaning more than one, i.e., most of the time translated pastors. The case suggests that it is a word that was having some action done to it. One might suggest receiving the action of the word "gave." The Ephesians 4 passage is used by many as the supporting data for the occupation of Pastor. It should be observed that the word is not singular. It is connected with the word "teacher." By using the plural, it does not seem to imply that Paul meant a multi-staffed organized church staff. It does imply that as the "giver" of the gracelet provides shepherding that Jesus followers are being trained to do the work of ministry as well as the Spirit flows gifts through them.

Lexical form *poimainō*. To grasp the significance of the different forms of the verbs in Greek, see Appendix 3 for a simple explanation.

4. Keener, *The IVP Bible Background Commentary (New Testament). Second Edition*, 477-478.

5. To act as a shepherd (*poiménas*) Noun: Masculine Plural Accusative from Lexical Form *poimén*.

Chapter 16

Acts 20:28

The kind of action of the word[6] Luke uses was the present infinitive. It was used to express progressive or an imperfective aspect of the word. It pictures the action expressed by the verb as being *in progress*, i.e., continue pastoring. As the gracelet is provided, continue your participation. It could be argued that the "elders" (elder, one is an elder when elding rather than sitting on a church board) to whom Paul was talking were those who were from Ephesus and maybe even the other cities around where churches had been birthed because of Ephesus. The flock, in its many forms, in the city of Ephesus, was who these elders were to function as "overseers." It is possible that each local house church had an overseer/elder and his/her job was to "feed" the folks who made up the body of Christ in that location. Their teaching duty, i.e., the pastor/teacher of Ephesians 4 is not a stretch, was to keep the local bodies in Ephesus healthy and to protect them from being ravaged by those who would distort the truth. Shepherding includes but is not limited to feeding the sheep and feeding the sheep includes providing a pasture for them to gain the food they need.

1 Peter 5.1-2

This command[7] from Peter for those functioning as elders was to do something once and complete it. If for example, someone told a person in the ancient world to ride your donkey and used an aorist to say that to you, they would say it in a way that expected you to finish that specific task. There is no indication that the task is ongoing or forever and, especially, not permanent. So, it just may be that the Spirit flows his gracelet of pastor/teacher to use on one occasion and expects you to complete that task. It is *not* something that you are continually called to do. It is not a position or a permanent call. It is *ad hoc* and ends when the task given is completed. It is one occasion at a time, not necessarily known ahead of time that it will happen over and over and over again.

John 21.16

This passage,[8] in the story John provides, is about the conclusion of the all night fishing event. Jesus tells Peter to "feed his sheep." The kind

---

6. To act as a shepherd (*poimaínein*) Verb: Present Active Infinitive from Lexical Form *poimainó*.

7. To act as a shepherd (*poimánate*) Verb: Aorist Active Imperative 2nd Plural from Lexical Form *poimainó*.

8. To act as a shepherd (*poímaine*) Verb: Present Active Imperative 2nd Singular from Lexical Form *poimainó*.

of action that is proposed by this word is that Peter is to actively be feeding his sheep. It was spoken directly to Peter to accomplish this. When he is feeding the sheep, he is a shepherd.

There is other material in the First Testament story, where the word "shepherd" occurs 173 times and relates to the feeding of sheep. This material may help us understand Paul's use of this word in Ephesians 4.11. We must say at the onset, the word should be translated "shepherd" rather than "pastor," and seen as a metaphor of function rather than carrying the idea of leadership and other ideas that have been imported into it in at a later timeframe.

The Psalms are Poetry

When I was in high school, there was one class that often caused me to have a gagging reflex. It was English Poetry. Just the idea of Poetry was unappetizing. I realize that lots of folks have a love for that area of literature, but I did not share it. Wouldn't you know that in my own journey of the study of Scripture, I was obliged to acknowledge that poetry is one of the major genres of the First Testament. Hebrew poetry covers approximately one-third of the writings of the First Testament. All of the book of Psalms is poetry and large sections of the Prophets and other parts of the narrative are also rendered in intricate and sometimes exquisite Hebrew Poetry. It should be noted that Hebrew Poetry cannot be read as if we were reading USAToday or some other international paper. C.S. Lewis once wrote, "The Psalms must be read as poems, as lyrics, with all the licenses and all the formalities, the hyperboles, the emotional rather than the logical connections, which are proper to lyric poetry."[9] That often takes a lot of re-education for those who have grown up on a versified Bible.

Psalm 23 is a lyric poem, which was originally meant to be sung. Imagine for a moment, David is hiding in a cave hoping not to be found by Absalom. He picks out his lyre and begins to compose what we call Psalm 23. A lyric poem usually expresses the thoughts and feelings of a single speaker. We must recognize that music is one of the main ways that we learn our theology in the church. This learning process can be seen in the conflict between Athanasius *and* Arius over the deity of Jesus in the fourth century AD where Athanasius argued his point through sermons and lectures while Arius sang his position by the music that he wrote and gave the church of his day. Here is a story that reflects this idea.

---

9. C. S. Lewis, *Reflections on the Psalms* (Chicago, IL: Mariner Books, 1965), 3.

Chapter 16

My sister was an accomplished piano player and played for her church for over fifty years. The church that we both grew up in was a brand of Pentecostalism where Southern gospel music was important. Each year at camp meeting time,[10] the denomination would print a new song book that was filled with new music written by pastors and musicians within the denomination. In their services, a large ad hoc choir would sing these new songs during the camp meeting time and then bring them back to their local churches. For the next year, the local congregation would sing a repertoire of camp meeting music each Sunday morning, evening, and Wednesday evening. The music was filled with their own brand of theology. For fifty-two weeks, until the next camp meeting, the theology of the songs was hammered into the heads of the congregants as they would sing them or listen to them.

On one occasion years later after I had moved to the West coast, my sister and family came for a visit. One day, out of the clear blue, my sister asked me what I thought about the "rapture" of the church. I spent the next forty or so minutes giving her the background of where that theological idea had come from, how it had been propagated, and why I didn't subscribe to it.

When I was finished, my niece, who was sitting in on the conversation asked my sister, "Mom, do you believe that?" To which my sister had a one word response, "No!"

I was not surprised. I suggested to her that her theological frame work was almost completely formed by the music that she had played and sung all those years. She had never thought of that and was not eager to accept that it was true. She thought she had received her belief from the three preaching sessions that she attended each week. I asked her if she could remember the last sermon her pastor had preached before her trip. She thought for a moment and said, "No, but it was good!" Then I asked her if she could remember the songs that she had played and sang in that same service and she rattled them off, singing lines from them, in a very short period.

I pointed out how many of the songs, which she played and sang week after week, talked about the rapture of the church and going

---

10. Camp meeting was a celebration time for a region of churches within the Church of God, Cleveland, TN, denomination. It was filled with music and preaching. The one that I attended on several occasions with my family was held in an open building called a "tabernacle." It was located on the Church of God Campgrounds in Wimauma, FL.

to heaven and that repetitiveness had formed her theological belief of that subject. I also shared how long it took me to unhook from that particular view of the end times.

So, to get a feel for the gracelet of pastor, let's take a look at Psalm 23 to get a vantage point of what Paul may have understood from his own Hebrew history about shepherding.

The Idea of Shepherd in Psalm 23

Psalm 23 is the most recognizable place in the First Testament to see the duties of a shepherd in relationship to the sheep. It is estimated that Psalm 23 may have been written in the wilderness during the time of David's flight from Absalom.[11] To get a grasp of where that conflict sets in the storyline, let me provide a short overview.

The whole Story of God could be seen as a six act play, which I have written about elsewhere,[12] where each of the following words describe each act from 1-6: Creation, Chaos, Covenant, Christ, Church, and Consummation. The first three, Creation, Chaos, and Covenant make up what we call the First Testament. The collection of Psalms appears in Act 3: Covenant, which is the storyline of Abraham to the Restoration after the Exile. In the Psalms collection, there are five sections; Psalms 23 appears at the beginning of the second section of Psalms, which has to do with how God relates to his creation. The storyline that provides the context out of which the Psalm arose is the story of Absalom, which is found in 2 Samuel 18. It is a sad story about a father and son who find themselves in opposition to each other in a military plot in which David, the father, had to oppose his third son, Absalom. Why? Because Absalom was leading a rebellion against David in order to take his throne. Out of his great concern for his son, he instructed his commander-in-chief to go easy on his son when he was captured. During this skirmish with his son, David had to hide in fear of his own capture and death. At the end of this short story within the overall story of Israel, Absalom got trapped by his long hair in the branches of a tree and some of David's soldiers who were chasing him killed him. It is thought that Psalm 23 was created during the timeframe of David hiding from Absalom.

Psalm 23

Psalm 23 pictures God as a shepherd. Its structure is simple. It is a

---

11. Jack R. Lundbom, "Psalm 23: Song of Passage," *Interpretation* 40, no. 1, (1986): 6.
12. Griffin, *God's Epic Adventure.*

catalog of God's acts of protection and provision as viewed by one who grew up shepherding. In order to comprehend the metaphor of shepherd, it is helpful to understand some of the background of shepherding in ancient Palestine. Shepherds were entrusted with finding narrow strips of green grass and springs of water in the middle of hot summer days. While leading their sheep there, they had to protect them from wild animals (i.e., remember the story of David with bear and lion). The narrow paths were very dangerous as those shepherding moved the sheep from one locale to another. So David begins his song with a metaphor: *The Lord is my shepherd.* Out of several possible thoughts and feelings inherent in the image of a shepherd, the poet chose only one: *I shall not lack anything.* The tricky word for the modern reader is "anything." Often read without the context of the rest of the Psalm, it is usually described as "anything that I ask for or even anything that I want." This line in the Psalm is thought then to mean: No matter what the present situation is, I shall not lack anything because God is my supplier. Unfortunately, this is not the meaning of this line of text.

The controlling metaphor is that God is shepherd and that he supplies David's needs according to the list of activities that God does that David shares in the rest of the Psalm. God is not at our beck and call to present us with everything that we think we need when we ask. He is not our servant, we are his. He is, however, ready and willing to provide what David writes and sings about.

The next three lines of the poem demonstrate the beginning of the catalog of acts of the shepherd toward the sheep:

He makes me lie down in green pastures,
he leads me beside quiet waters,
he restores my being.

God cares for his sheep and provides them with:

- **Rest:** The shepherd's duty was to take the sheep on a journey to provide them with lush green grass. This journey was sometimes daily and sometimes took longer. To provide the sheep with lush green grass, he would seek out *rough herbage* early in the day for them to eat, then *richer sweeter grass* as the morning progressed, and, finally, a *shady lush green place* at noontime. This pattern of life brought rest to the nervous sheep. It also suggests that the sheep could not handle the shady lush green place until it had been prepared by the rough herbage. In short, the shepherd knew how to feed the sheep, which was his major function. Here's a thought: Often our desire is to bypass the rough stuff wanting the lush green stuff quickly. Rough stuff provides the capacity for us to handle the lush green stuff properly. Our own narcissistic drive is to have things quickly and then blame God when he does not perform; our own dog and pony show is driven by the consumeristic drive of the Western World.

- **Refreshment:** The word *quiet* equals a *peaceful rest*. Sheep would not drink from a fast moving stream. However, sheep would often drink from pot holes along the path on the way to the peaceful water. These pot holes were filled with dung and urine from the previous group of sheep that had passed by. Sheep sometimes had an inability to wait for the cool, clear, sparkling water provided by the shepherd. Sheep are sometimes impatient, aren't we?

- **Restoration:** The shepherd now provides *restoration* for the total person. (*being:* translated *soul* in a lot of translations and does not mean some third part of a person as in body, soul, and spirit, but means the totality of the life of an individual, the *mental, physical, emotional, social,* and *spiritual* self. In the Hebrew mindset and theology proper, you don't have a soul, you are a *soul.*)

Next, the text says that he *guides me in paths of righteousness for his name's sake.*

The catalog of acts of the shepherd continues. The shepherd leads in "right" paths vs. "dangerous" paths. And he does this leading for "his name's sake." The psalmist assures us that we can depend on these provisions because God provides them for his name's sake. Why? Because God's reputation was at stake. David as a functioning shepherd knew that God's reputation was at stake. This made him understand that as a living member of the family, God would take care of him. It is a difficult reflection to grasp, but God takes care of his sheep so that no shame can be placed at his feet.

Next, the text continues with even though I walk through the valley of the shadow of death,

> I will fear no evil,
>   for you are with me;
> your rod and your staff,
>   they comfort me.

Christian tradition has taken these words and applied them to physical death. These words are often read at funerals. Physical death was probably not the mindset of David when he first wrote this song. In reality, there was a valley by the name *valley of the shadow of death.* The shepherd would move the sheep through the valley, which was made up of a narrow path, so narrow that the sheep could not turn around. Beside the path was a gully with a drop of seven to eight feet. Half way through the canyon the path changed sides. The sheep were forced to jump from one side to another. The side being jumped to was about eleven inches higher. The shepherd would stand and coax the sheep to make the leap. If the sheep fell, the rod was there to pick him up while the staff was ever ready to keep the wild animals away.[13]

The Dictionary of Biblical Imagery suggests the following about the rod and staff:

But the rod and staff can also be images of comfort, protection and security. This is preeminently true of the shepherd's rod and staff. One of these was the familiar crook, used for disciplining a wandering sheep, encircling a sheep's neck or belly to rescue it from a gully and laying across the backs of sheep for purposes of counting (the so-called rodding of the sheep) as they entered the sheepfold (Lev 27.32; Ezek 20.37). The other half of the "rod and staff" pair was a clublike weapon used for warding off predators. The picture has been rendered forever famous by the detail in Psalm 23 that in the valley of deepest darkness, the place of treacherous gullies and lurking predators, the sheep will "fear no evil; … thy rod and thy staff, they comfort me" (Ps 23.4 RSV).[14]

This article is not specific about whether the rod or the staff is the one with the "familiar crook." Most visuals that we have received through the years have promoted the "staff" as being the one with the "crook." It may well be that the "rod" was that instrument. The *rod* was the familiar crook used to rescue the sheep from the gullies or was placed over the sheep's back to count them as they entered the fold (Lev. 27.32).[15] It was "a club-like weapon" (Ex. 21.20; 1 Sam. 14.27; Ps. 23.4), with "a shepherd's crook" (Ezek. 20.37).[16] The rod was for protection.[17] The staff was also a protective weapon about the size of a club often ladled with rocks, etc. It was used to fight off attacking wild dogs or other wild animals.[18] As a passing

---

13. Leland Ryken, *The Bible as Literature* (Grand Rapids, MI: Zondervan, 1974), 132-133.

14. Leland Ryken, James C. Wilhoit, and Tremper Longman III, *Dictionary of Biblical Imagery* (Downers Grove, IL: InterVarsity Press 1998), 733-734.

15. Ryken, *The Bible as Literature*, 132.

16. Ronald F. Youngblood. General Editor, *Nelson's New Illustrated Bible Dictionary*, 989.

17. D. A. Carson. Consulting Editor, *New Bible Commentary: 21st Century Edition*, 500.

18. Ryken, *The Bible as Literature*, 132.

thought, one might want to think about the text "spare the rod and spoil the child," while it may be inspired by some verses in proverbs, the saying does not come from the Bible itself. It comes from the poem *Hudibras*[19] written by Samuel Butler (1612-1680) in the seventeenth century. It was a poem that may actually be mocking the religious extremist.

It is fair to say that part of shepherding was protecting the sheep, not beating the sheep.

You prepare a table before me in the presence of my enemies.

Here the metaphor changes, but, by extension of the overall shepherding metaphor, still controls the poem. The preparing of the table is what the shepherd did when the sheep got to the other side of the canyon. The protection from enemies included the shepherd finding grass that did not have poisonous plants or wild animals nearby. It is helpful to note that this is done in the presence of enemies not devoid of enemies. Our tendency is to think that peace is the eradicating of all enemies. Such is not the case in this present evil age. This may be a visual picture of "peace" in the midst of trouble, not peace by the absence of trouble (Psalm 3).

You anoint my head with oil;

In the yearly life of the sheep, summer time was "fly" time for shepherd and sheep. The nuance of flies in the summer was a problem. But, the shepherd knew what to do for the sheep according to the symptoms the sheep was displaying. There were three basic treatments the shepherd would use. David uses the word *anoint*, which basically is defined as "to smear something on an object," in this case, different kinds of oil for different purposes. The three conditions that shepherds had to deal with in this arena were: the nose fly, scab, and mating.

First, let's look at the nose fly. These little flies would buzz around the nose of the sheep attempting to deposit their eggs on the damp, mucous membranes of the nose. If successful, the eggs would hatch and form small, slender worm-like larvae. They would work their way up the nasal passage into the sheep's head. They would burrow into the flesh, which caused intense irritation accompanied by severe inflammation.

For relief from this agonizing annoyance, sheep would deliberately beat their heads against trees, rocks, or posts. They would rub their nose in the soil and thrash around against anything rough. Some extreme cases

19. Wikipedia, "Hudibras " Wikipedia https://en.wikipedia.org/wiki/Hudibras (accessed September 12, 2015).

could cause a sheep to kill itself in a frenzied endeavor to gain a respite from the aggravation. Advanced stages of this infection could cause blindness. Some sheep would race from place to place until dropping from sheer exhaustion. Others would toss their heads up and down for hours. Sometimes they would hide and not eat.

What was the cure for this condition? It was a mixture of oil, sulphur, and spices. This solution was smeared over the sheep's nose and head as a protection against the nose fly. The attentive shepherd applied this solution as a preventative measure rather than a curing one. It was applied so that sheep did not get nose flies. Often in churches that practice anointing, it is something applied after the fact. A brother or sister gets sick with some disease and the "shepherd/pastor" anoints with oil and prays for deliverance. What might it be like if one who is practicing pastoring would anoint her/his congregants as a preventative measure, say before the flu season hit? Just wondering...

The second condition the shepherd had to deal with was scab. Scab was a highly contagious disease common among sheep. It was caused by a minute, microscopic parasite that grows in warm weather. It spreads throughout a flock by direct contact between infected and non-infected sheep. Sheep loved to rub heads in an affectionate and friendly manner. As with the nose fly, the head had to be anointed with an oil mixture to keep the animal from becoming infected by the disease and, in this case, a precautionary step to keep from catching the disease. This action is often not the conventional way that those practicing "anointing with oil," participate, which is the disease comes first, the anointing occurs with prayer for healing. Maybe one might practice it the other way around.

Finally, sheep mated. In so doing, the typical activity of the rams was to butt heads with each other as they sparked out their territory of ewes. To keep the rams from hurting each other, shepherds would grease the heads and noses so that when they rammed each other, they would simply slide off each other and not hurt each other.[20] One wonders what would happen in so-called "church fights" if the butt heads were anointed before butting heads.

My cup overflows

Typically this phrase has been interpreted as "having more than enough" for any need that comes along. To that traditional meaning,

20. Phillip Keller, *A Shepherd Looks at Psalm 23* (Grand Rapids: Zondervan Publishing House, 1970), 110-117.

John Goldinggay, in his commentary on Psalms, suggests that the line be translated: "My cup amply satisfies,"[21] which may convey an idea that the sheep may enjoy the best and fullest that the shepherding has to offer. John Calvin says as much: "...this overflowing cup, ought to be explained as denoting the abundance, which goes beyond the mere supply of the common necessaries of life...."[22]

> Surely goodness and love will follow me
>   all the days of my life,
> and I shall return to the house of the Lord
>   at the close of my days.

In the final four lines of David's poem, he suggests that shepherding provides security as the sheep are returned to God's house (i.e., his fold, for protection and provision) over and over.

So, in shepherding, Psalm 23 provides a catalog of sorts that describes what shepherding is. Shepherding provides:

- Provision
- Rest
- Refreshment
- Restoration
- Direction/guidance
- Freedom from fear
- Protection/comfort
- Protection from enemies
- Care/more than enough/enjoying the best and fullest of what shepherding offers

So, notice how the shepherd acts as portrayed in this Psalm. Surely, there are others provisions, but the gracelet of shepherding is far removed from what has become the dominant idea of a pastor/senior pastor/lead pastor in the twenty-first century. Rather, when God flows this gracelet through an individual, male or female, he may be providing provision, rest, refreshment, restoration, direction/guidance, freedom from fear, protection/comfort, protection from enemies, care/ more than enough, and, finally, security. Most likely the gracelet could include one or a combination of items above as the situation requires. All Jesus followers

---

21. John Goldingay, *Psalms, Vol. 1, Baker Commentary of the Old Testament Wisdom and Psalms* (Grand Rapids, MI: Baker Academic, 2006), 43.

22. John Calvin, "Commentary on Psalms - Volume 1," Bible Hub http://biblehub.com/library/calvin/commentary_on_psalms_volume_1/psalm_23_5-6.htm (accessed September 12, 2015).

are pastors when they are pastoring; when they are not pastoring, they are Bill, Maude, Jimmy, or Sarah. The gracelet is more about what is being received than through whom it is being sent.

Evangelizing and Pastoring-Teaching

In today's medical world, we have two kinds of functioning doctors that may offer us a clue as to how these gracelets may work out. The two doctoring techniques are obstetrician, one who brings the child into the world, and a pediatrician, who takes care of the child once born into the world. Evangelizing is like the function of an obstetrician, while pastoring is like the function of a pediatrician.

When evangelizing is at work as a gracelet, it is among those that are new to what the Gospel of John calls being born from above.[23] The working of this gracelet occurs in the proclamation of the gospel, in words and works. Often the result of this gracelet is that God brings folks to a new humanity lived out in the present evil age, bringing folks from darkness to light.

When pastoring is at work as a gracelet, it is among those who are followers of Jesus living in their new humanity. The teaching part of this gracelet is a training of Jesus followers to learn the Story of God and to live into it in this present evil age.

So What?

We might summarize at this point by saying as we have of other gracelets in Ephesians 4, that one is an evangelist when one is actually evangelizing. One is a pastor-teacher when one is actually pastoring-teaching. When these activities are not in operation, the person is none of these. To make the point clear: when Jane or Jim, who has the title of Pastor is home at night sleeping, s/he is not a pastor, s/he is a sleeper. A person is what they are when they are functioning as conduits of a gracelet of the Spirit.

Let's Have a Conversation

- In what way does this teaching on the so-called "office gifts" differ from the conventional teaching? What difference does it make?
- How does the phrase "when you are pastoring, you are a pastor" strike you in light of the common way of using the term pastor for a position in a church?

213

...everyone teaching a Spiritual Gifts course should cancel it and replace it with a course entitled something like "Gracelets: Being Conduits of the Extravagant Acts of God's Grace to Others."

Conclusion | Appendices

⇒ **Check Your GPS: Where You Are Going**
- Conclusion
- Appendix 1: Alphabetical List of Gracelets
- Appendix 2: Word of Faith Teaching
- Appendix 3: Greek Verb and Noun System

Conclusion

I have worked on this book off and on since 2007. Mostly off. In the last few months, I set my mind to finish it. When this Conclusion has been written, it will be done. As a publisher, I have often told authors that at some point, they have to stop writing and let it go to the publisher. I now have to follow my own advice. I know well what they experienced when they finally had to let it be born to the public.

I congratulate you if you have read this far. I realize that most readers will not agree with me on all the conclusions that I have drawn. That's okay. Hopefully, however, some of the conclusions have caused you to stop and think about what you have always been taught about this subject and maybe even seeped into your theological thought process. I also realize that some of this material that you have been presented is rather new to your own theological intake and you may need time to resolve things that you have been taught with things you have read here. That is surely an okay place to find yourself.

One of the cases that we have tried to build is that what we have traditionally called spiritual gifts could better be called gracelets and that ownership, i.e., that we possess them, may not be as real as we have been led to believe. In order to produce a different thesis, we considered how words work in the English language, then we looked at the words that are often translated "spiritual gifts." My hope is that while that chapter was a bit on the technical side, if you chose to jump past it, that sometime you will go back and engage it.

We presented you with information to try and delineate between the "gift" of the Spirit and the "gifts" of the Spirit, since those are two different concepts and sometimes get conflated. An important consideration when studying this kind of information is to offer clues about how to read. We took a stab at offering two different clues "context and hierarchy" in Chapters 6 and 12. These are extremely important in your own formation of what and how you think gracelets should be operating in our present culture.

The heart of the information, although not the heart/center of the book, is the chapters in which we discussed the different gracelet lists. I trust that your comprehension level went up as you read and munched on that information. Hopefully, you didn't find any bones that choked you.

I trust that reading this book has been insightful to you and that you might return to it again and again when the concepts presented here grow fuzzy.

I leave you then with a list of ideas that I began with. They are:

1. That the Greek word *charisma* often translated by the English word "gift" does not intrinsically mean a Spirit-given ability given to an individual, i.e., s/he is a prophet.
2. That *charisma* should be defined in its own context and that definition should not necessarily be transported to all other contexts.
3. That *charisma* means a concrete way that God expresses his grace. For that Spirit activity, I have chosen to call these concrete events *gracelets*, i.e., small drops of grace distributed by God to others through a human conduit.
4. That the gifts list passages in Paul (1 Cor 12; Rom 12.3–8; Eph 4.11–13) discuss Spirit activities rather than individual abilities, which an individual possesses.
5. That Jesus followers should not sit around waiting until they have figured out "what" special ability they have or don't have because they have taken a "Spiritual Gift" test or appraisal. There are no special abilities delivered, only functions for the moment.
6. That there should be an Acts-like event in which all the "Spiritual Gifts tests/assessments" are burned. I know that sounds a bit abrupt, but I stick by that statement.
7. That followers of Jesus should stop using the word "gift" or "spiritual gifts" and start talking about gracelets as a Spirit activity, which flows through a person to another for the latter's benefit.
8. That everyone teaching a spiritual gifts course should cancel it and replace it with a course entitled something like

Conclusion

GRACELETS: Being Conduits of the Extravagant Acts of God's Grace.

The result of all this reading and comprehending is that you actually allow the Spirit to flow through you for the sake of others around you. My prayer then is: "Lord, let it be so!"

∽

It is important to remember that the authors of the text did not provide definitions.

GRACELETS

Appendix 1: Alphabetical List of Gracelets

The following is a list of all the gracelets that we have presented in this book in alphabetical order for easy access to the gracelets name and its possible definition. It is important to remember that the authors of the text did not provide definitions. Thus, these are the definitions that I have attributed to these gracelets based on my own biblical study of them.

Administrations (*kuberneseis*): 1 Cor. 12.28

To steer or direct the affairs of the church by giving direction, which results in the effective accomplishment of spreading the gospel, i.e., the message of the kingdom of God.

Aiding (*proistamenos*) Rom. 12.8

To care for others in the community such as widows, orphans, slaves, and strangers, i.e., those vulnerable within the community.

Apostles (*apostolos*): Eph. 4.11; 1 Cor. 12.28

One who is commissioned by God to bring the gospel to new places and provides spiritual care for the new humanity gatherings that he/she has birthed.

Celibacy: (*thelō de pas anthrōpos eimi hōs kai emautou*) 1 Cor. 7.7, 25–40

The spontaneous proficiency for married or single, male or female, to have one's sexual appetite lowered to a hibernation status in times of being apart: In the case of those who are married, or in close encounters with those who are not married. It is the gift, which provides the Jesus follower a way to escape sexual sins.

Discernings of Spirits (*diakriseis pneumaton*): 1 Cor. 12.10

Perception empowered by the Spirit to judge the source of prophetic words, whether divine, human, or demonic.

Evangelists (*evangelistas*): Eph. 4.11

The function of sharing the good news about Jesus and the kingdom and trains others to do the same.

Exhortation (*parakaion*): Rom. 12.8

The sensitivity to draw close to others in their time of need in order to encourage and motivate them to conquer the experiences of life.

Faith (*pistis*): 1 Cor. 12.9, 13.2

The confidence that is infused by the Spirit that a specific situation or need is going to be met by God.

Gifts of Healings (*charismata iamaton*): 1 Cor. 12.9

The gracelets of healings are the actual outcomes of healing, which a sick person receives.

Giving (*metadidous*) Rom. 12.8

The act of sharing food or possessions within the community with generosity (aploteti). It is giving, but it is not necessarily currency/money that is in the definition of this word.

Interpretation of Tongues: (*hermēneia glōssa; diermēneuō*) 1 Cor. 12.10

Human speech in the listener's language that brings edification to the group that interprets what has been spoken with the gracelet of tongues.

Knowledge, Issuance of (*logos gnoseos*): 1 Cor. 12.8

A message of inspired teaching or instruction given by the Spirit that brings a new level of maturity in following Jesus to the receiver of the gracelet.

Miracles, Effects of (*energemata dunameon*): 1 Cor. 12.10, 29

The effect of an extraordinary event in which the power of God has been displayed.

Appendix 1

Pastors-Teachers (*poimenas kai didaskalous*): Eph. 4.11

The function of caring for the needs of others by tending, feeding, and teaching.

Philanthropy (*psōmizō pas*) 1 Cor. 13.3

Acquiring wealth and freely giving it away for the proclamation of the kingdom.

Prophecy (*propheteia*): 1 Cor. 12.10, 12.28

Communicating the pulse of God's heart for the purpose of edifying.

Prophets (*prophetas*): Eph. 4.11; 1 Cor. 12.28

One who functions as a frequent spokesperson of prophecies and is a prophet when s/he is prophesying.

Service (*diakonian*): Rom. 12.8

The divine recognition and response to specific needs in the Body of Christ.

Showing Mercy (*eleon*) Rom. 12.8

The giving of financial assistance to the "poor" in the church.

Teachers (*didaskalous*): Rom. 12.8; 1 Cor. 12.28

The natural function of communicating spiritual truth and information that is infused by the Spirit, which benefits the ministry and health of the body of Christ.

Tongues, Kinds of (*gene glosson*): 1 Cor. 12.10, 28

The human phenomena of speech infused by the Spirit that is sometimes a known language, sometimes an unknown language that is spoken and should be accompanied by the gracelet of interpretation so that the community can be edified as well as the individual.

Conclusion

Wisdom, Utterance of (*logos sopias*): 1 Cor. 12.8

The proclamation of the good news as the Spirit imparts a depth of understanding of the truth of the gospel that may not have been understood before by the recipient of the gracelet.

∽

GRACELETS

Appendix 2: Word of Faith Teaching

The Word of Faith Teaching

Sometimes to understand what something is, it is helpful to understand what it is not. Because in certain facets of the church, faith is held in primacy, not unlike tongues in the Corinthian congregation or in the modern Assemblies of God movement or word of knowledge in the newer Vineyard movement, it may be helpful to take an interlude in our discussion about the diversity of gracelets to dispel some misguided information about faith.

The so-called "word of faith" teaching has been popular through the writings of the late Kenneth Hagin and has had a wide influence in the Charismatic church. The following information is not an assault on the person of Kenneth Hagin but on his teaching about faith. It is fair to point out that close to the end of his life, he took a different position and somewhat rebuked his followers about how extensive they had perverted his own teaching.[1] However, that warning by him does not seem to have taken effect in the visible churches that follow his teaching.

What is the Prayer of Faith?

In many Pentecostal/Charismatic churches today, there is a teaching, which uses James 5.15 as a prooftext that is often believed to be a part of, if not, the *gracelet of faith*. When this subject is discussed in some Christian circles, it often produces a lot of heat and not very much light.

We propose the following question and then give two possible answers.

The question: Is there such a category of prayer that is often called by some in the Charismatic church "The Prayer of Faith?" First, it seems obvious that all prayer is attached to faith in some fashion.

---

1. J. Lee Grady, "Kenneth Hagin's Forgotten Warning," CBN.com http://www.cbn.com/spirituallife/churchandministry/grady_hagan_prosperity.aspx (accessed July 20, 2015).

Otherwise, why would one pray at all. Second, to comprehend the answer that we will propose, the reader should review how he or she reads and interprets Scripture. It seems a given in this culture and other cultures before this one, beginning with the invention of the Guttenberg press, that every Jesus follower has the right to read and interpret the sacred text. It should be noted that the execution of that right often causes a lot of anxiety between church folks.

At the core of this discussion seems to be the disregard of a basic concept. When the original writers of the text took their writing utensil or began to dictate what they wanted to say to another who wrote for them, they were communicating to a real live audience living in a specific timeframe and geographic area. It is assumed that the readers would have known the writer and that the subject matter would have been familiar to them within their culture. We now refer to it as history; they would have referred to it as daily life. The most important result that can occur when we study Scripture is to try to hear what the first hearer heard when they heard or read the words we call Scripture.[2]

Different current church cultures read Scripture with a different starting point. Within current congregations, if they are reading the text at all, they are most likely reading it subjectively without any regard for grammar or history. I have heard the following scenario hundreds of times in my life. "Today, as we come to the Word of God, we are going to put it first. We are not going to tell you what we think it says, we are going to tell you what it is actually saying." When that kind of language is used to preface a time of teaching, the speaker is communicating to his or her audience that any interpretation that the listeners have heard that contradicts what is about to be said is based on opinion of another, while the one that is going to be presented is based on the plain meaning of the text at hand.

Several years ago while on a road trip through the high desert of Southern California, I was listening to the radio; yes, you read that right, the radio. It was early in the morning. The radio preacher had just preached a stirring sermon in which he told his listening audience that if they did not have faith, they could not receive what they deserved from God and that one way of raising their faith was to send the preacher's ministry a prescribed amount of money making sure that the hearer referenced "offer number 313." I had heard this marketing approach many times before that occasion and many times since that occasion. The bewitching hour of his program ended and at the turn

2. Griffin, *God Has Spoken*, Location 43.

of the hour a new voice began sharing. Right out of the box, the new radio preacher said that if you believed a certain way about faith you were doomed. What way was that "certain way"? It was the very way the previous radio preacher had just prescribed as being *the way* to have faith. Each was delivering what they called the *plain meaning* of the text. My immediate thought: no wonder so many folks are confused and not just from listening to two dueling radio preachers but from a steady diet of *plain meaning* teaching Sunday after Sunday in their own community of faith. Anemic preaching leads to anemic Jesus followers.

The goal of interpreting is obviously to make the text plain. If we were to comprehend that the phrase plain meaning meant what would have been plain to the first hearer or reader, then, we are on a more believable path to understand. But, that is not what that phrase has come to mean. It has become a concrete phrase that endorses the speaker's point of view and often has nothing to do with what the original author knew to be plain, but rather the text has been sifted through a twenty-first century cultural view whose message is carried along by the vehicle of the distorted prism of a seventeenth-century language.

Worldview surely comes into play with the prevalent way of reading, reflecting, and thinking. In my opinion, a weak way of exploring the text of Scripture has come to some pretty radical interpretations of the sacred text. One of those is surely the teaching on faith within one segment of the charismatic church life. So, let's turn to some specific texts that are often used to talk about faith and see what conclusions we come to.

Mark 11.20-24

The most popular teaching comes from the words of Jesus in Mark 11.20-24 that reads:

> In the morning, as they went along, they saw the fig tree withered from the roots. Peter remembered and said to Jesus, "Rabbi, look! The fig tree you cursed has withered!"

> "Have faith in God," Jesus answered. "Truly I tell you, if anyone says to this mountain, 'Go, throw yourself into the sea,' and does not doubt in their heart but believes that what they say will happen, it will be done for them. Therefore I tell you, whatever you ask for in prayer, believe that you have received it, and it will be yours."

From these verses, the late Kenneth Hagin taught the concept of *positive confession*, which in turn was popularized by the Word of Faith churches. The idea of the plain meaning of the English words is used to offer his interpretation, which implies that the interpretation comes at the expense of reading without context. What one is then led to believe is that when a Jesus follower has a specific desire and then claims it, that God will oblige and give what is being asked for. So, asking in belief, i.e., claiming, will surely come to pass in the future because one has claimed it in the present.

With a bit of context, here is an alternative way to view this passage. The text of verse 22 that is translated above by the NIV reads "Have faith in God." Another way to translate that would be: "You have the faithfulness of God. This translation provides a clearer understanding of what Mark is getting at. The word "faith" is not a declarative word, i.e., something that you have. Mark alludes to Habakkuk 2.4, where Habakkuk tells his readers that the righteous person lives because of his or her faithfulness to the covenant of God, which is based on God's faithfulness to bless those who keep his covenant. Mark's passage is an echo of the Habakkuk passage.

The Hagin interpretation suggests that if one has faith "in" God and believes, what is asked for will be given. What enters into the discussion is the idea of certainty, i.e., the abolishment of doubt. So the prayer has to somehow abolish and resist doubt to gain the prize of what is being asked for. Controlling doubt was most likely not in the mind of Jesus. Rather, he was telling the folks to whom he was talking and reminding them that asking and receiving has to do with the faithfulness of God, not the human ingenuity of lynching doubt.

In verse 23, when Jesus speaks of "this mountain," it is most probable that he is referring to the Mount of Olives. He may be making an allusion to Zechariah 14, which suggests that when the future (eschatological) day of the Lord arrives, the Mount of Olives will be split in two (Zech 14.4) and the whole land will be turned into a plain (Zech. 14.10). The picture is of the coming of the king (Messiah) to set up his rule (kingdom). Mark was using Apocalyptic (symbolic) language from Zechariah 14.4, 10.[3] To literalize this passage using "plain English meaning of words" is to miss the point of what Jesus was saying. The "plain meaning" is controlled by the context and historical background, not an English translation in the present era.

Verse 24 then becomes a prayer for God to bring his rule/kingdom.

---

3. As readers, we should always be reminded that knowing the Old/First Testament allows the reader of the Second Testament to have a better grasp of what is being written.

What is declared by Jesus is the absolute readiness of God to respond to bring about his kingdom. When prayer becomes the source of faith's power and means of its strength, the only restriction is the sovereignty of God. This kind of prayer resembles the disciple's prayer in Matthew 6. This saying in Mark then may be something like, "Keep believing in God's faithfulness and his rule will come sooner than you think."

The teaching of this passage is that God is ready to respond because of his faithfulness to bring about the kingdom/rule here and now, not on an individual's ability to conjure up faith so that God will work on his/her behalf.

An Illustration

What the writers of the Gospels tell us about the teaching of Jesus is often taught elsewhere in the Second Testament by other authors. One clear portrait of the Mark passage may be found in the writing of Paul presented to us at Romans 4.13-25. Herein, Paul tells a story about the faith of Abraham whose faith was not some abstract idea but was grounded in his understanding of the faithfulness of God to do what he said he would do rather than the idea that faith is something that one musters up (v. 21). We are not to imagine that Abraham, upon hearing God, began to proclaim that he was a father or that Sarah was pregnant. Neither of those statements would have been true. What he considered was that in reality his and Sarah's bodies were beyond the age of producing children. What he chose to believe was that God was faithful to bring about what he said he would do. That's a far cry from, "God, I want a brand new car and I believe that you will give me one. I will not doubt! I claim it in Jesus name."

The Romans 10.17 passage has often been used to substrate a misnomer about faith. Just ask almost any Jesus follower about this passage and you will likely hear that a person's faith grows as that person grows in the knowledge of Scripture. I know, I have written it somewhere in all these pages before, that pulling a single verse out of context and expounding on what seems like the "plain meaning" of the English sentence is simply just "plain wrong," as a procedure of hearing what the text is saying. The NIV offers the following translation: "faith comes from hearing the message, and the message is heard through the word about Christ." But even that translation leaves some wiggle room for "plain meaning people" to forge a message that is not Paul's intent. The very little known and read *God News Bible* puts it this way: "So then, faith comes from hearing the message, and the message comes through preaching Christ." Paul seems to be implying that telling the story of Jesus is the path that leads a non-follower of Jesus to having faith in Jesus.

In the Haginian tradition, the James 5.13-16 passage seems to play a central role in coming to grips with understanding faith by naming the kind of prayer that is prayed a "Prayer of Faith," another "plain meaning" faux pas. James seems to be talking to the diaspora church about being good Jesus followers. In chapter 5, he makes some suggestions about the elders[4] praying. Different translations handle these verses differently. But, there is no indication anywhere that the words "prayer of faith" is a phrase that signifies a kind of prayer. It seems more likely that all prayers have the ingredient of faith.

So What?

In many traditions, this concept popularized by Hagin seems to hold the attention of Jesus followers, i.e., that "faith" in the "prayer of faith" is the gracelet of faith. That further leads to the assumption, as in Hagin theology, which is sometimes shared by other Pentecostal and Charismatic churches, that the gracelet of faith produces the desired thing prayed for. That concept seems too foreign for the concept of faith in the Second Testament, especially the gracelet of faith. It seems that because of the Enlightenment that humankind has come to believe that a person can make things work out for their own good. We've heard it before and will no doubt hear it again, "you can achieve what you believe." Surely goals are important. Belief is also important. But, it doesn't seem that the gracelet of faith works on that plane. Like all other gracelets, the gracelet of faith is received by a recipient; the recipient does not have to have faith in order to receive the gracelet of faith.

Let's Have a Conversation

- Have you been exposed to the "word of faith" teaching in person or on TV and how has it affected you?
- Why do you think this kind of teaching resonates so well in the Western culture?

ꞏꝏꞏ

---

4. Most likely the elders mentioned here represent the leadership brand from that part of the church of Jerusalem that followed the synagogue model of governance. See chapter 12 for a brief discussion of this model.

GRACELETS

Appendix 3: Greek Verb and Noun System

The following material comes from a course on beginning Greek that I taught over the years to help explain the basics of how the Greek language worked.[5]

The Greek Noun System

The function of the word is signaled by its inflection. Words belonging to the noun system will indicate three separate messages by the ending added to the stem.

Number

The patterns of endings used on any particular word will either be singular (only one) or plural (more than one).

Gender

There are three endings, which will be either masculine, feminine, or neuter.

You will often find these abbreviated as follows:

m., or masc. = masculine
f., or fem. = feminine
n., or neut. = neuter

Gender refers to a pattern of inflectional endings. Usually the gender of a noun has no relationship to the sexual gender of the object it refers to.

Therefore, the Greek inflection system for nouns, etc., will have three possible patterns (m. f. n.), which will include endings that are singular or plural.

5 Winn Griffin, *How to Expand Your Biblical Took Kit* (Woodinville, WA: SBL Ministries, 1996), 26-27, 30-31. The material presented above is from Lesson Five: The Greek Noun System and Lesson Six: The Greek Verb System.

GRACELETS

Case

There are five sets of endings in this pattern. These endings will have both a singular and plural form and can be identified in each gender. They are:

1. Nominative
2. Genitive
3. Dative
4. Accusative
5. Vocative

The purpose of case is to show the relationships between various words in a sentence. In English, we tend to use different types of helping words or phrases to express the message of case, which we find in Greek. Sometimes word order is the English way of expressing the role of a particular Greek case form.

Nominative

The nominative case form usually signals the subject of the sentence. English will indicate the subject of the sentence by word order: The subject comes before the verb. *Orval sees Hector* does not mean the same thing as *Hector sees Orval*. In the Greek sentence, word order has more to do with *emphasis* than function.

Genitive

The genitive case expresses description. It is employed to qualify the meaning of a preceding noun and to show in a more definite sense how the noun is to be understood. There are other uses, but they must be learned by observation and by having a basic grammar by your side.

The root meaning of the genitive is attribution. It may employ relationship. Thus, the kingdom of God is the kingdom, which has as its distinguishing attribute its relationship to God. Or, the genitive may employ an essential quality. Thus, *unbelieving heart* is a heart, which has as its distinguishing attribute the quality of unbelief. The Genitive defines by attributing a quality of relationship to the noun, which it modifies.

Dative

The dative case is used to mark the indirect object of the sentence. Usually in English, we use words like *to, for,* or *by,* to do the same thing.

Appendix 3

It is that which the action of the verb is done to, for, by, or with. Like the genitive, the dative case can be used to express various kinds of *meanings*.

Accusative

The accusative usually marks the object of the sentence. The object of the sentence is that which is immediately acted upon. The original function of the accusative was to limit the extension of the verb.

Vocative

This is the case of direct address and is used infrequently.

The Greek Verb System

A Greek verb has five properties. They are: *Tense, Voice, Mood, Person,* and *Number*. Each one is vital to the understanding of a verb and its function in a sentence.

Tense

There are six possible tenses, which the Greek language uses. They are: *Present, Future, Aorist, Imperfect, Perfect,* and *Pluperfect.* In English, a verb usually signifies *time*, while in Greek a verb primarily signifies *kind of action.* The *time* element is present only when a tense is found in the Indicative Mood.

There are basically three kinds of action, which you should be aware of: *Simple, Continuous,* and *Completed.* Each one of the six tenses shows one of these kinds of action. Let's examine each of these kinds of action.

Simple Action

A verb with this action simply states that something happened. It is like a *snapshot* with a camera. It locks the action to a specific time and space. It does not imply any preceding or following results of the action. An illustration: I tied my shoe. The action of *tied* is like a snapshot picture. It occurred. In Greek, this kind of action is called *Aorist.* While the action is a snapshot, the action can actually take place over a period. In the indicative mode, the aorist simply denotes that the action occurred in the past time.

Continuous Action

A verb with this action states that something is happening or in the process of happening. The beginning and end of the action is not in view. In Greek, there are three tenses, which have this kind of action: *Present, Imperfect,* and *Future.* This action is like viewing a *movie* versus looking at a *snapshot.*

- *Present:* I am tying my shoe.
- *Imperfect:* I was tying my shoe.
- *Future:* I shall tie my shoe.

Completed Action

A verb with this action states that something has happened and the result continues. In Greek, there are two tenses, which have this kind of action: *Perfect* and *Pluperfect.*

- *Perfect:* I have tied my shoes and they remain tied.
- *Pluperfect:* I had tied my shoes and they remained tied for a while, but the result of that action is not now apparent.

Voice

The voice in Greek shows the relationship between the subject and the action of the verb. There are three voices: *Active, Middle,* and *Passive.*

Active Voice

In the active voice, the subject is doing the action to the verb. An illustration: I tied my shoe. The "I" is accomplishing the action.

Middle Voice

In the middle voice, the subject is either acting upon or on behalf of the subject. An illustration: I tied my shoe for myself.

Passive Voice

In the passive voice, the subject is receiving the action of the verb. An illustration: I am being tied.

Mood

Mood demonstrates how the action of the verb was or is accomplished.

There are only two viewpoints: *that which is actual* and *that which is possible.* There are four moods in Greek: *Indicative, Subjunctive, Optative,* and *Imperative.* The *Indicative* is the mood that suggests that the verbal idea is actual. Possible action may be one of the other three moods:

- *Subjunctive:* probability
- *Optative:* possibility
- *Imperative:* volitionally possible

Indicative Mood

The Indicative shows that there is no doubt in the mind of the writer or speaker. It is the mood of certainty. Illustrations:

- I tied my shoe. When the verb *tied* is indicative, it means that there was no doubt in the speaker's mind that the shoe was tied.
- *In the beginning **was the word.*** (John 1.1) A statement of simple fact in the mind of the author.

Subjunctive Mood

The Subjunctive Mood shows probability. While the Indicative assumes reality, the subjunctive assumes unreality. It is a step away from the actual to that which is only conceivable. Illustrations:

- I should be tying my shoe.
- *Let us **hold firmly** to the faith we profess* (Heb. 4.14) is not a command to do so but a hope of probability that the author and his readers can firmly hold their confessed faith.

Optative Mood

The Optative is the mood of strong contingency; the mood of possibility. It contains no definite anticipation of realization, but merely presents the action as conceivable. Illustrations:

- I should possibly be tying my shoe.
- *May the Lord **direct** your hearts...* (2 Thess. 3.5) suggests that it is possible for God to direct the hearts of the Thessalonians. It is the expression of a wish.

Imperative Mood

The Imperative is the mood of command. It expresses intention. One may choose or choose not to follow the command. Illustrations:

- Tie your shoe.
- *Love* *your* *enemies...* (Matt. 5.44). The degree of authority involved in the command, and the degree of probability that the one addressed will respond are matters, which are incidental to the Imperative. The Imperative itself denotes only the appeal to the will for choice.

Person and Number

Person in Greek is like *person* in other languages. There are three: *First, Second,* and *Third.* There are two numbers: *Singular* and *Plural.*

∞

GRACELETS

Bibliography

Arndt, William, F. Wilbur Gingrich, Frederick W. Danker, and Walter Bauer. *A Greek-English Lexicon of the New Testament and Other Early Christian Literature.* 2d ed. Chicago, IL: University of Chicago Press, 1979.

Assemblies of God, "Modern Day Manifestations of the Spirit," aog. org http://ag.org/top/Beliefs/topics/sptlissues_manifestations.cfm (accessed February 26, 2013).

Banks, Robert. *Going to Church in the First Century.* Beaumont, TX: Christian Books Publishing House, 1980.

Barclay, William. *The Revelation of John, Vol. 1 (New Daily Study Bible) 3rd Edition (April 1, 2004).* Louisville, KY: Westminster John Knox Press.

_____. *The Letter to the Romans.* [2d ed. The Daily Study Bible Series. Philadelphia, PA: Westminster Press, 1957.

_____. *The Letters to the Galatians and Ephesians.* Philadelphia, PA: Westminster Press, 1959.

_____. *The Acts of the Apostles (The New Daily Study) 3 Edition (November 30, 2003).* Louisville, KY: Westminster John Knox Press, 1975, 2003.

Barna, George, "Awareness of Spiritual Gifts Is Changing," Barna Group https://www.barna.org/barna-update/5-barna-update/32-awareness-of-spiritual-gifts-is-changing#.UkjneDaTh8E (accessed September 29, 2013).

_____, "The Year's Most Intriguing Findings, from Barna Research Studies," Barna Group https://www.barna.org/barna-update/5-barna-update/64-the-years-most-intriguing-findings-from-barna-research-studies#.UkjjIDaTh8E (accessed September 29, 2013).

_____, "Survey Describes the Spiritual Gifts That Christians Say They Have," Barna Group https://www.barna.org/barna-update/faith-spirituality/211-survey-describes-the-spiritual-gifts-that-christians-say-they-have#.UkjkXDaTh8E (accessed September 29, 2013).

Barna Group, "Survey Describes the Spiritual Gifts That Christians Say They Have," The Barna Group http://www.barna.org/barna-update/article/12-faithspirituality/211-survey-describes-the-spiritual-gifts-that-christians-say-they-have (accessed July 27, 2009).

Barnett, John, "Ephesus: The Jealousy of Jesus," 947krks.com http://www.947krks.com/devotionals/discoverthebook/11603927/ (accessed Novebmer 20, 2012).

Barr, James. *The Semantics of Biblical Language*. 2004: Wipf and Stock Publishers, 2004.

Barrett, C. K. *The First Epistle to Corinthians*. Peabody, MA: Hendrickson Publishers, Inc, 1993.

Barth, Markus. *Ephesians*. Vol. 1. Garden City, NY: Doubleday & Company, 1974.

_____. *Ephesians: Introduction, Translation, and Commentary on Chapters 1-3 (Anchor Bible, Vol. 34)*. 1st ed. Garden City, NY: Doubleday, 1974.

Bauder, W. Link, *The New International. Dictionary of New Testament Theology*. Grand Rapids, MI:Zondervan, 1975.

Bauer, Walter. *A Greek-English Lexicon of the New Testament*. Chicago, IL: University of Chicago Press, 1957.

Beare, Francis Wright. *The First Epistle of Peter*. Oxford: Basic Blackwell, 1958.

Berding, Kenneth. *What Are Spiritual Gifts? Rethinking the Conventional View*. Grand Rapids, MI: Kregel Publications, 2006.

Best, Ernest. *New Century Bible Commentary: 1 Peter*. Grand Rapids, MI: Eerdmans, 1982.

BibleStudyTools.com, "Dictionaries," BibleStudyTools.com http://www.biblestudytools.com/dictionaries/ (accessed January 30, 2015).

Biblica. *The Books of the Bible*. Colorado Springs, CO: Biblica, 2011.

_____, "1 Peter: Introduction to NIV Study Bible," Biblica http://www.biblica.com/en-us/bible/online-bible/scholar-notes/niv-study-bible/intro-to-1-peter/ (accessed May 18, 2014).

Bilezikian, Gilbert G. *Community 101: Reclaiming the Church as Community of Oneness*. Grand Rapids, MI: Zondervan Publishing House, Willow Creek Resources, 1997.

Bleijenberg, Linda, "What Is Primitivism? Lovejoy & Boas, Gauguin and the Myth of Tahiti," originsofarchitecture. wordpress.com https://originsofarchitecture.wordpress.com/2013/03/16/what-is-primitivism-lovejoy-boas-gauguin-and-the-myth-of-tahiti/ (accessed February 22, 2015).

Blumhofer, Edith L., Russell P. Spittler, and Grant A. Wacker. *Pentecostal Currents in American Protestantism*. Urbana and Chicago: University of Illinois Press, 1999.

Bibliography

Boas, George, "Primitivism," University of Virginia Library http://xtf.lib.virginia.edu/xtf/view?docId=DicHist/uvaBook/ tei/DicHist3.xml;chunk.id=dv3-72;toc.depth=1;toc.id=dv3-72;brand=default (accessed July 30, 2015).

Brown, Colin. *New International Dictionary of New Testament Theology (DNTT: 4 Volume Set)* Edited by Colin Brown. Grand Rapids, MI: Zondervan, 1986.

Brown, Raymond Edward. *The Gospel According to John.* Vol. I-XII. 2 vols. [1st ed. Garden City, NY: Doubleday, 1966.

Bruce, F. F. *The Epistle to the Ephesians.* London: Pickering & Inglis ltd., 1962.

_____. *1 and 2 Corinthians* New Century Bible Commentary. Grand Rapids, MI: Eerdmans, 1980.

_____. *The Book of the Acts.* Rev. ed. The New International Commentary on the New Testament. Grand Rapids, MI: Eerdmans Publishing Company, 1988.

_____. *The Book of the Acts.* Grand Rapids, MI: Wm. B. Eerdmans Publishing Company, 1988.

_____. *The Epistle to the Ephesians: Kindle Edition.* Cleaverton Down, UK: Creative Communications, Ltd, 2012.

Burge, Gary M. "The Greatest Story Never Read." *Christianity Today*, August 9, 1999, 45-49.

Burke, Daniel, "Nicodemus, the Mystery Man of Holy Week," RNS (Religious News Service) http://www.religionnews. com/2013/03/27/nicodemus-the-mystery-man-of-holy-week/ (accessed August 2, 2013).

Butler, Trent C., "Tyrannus," Broadman & Holman Publishers http://www.studylight.org/dic/hbd/view.cgi?number=T6335 (accessed September 11, 2013).

Calvin, John, "Commentary on Psalms - Volume 1," Bible Hub http://biblehub.com/library/calvin/commentary_on_psalms_ volume_1/psalm_23_5-6.htm (accessed September 12, 2015).

Carson, D. A., (Consulting Editor). *New Bible Commentary: 21st Century Edition.* Downers Grove, IL: InterVarsity Press, 1994.

Charles E. Fuller Institute of Evangelism and Church Growth, "Wagner-Modified Houts Questionnaire," Charles E. Fuller Institute of Evangelism and Church Growth http://exchristian.net/ images//wagner_modified_houts.pdf (accessed September 28, 2013).

Coggins, James R. and Paul G. Hiebert. Eds. *Wonders in the World.* Hillsboro, KS: Kindred Press, 1989.

Conzelmann, Hans. *1 Corinthians: A Commentary on the First Epistle to the Corinthians* Hermeneia--a Critical and Historical Commentary on the Bible. Minneapolis, MN: Fortress Press, 1975.

Cornwall, Robert D. *Unfettered Spirit: Spiritual Gifts for the New Great Awakening.* Gonzalez, FL: Energion Publications, 2011.

Dawn, Marva J. *A Royal Waste of Time: The Splendor of Worshiping God and Being Church for the World.* Grand Rapids, MI: Wm. B. Eerdmans Publishing Co, 1999.

Dictionary.com, "Supernatural," Dictionary.com http://dictionary.reference.com/browse/supernatural?s=t (accessed February 8, 2015).

Douglas, J. D. *The New International Dictionary of the Christian Church.* Grand Rapids, MI: Zondervan Publishing Company, 1974.

Dunn, James D. G. *Baptism in the Holy Spirit: A Re-Examination of the New Testament on the Gift of the Spirit.* Philadelphia, PA: Westminster John Knox Press, 1977.

_____. *Unity and Diversity in the New Testament: An Inquiry into the Character of Earliest Christianity.* Philadelphia, PA: The Westminster Press, 1977.

_____. *Jesus and the Spirit: A Study of the Religious and Charismatic Experience of Jesus and the First Christians as Reflected in the New Testament.* Grand Rapids, MI: W.B. Eerdmans Publishing Company, 1997.

_____. *Unity and Diversity in the New Testament: An Inquiry into the Character of Earliest Christianity.* Norwich, UK: SCM Press, 2006: Third Edition.

Eiderman, B. Van, *Zondervan Pictorial Encyclopedia of the Bible.* Grand Rapids, MI:Zondervan.

ESPN, "Jermaine Kearse's Bobbling Catch Was a Miracle (Even Though It Didn't Matter in the End)," ESPN http://ftw.usatoday.com/2015/02/jermaine-kearse-catch (accessed June 3, 2015).

Fee, Gordon D. *The First Epistle to the Corinthians.* The New International Commentary on the New Testament. Grand Rapids, MI: W.B. Eerdmans Publishing Company, 1987.

_____, *Dictionary of Paul and His Letters.* Downers Grove, IL:InterVarsity Press, 1993.

_____. *God's Empowering Presence: The Holy Spirit in the Letters of Paul.* Peabody, MA: Hendrickson Publishers, Inc., 1994.

_____. *Revelation.* Eugene, OR: Cascade Books, 2011.

_____. *The First Epistle to the Corinthians: The New International Commentary on the New Testament: Revised Edition.* Grand Rapids, MI: W.B. Eerdmans Publishing Company, 2014.

Fee, Gordon D., and Douglas Stuart. *How to Read the Bible for All Its Worth (3rd Edition).* Grand Rapids, MI: Zondervan, 2003.

Flynn, Leslie B. *19 Gifts of the Spirit.* Wheaton, IL: Victor Books, 1974.

Frazee, Randy. *The Connecting Church.* Grand Rapids, MI: Zondervan 2001.

Bibliography

Gainey, Henry, "The Afterglow," The Word for Today http://www.amazon.com/Afterglow-Calvary-Basics-Henry-Gainey/dp/0936728760/ (accessed July 8, 2015).

Goldingay, John. *Psalms, Vol. 1, Baker Commentary of the Old Testament Wisdom and Psalms*. Grand Rapids, MI: Baker Academic, 2006.

Grady, J. Lee, "Kenneth Hagin's Forgotten Warning," CBN.com http://www.cbn.com/spirituallife/churchandministry/grady_hagan_prosperity.aspx (accessed July 20, 2015).

Green, Michael. *I Believe in the Holy Spirit*. Grand Rapids, MI: Eerdmans, 1975.

Grenz, Stanley J. *A Primer on Postmodernism*. Grand Rapids, MI: William B. Eerdmans Pub. Co., 1996.

Griffin, Winn. *How to Expand Your Biblical Took Kit*. Woodinville, WA: SBL Ministries, 1996.

_____. *Learning to Think and Teach Biblically*. Woodinville, WA: Seeing the Bible Live Publishing, 1998.

_____. *Wordwise: Healing*. Woodinville, WA: SBL Ministries, 1999.

_____. *God's Epic Adventure*. Woodinville, WA: Harmon Press, 2007.

_____. *God Has Spoken: But What Has He Said? 3 Reasons for and 3 Approaches to Hearing God in Scripture*. Woodinville, WA: Basilia Press: An Imprint of Harmon Press, 2013.

_____. *God's Epic Adventure [The Reader Edition]*. Woodinville, WA: Harmon Press, 2014.

Griffiths, Michael. *Grace-gifts*. Grand Rapids, MI: Eerdmans, 1979.

Guder, Darrell L., (Editor). *Missional Church: A Vision for the Sending of the Church in North America (The Gospel and Our Culture Series)* Grand Rapids, MI: Wm. B. Eerdmans Publishing Co, 1998.

Gundry, Robert H. *A Survey of the New Testament*. 4th ed. Grand Rapids, MI: Zondervan, 2003.

Harry, J. E., "Corinth," Wm. B. Eerdmans Publishing Co. http://www.internationalstandardbible.com/C/corinth.html (accessed July 10, 2015).

Henderson, Jim. *Evangelism without Additives: What If Sharing Your Faith Meant Just Being Yourself?* Colorado Springs, CO: WaterBrook Press, 2007.

Hollenweger, W.J., *The International Dictionary of Pentecostal Charismatic Movements (Revised and Expanded Edition)*. Grand Rapids, MI:Zondervan, 2003.

Horton, Stanley M. *What the Bible Says About the Holy Spirit*. Springfield, MO: Gospel Publishing House, 1976.

Hummel, Charles E. *Fire in the Fireplace: Contemporary Charismatic Renewal*. Downers Grove, IL: InterVarsity Press, 1978.

Hunter, Harold D., "A Portrait of How the Azusa Doctrine of Spirit Baptism Shaped American Pentecostalism," Enrichment Journal: Assemblies of God http://enrichmentjournal. ag.org/200602/200602_078_azusadoctrine.cfm (accessed November 3, 2015).

Hurtado, Larry, "50th Anniversary: Barr's "Semantics of Biblical Language," Larry Hurtado (accessed October 24, 2013).

Hybels, Lynne, and Bill Hybels. *Rediscovering Church: The Story and Vision of Willow Creek Community Church*. Grand Rapids, MI: Zondervan Publishing House, 1995.

Indiana, University of, "Temple Cures," University of Indiana http://www.indiana.edu/~ancmed/curecult.htm (accessed July 20, 2015).

infoplease, "Middle Ages: Transition to the Modern World," infoplease http://www.infoplease.com/encyclopedia/history/middle-ages-transition-to-modern-world.html (accessed November 11, 2015).

israeljerusalem.com, "Ephesus - School of Tyrannus," israeljerusalem. com http://www.israeljerusalem.com/school-of-tyrannus.htm (accessed September 2, 2015).

Jamieson, Fausset, Brown,, "Commentary Critical and Explanatory on the Whole Bible," Christian Classics Ethereal Library http://www.ccel.org/ccel/jamieson/jfb.xi.v.xx.html#xi.v.xx-p2.1 (accessed September 9, 2013).

Jones, Bob, "New Apostolic Government in Place by 2012," bobjones. org http://bobjonesnew.unionactive.com/Docs/Words%20of%20 2008/2008-11-Apostolic_Govt_By_2012.htm (accessed February 17, 2014).

Kansas Historical Society, "Stone's Folly, Topeka, Kansas," Kansas Historical Society http://www.kansasmemory.org/item/216413 (accessed November 23, 2012).

Katz, Jack. "Cooks Cooking up Recipes: The Cash Value of Nouns, Verbs and Grammar." *The American Sociologist*. Vol. Volume 43, No. 1, (2008).

_____. "Cooks Cooking up Recipes: The Cash Value of Nouns, Verbs and Grammar." *The American Sociologist*. Vol. 43, No. 1, (2008).

Keener, Craig S., *The IVP Bible Background Commentary: New Testament*, InterVarsity Press. 2014.

_____, "John Macarthur's Strange Fire, Reviewed by Craig S. Keener," The Pneuma Review http://pneumareview.com/john-macarthurs-strange-fire-reviewed-by-craig-s-keener/ (accessed November 2, 2015).

_____. *The IVP Bible Background Commentary (New Testament)*. *Second Edition*. Downers Grove, IL: IVP Academic, 2014.

Keil, Carl Friedrich, and Franz Delitzsch. *Biblical Commentary on the Old Testament*. Peabody, MA: Hendrickson Publishers, 1996.

Bibliography

Keller, Phillip. *A Shepherd Looks at Psalm 23*. Grand Rapids: Zondervan Publishing House, 1970.

Keller, Tim, "How Can Christianity Be Both Monotheistic and Trinitarian?," YouTube https://youtu.be/UuMepL0tktc (accessed July 20, 2015).

Kinghorn, Kenneth Cain. *Gifts of the Spirit*. Nashville, TN: Abingdon Press, 1976.

_____. *Discovering Your Spiritual Gifts: A Personal Inventory Method*. Grand Rapids, MI: Zondervan, 1981.

Koch, Kurt. *Charismatic Gifts*. Grand Rapids, MI: Kregel Publications, 1975.

Kurian, George Thomas, Ed. *Nelson's New Christian Dictionary: The Authoritative Resource on the Christian World*. Nashville, TN: Thomas Nelson, 2001

Ladd, George Eldon. *A Theology of the New Testament*. Rev. ed. Grand Rapids, MI: Eerdmans, 1993.

Laing, Mark T. B. *From Crisis to Creation: Lesslie Newbigin and the Reinvention of Christian Mission*. Eugene, OR: Wipf & Stock Publishers, 2012.

Lewis, C. S. *Reflections on the Psalms*. Chicago, IL: Mariner Books, 1965.

Lindsay, Gordon. *Gifts of the Spirit*. Dallas, TX: Christ for the Nations, 1963.

Lundbom, Jack R. "Psalm 23: Song of Passage." *Interpretation* Vol. 40, no. 1, No. 1986): 6.

Luther, Martin. *Luther's Works*. St Louis, MO: Concordia Publishing House, 1958.

MacArthur, John. *The Charismatics: A Doctrinal Perspective*. Grand Rapids, MI: Zondervan Publishing House, 1978.

MacNutt, Francis. *Healing*. Notre Dame, IN: Ave Maria Press, 1999.

Marshall, I. Howard, Stephen Travis, Ian Paul. *Exploring the New Testament: A Guide to the Letters & Revelation*. Vol. 1. Downers Grove, IL: InterVarsity Press, 2002.

Martin, Ralph P. *The Epistle of Paul to the Philippians: An Introduction and Commentary*. Rev. ed. The Tyndale New Testament Commentaries. Grand Rapids, MI: Wm. B. Eerdmans Publishing Company, 1987.

McGarvey, J. V., "A Commentary on Acts of Apostles," StudyLight.com http://www.studylight.org/com/oca/view.cgi?bk=43&ch=3 (accessed September 28, 2013).

Merriam-Webster, "Apostle," Merriam-Webster http://www.merriam-webster.com/dictionary/apostle (accessed October 1, 2015).

Morris, Leon. *The Gospel According to John*. Grand Rapids, MI: Eerdmans Publishing Company, 1971.

_____. *The Gospel According to John*. Grand Rapids, MI: William B. Eerdmans Publsihing Co., 1971.

Moule, H. C. G. *The Epistle to the Ephesians: With Introduction and Notes.* Cambridge: The University Press, 1902, 1886.

Nathan, Rich, and Ken Wilson. *Empowered Evangelicals: Bringing Together the Best of the Evangelical and Charismatic Worlds.* Boise, ID: Ampelon Publishing, 1995 Reprint edition (March 3, 2009).

Nida, Eugene A. and Daniel C. Arichea. *Translator's Handbook on the First Letter from Peter.* New York, NY: United Bible Society, 1980.

Olson, Roger E., "Can 'Authentic Christianity' Be Found Today?," Patheos.com http://www.patheos.com/blogs/rogereolson/2015/03/can-authentic-christianity-be-found-today/ (accessed July 30, 2015).

Osborne, Grant R. *The Hermeneutical Spiral: A Comprehensive Introduction to Biblical Interpretation, 2nd Ed.* Downers Grove: InterVarsity Press, 2006.

Peterson, Eugene. *A Long Obedience in the Same Direction: Discipleship in an Instant Society.* Grand Rapids, MI: InterVarsity Press, 2000.

Price, Robert M., "Evangelism as Entertainment," religion-online.org http://www.religion-online.org/showarticle.asp?title=1714 (accessed February 18, 2014).

Robeck Jr., Cecil M. *The Azusa Street Mission and Revival.* Nashville, TN: Thomas Nelson, 2006.

Robeck, Mel. "The Gift of Prophecy in Acts and Paul." *Studia Biblica et Theologica, Part 1 and 2.* Vol. Vol 4 and 5, No. 1974 and 1975).

Ryken, Leland. *The Bible as Literature.* Grand Rapids, MI: Zondervan, 1974.

Ryken, Leland, James C. Wilhoit, and Tremper Longman III. *Dictionary of Biblical Imagery.* Downers Grove, IL: InterVarsity Press, 1998.

Schmoller, Alfred. *Concordantiae Novi Testamenti Graeci: Hankonkordanz Zum Griechischen Neuen Testament.* Stutgart: Wurttembergische Bibelanstalt, 1968.

Schweizer, Eduard. *Church Order in the New Testament.* Norwich, UK: SCM Press, 2011: Revised Edition

Scott, W. M. F. "Priesthood in the New Testament." *Scottish Journal of Theology.* Vol. 10, No. 4, (1957): 399-415.

Smith, Christopher R. *The Beauty Behind the Mask: Rediscovering the Books of the Bible.* Toronto: Clements Publishing, 2007.

Smith, James K. A. *Who's Afraid of Postmodernism?: Taking Derrida, Lyotard, and Foucault to Church.* Grand Rapids, MI: Baker Academic, 2006.

Smith, Maximilian Zerwick and Joseph. *Biblical Greek, Illustrated by Examples, English Edition, Adapted from the Fourth Latin Edition by Joseph Smith S.J.* Rome: Pontificio Istituto Biblico, 1963.

Snyder, Howard. *The Community of the King.* Grand Rapids, MI: InterVarsity Press, 1977.

Spittler, Russell P. *Perspectives on the New Pentecostalism.* Grand Rapids, MI: Baker Book House, 1976.

Bibliography

SPWBooks, "Questions About Seagulls," SPWBooks http://www. spwickstrom.com/gullfaq/ (accessed October 20, 2013).

Storms, Sam. *The Beginner's Guide to Spiritual Gifts*. Ventura, CA: Regal Books | Gospel Light, 2012.

Stovell, Jon, "Society of Vineyard Scholars Facebook Group [Conversation on Theological Dictionary of New Testament]," Facebook https://www.facebook.com/groups/102214556490936/ permalink/601544656557921/ (accessed November 9, 2013).

Tenney, Merrill Chapin. *The Zondervan Pictorial Encyclopedia of the Bible*. Grand Rapids, MI: Zondervan Publishing House, 1975.

Tenney, Merrill Chapin, and J. D. Douglas. *The New International Dictionary of the Bible*. Pictorial ed. Grand Rapids, MI, U.S.A.: Regency Reference Library, Zondervan Pub. House, 1987.

Thiselton, Anthony C. *The First Epistle to the Corinthians: A Commentary on the Greek Text (NIGTC)*. Grand Rapids, MI: William B. Eerdmans Publishing Company, 2000.

Traveler, Condé Nast, "Explainer: Why Do Airplanes Take Off into the Wind?," Condé Nast Traveler http://www.cntraveler.com/daily-traveler/2012/06/airplane-flying-wind-storm (accessed September 21, 2013).

USA, National Coffee Association, "Ten Steps to Coffee," National Coffee Association USA http://www.ncausa.org/i4a/pages/index. cfm?pageid=69 (accessed June 17, 2014).

Vanhoozer, Kevin, *New Dictionary of Biblical Theology*. Downers Grove, IL:InterVarsity Press, 2000.

_____. *Is There a Meaning in This Text?* Grand Rapids, MI: Zondervan, 2009.

Vincent, M. R. *Vincent's Word Studies in the New Testament*. Peabody, MA: Hendrickson Publishers, 1985.

Vincent, William. *The Origination of the Greek Verb. An Hypothesis, Volume 2*. London, 1794.

_____. *The Origination of the Greek Verb: An Hypothesis*. London, 1794.

Wagner, C. Peter. *Your Spiritual Gift*. Ventura, CA: Regal Books, 1979.

_____. *Discover Your Spiritual Gifts*. Ventura, CA: Regal, 2002.

Walton, John H., Victor H. Matthews, and Mark W. Chavalas. *The IVP Bible Background Commentary: Old Testament*. Downers Grove, IL: InterVarsity Press, 2000.

Warfield, Benjamin Breckinridge. *Counterfeit Miracles* Thomas Smyth Lectures, Columbia Theological Seminary, Decatur, Ga. [London]: Banner of Truth Trust, 1972.

Webster, "Merriam-Webster Dictionary," Merriam-Webster, Inc. http://www.merriam-webster.com/dictionary/gift (accessed October 21, 2015).

Wikipedia, "Die Hard," Wikipedia (accessed September 21, 2013).

_____, "Hudibras" Wikipedia https://en.wikipedia.org/wiki/ Hudibras (accessed September 12, 2015).

_____, "Paul the Apostle," Wikipedia http://en.wikipedia.org/wiki/ Paul_the_Apostle (accessed January 5, 2015).

Willans, Jean Stone. *The Acts of the Green Apples: The inside Story of the Beginning of the Charismatic Renewal.* Hong Kong: Society of Stephen, 1973.

Witherington, Ben. *New Testament History: A Narrative Account.* Grand Rapids, MI: Baker Academic, 2001.

_____. *The Indelible Image: The Theological and Ethical Thought World of the New Testament.* Grand Rapids, MI: InterVarsity, 2010.

_____. *The Indelible Image: The Theological and Ethical Thought World of the New Testament (Volume 2).* Downers Grove, IL: InterVarsity, 2010.

Wood, D. R., W. A. R. Millard, J. I. Packer, D. J. Wiseman, and I. Howard Marshall. *The New Bible Dictionary.* 1st ed. Grand Rapids, MI: InterVarsity Press, 1996.

Wright, N. T. *Paul for Everyone: The Prison Letters: Ephesians, Philippians, Colossians, Philemon (New Testament for Everyone).* Louisville, KY: Westminster John Knox Press, 2002.

_____, "Ask. N. T. Wright: April Q & a Response," Facebook: N.T. Wright Discussion Group https://www.facebook.com/notes/n-t-wright/ask-n-t-wright-april-q-a-response/644725545580506 (accessed November 4, 2015).

_____. *Simply Good News: Why the Gospel Is News and What Makes It Good.* San Franscisco, CA: HarperCollins, 2015.

Youngblood, Ronald F. General Editor. *Nelson's New Illustrated Bible Dictionary.* Nashville, TN: Thomas Nelson Publishers, 1986

Yorn, Rick. *Discover Your Spiritual Gift and Use It.* Wheaton, IL: Tyndale, 1974.

∽

Other Books by Winn Griffin

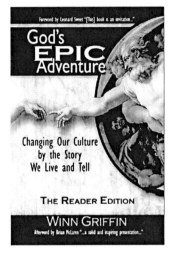

God's EPIC Adventure uses a six-act-play model as a way of presenting Scripture as a full-length Story in order to assist the reader toward a better reading experience of Scripture's text. The author presents the gluing themes of Covenant in the Old Testament and Kingdom of God in the New Testament as two ways of saying the same thing, namely that God has invaded this present evil age with his rule. The intended results of reading the Bible with its storyline is to learn the art of living into the Story that Scripture presents. Readers will find ways to use this book that they have never thought of before!

∽

Readers of Scripture...will learn here how to step right into the big picture of God's story. If you want to understand the buzz about "narrative" and Scripture, Winn's book is a surefooted and up-to-date guide.

- Kent L. Yinger, George Fox Evangelical Seminary

God Has Spoken, But What Has He Said?
3 Reasons For and 3 Approaches to Hearing God in Scripture (eBook)

God has spoken; we can read what he has said in the Bible. The question is not if he has spoken, but when he did, what did he say? And more to the point, if he can be heard in the sacred text, is anyone listening? In this eBook, the author shares three (3) reasons for and three (3) approaches to hearing God's voice from the pages of the Bible. The reader will surely be able to read with fresh eyes and hear with fresh ears after reading this short eBook.

googling God's Will: Why Keep Searching for It When It's Not Lost?

Tired of googling God's Will in all the wrong places? It's a habit that consumes valuable time and often produces tragedy and frustration instead of fulfillment. Can you really find something, in this case, the will of God, which is not lost?

The whole concept of "searching" suggests that something is lost, but is it really? What should you do? Stop "googling God's Will" and spend that precious time living into it. It's doable and the aim of this book is to dispel some of the theological sacred cows about the will of God and help you learn a new way of thinking and reflecting that can free you up to live into his will.

Asking questions is often at the root of learning, but asking the wrong questions takes us on a journey along a path to nowhere. Have you ever asked questions like:

- Does God have a "perfect or permissive will" for my life?
- Can I "put out a fleece" to discover his will?
- How does the Spirit interact with me in living into the will of God?

The bottom line: well, you will have to read *googling God's Will* to see what this book offers as possible solutions.

About Veilless in Corinth:
An Interpretative Read of 1 Corinthians 11.2-16 (eBook)

In the traditional reading of 1 Corinthians 11.2-16, Paul is seen as interacting with a problem within the worship service in the Corinthian church: Should women wear or not wear veils when they pray or prophesy? Most commentaries follow this reading, working with the text as it stands within the customs of the day. Most readers seem to come away from the traditional reading thinking that Paul is a woman-hater because this text presents his prejudice on the subject. If this is true of Paul, then he has varied from the story that underlies his telling in his writings.

About Harmon Press

HarmonPress is a publishing company dedicated to helping authors get their works into print, using cutting edge design technology, lightning-fast printing, and distribution of an author's book to the marketplace. For information go to http://www.harmonpress.com

CPSIA information can be obtained
at www.ICGtesting.com
Printed in the USA
FSOW01n2259250116
16180FS